HUMAN DIGNITY AND WELFARE SYSTEMS

Chak Kwan Chan and Graham Bowpitt

To our Lord, who gave us the strength and wisdom to
complete this project

First published in Great Britain in October 2005 by

The Policy Press
University of Bristol
Fourth Floor
Beacon House
Queen's Road
Bristol BS8 1QU
UK

Tel +44 (0)117 331 4054
Fax +44 (0)117 331 4093
e-mail tpp-info@bristol.ac.uk
www.policypress.org.uk

British Library Cataloguing in Publication Data
A catalogue record for this book is available from the British Library.

Library of Congress Cataloging-in-Publication Data
A catalog record for this book has been requested.

ISBN 1 86134 431 7 hardback

Chak Kwan Chan is Senior Lecturer in Social Policy and
Graham Bowpitt is Senior Lecturer in Social Policy, both at Nottingham
Trent University.

Cover design by Qube Design Associates, Bristol.
Printed and bound in Great Britain by MPG Books, Bodmin.

Contents

List of tables and figures

Tables

Figures

Preface

Writing a book about human dignity is a moral rather than a professional duty. It is also a responsibility to the poor and weak, with whom we meet and about whom we read. The Universal Declaration of Human Rights and the Geneva Convention Relative to the Treatment of Prisoners provide all societies with the same guidance for safeguarding human dignity. Based on the principles on human rights enshrined in these documents, we can condemn the Nazis' 'final solution' – the extermination of Europe's Jews during the Second World War – the Japanese army's Nanking massacre of 1937 and its sexual enslavement of Chinese and Korean women, and more recently American soldiers' abuse of Iraqi prisoners. Unfortunately, a government's systematic abuse of welfare recipients through its deliberate portrayal of claimants as lazy and abusers of welfare, its exercising control over their behaviour through 'compulsory voluntary work', the publication of social assistance recipients' names, and the limitation of lifetime welfare rights to a few years have never been treated as illegal actions. On the contrary, such welfare measures are being practised in both developed and developing countries, embellished with titles like 'welfare-to-work', 'workfare' and 'active labour market policies'. This is the issue that our project addresses, and we hope that the project contributes to framing welfare policies that can effectively enhance the dignity of unemployed citizens.

We are grateful to Mr Nigel Horner of the School of Social Sciences at Nottingham Trent University for providing Dr Chan with an opportunity to gather key literature and to conduct interviews in Hong Kong. Through the visit he gained an up-to-date understanding of unemployment issues in Hong Kong and China following interviews with several university and government researchers and a member of the Hong Kong Legislative Council.

Our gratitude also goes to Dawn Rushen, Rowena Mayhew, Laura Greaves, Helen Bolton and Natasha Ferguson at The Policy Press. Because of their patience, support and effective work, we are able to publish the result of our project while facing tremendous teaching and family commitments.

Most gratitude should go to our families for their understanding as we worked at midnight and during holidays, and for their unfailing support for our academic exploration.

Chak Kwan Chan and Graham Bowpitt
March 2005

List of abbreviations

AEA	Active Employment Assistance
AG	Activity Guarantee
ALMP	Active labour market policies
AMS	National Labour Market Board
AMV	Labour Market Administration
APW	Average Production Worker
BI	Basic insurance
BLGS	Basic livelihood guarantee system
BNA	Basic needs approach
CCP	Chinese Communist Party
CLB	County Labour Board
CPPCC	Chinese People Political Consultative Conference
CE	Chief Executive
CSSA	Comprehensive Social Security Assistance
CTC	Child Tax Credit
CW	Community work
DE	Disregarded Earnings
DTI	Department of Trade and Industry
DWP	Department for Work and Pensions
EEP	Ending Exclusion Project
ERB	Employee Retraining Board
ES	Employment Service
ESC	Employment Services Committee
ESW	Employment Support Worker
FUIF	Federation of Unemployment Insurance Funds
GDP	Gross domestic product
GETS	Graduate Employment Training Scheme
GNP	Gross national product
HKSAR	Hong Kong Special Administrative Region
IB	Incapacity Benefit
IEAF	Intensive Employment Assistance Fund
IS	Income Support
IWEP	Initiatives for Wider Economic Participation
JC	Jobcentre
JCP	Jobcentre Plus
JSA	Jobseeker's Allowance
LAN	County Labour Council
LC	Legislative Council

LCA	Low cost but acceptable
LDH	Incentive Allowance Scheme for Local Domestic Helpers
LMI	Labour Market Institute
LO	Swedish Trade Union Confederation
LSDA	Learning and Skills Development Agency
MAS	National Board of Health and Welfare
MLA	Minimum living allowance
MLSG	Minimum living standard guarantee
NC	National Congress
NCSR	National Centre for Social Research
NDYP	New Deal for Young People
NGO	Non-governmental organisation
NHS	National Health Service
NLG	New Labour government
NPC	National People's Congress
NVQ	National Vocational Qualifications
PA	Personal Adviser
PES	Public Employment Service
PESO	Public Employment Service Office
PRC	People's Republic of China
RA	Residents' association
RETPMA	Re-employment Training Programme for the Middle-Aged
RSC	Re-employment service centre
SA	Social Assistance
SAR	Special Administrative Region
SARS	Severe acute respiratory syndrome
SC	Street committee
SCPB	Standing Committee of the Political Bureau
SDP	Social Democratic Party
SFS	Support for Self-reliance Scheme
SJAP	Special Job Attachment Programme
SOE	State-owned enterprise
TANF	Temporary Assistance for Needy Families
VIRI	Voluntary income-related insurance
WFI	Work-focused interview
WTC	Working Tax Credit
YG	Youth Guarantee
YPTP	Youth Pre-employment Training Programme
YSSS	Youth Self-employment Support Scheme
YWETS	Youth Work Experience and Training Scheme

Part One:
Background

ONE

Human dignity and social policy

*In the twentieth century, more than a hundred million in Europe
alone died by violence, often in a way they could not have foreseen
even in their worst nightmares. In our century, history has been a
butcher's bench, and the words* human dignity *have often sounded
empty.*

(Michael Novak, 1998)

The importance of human dignity always emerges from the torture
and abuse of human beings. In 2004, the abuse of Iraqi prisoners by
American soldiers in Abu Ghraib prison was widely reported.
Newspaper photographs show a hooded prisoner with wires fixed to
his body, a dog attacking a prisoner and nude inmates piled in a human
pyramid, forced to simulate sex with each other. In response to these
abuses, General Mark Kimmitt, Deputy Director of Operations for
the US military in Iraq, urged the US army to 'treat people with
dignity and respect' (*Guardian*, 2004a). The Church of England also
urged the US government to treat Taleban and Al-Qaeda prisoners in
Guantanamo Bay with 'humanity and dignity' (BBC News, 2002).
The rights of the prisoners are protected by the Geneva Convention,
which clearly states:

> Persons taking no active part in the hostilities, including
> members of armed forces who have laid down their arms and
> those placed *hors de combat* by sickness, wounds, detention, or
> any other cause, shall in all circumstances be treated humanely,
> without any adverse distinction founded on race, colour,
> religion or faith, sex, birth or wealth, or any other similar
> criteria. (Geneva Convention, 1950, Article 3)

Based on this international treaty, we can easily judge that the actions
of the soldiers involved were illegal and violated the dignity of the
prisoners. Yet the number of prisoners of war is relatively small
compared with the hundreds of thousands of poor people who are
living on various types of public benefits. Welfare recipients typically
suffer, not from physical abuse, but from psychological and social abuse

as a result of abusive welfare practices such as compulsory birth control, the publication of the names of welfare recipients, the restriction of financial support to limited periods and the termination of welfare benefits for a household when only one of its members fails to fulfil work requirements (see Chapters four and five). The abuse of welfare recipients receives less attention than the maltreatment of prisoners, and these types of welfare practices are not treated as illegal but are widely practised in many countries. Academics use terms such as 'residual welfare system' or 'liberal welfare regime' to describe the type of welfare system where such practices continue, and 'stigma' is the strongest word used to describe an abusive welfare measure. Rather than being considered to be problematic or criminal, stigmatising welfare practices have been widely adopted in both developed and less developed countries.

Our concern for the dignity of welfare recipients immediately presents us with a big question: 'What is human dignity?' The concept of dignity is vague and confused (Harris, 1997; Heyd, 1999). A historical analysis of the concept found that it has 'diverse grounds, diverse subjects and diverse degrees' (Miguel, 2002). Today, human dignity is said to be based variously on financial security (Shipman, 1995), the universal provision of a minimum income (Wilson, 1994), user involvement in the caring process (Carpenter and Sbaraini, 1997), and the free expression of sexual orientation (Dignity USA, 2003). As a result, dignity is serving different masters for different purposes (Chan, 2004, p 228). Moralists and professional philosophers use the terms 'human dignity' and 'human worth' for 'little more than rhetorical effect' (Harris, 1997, p 1), while politicians employ it as 'an elastic, all-purpose justification' for their policies (Stetson, 1998, p 10). Although Chan (2004) has pointed to equal human value, self-respect, autonomy and positive mutuality as four dimensions of human dignity, more work needs to be done to examine the theoretical basis of these principles and their interrelationships. In this way, a more coherent and solid framework for human dignity can be developed. In short, a clear concept of human dignity is fundamental to human welfare because 'the principle of human dignity makes normative demands on the state' and 'informs the scope and meaning of all the rights and guarantees of the Basic Law' (Donald Kommers, quoted in Goolam, 2001). Against this background, this study tries to define the concept of human dignity and uses it as a tool to assess the dignity of welfare recipients.

The study of dignity can help evaluate whether the current direction of social policy can truly promote human well-being. Many developed economies such as the United States, the United Kingdom, Canada and Hong Kong have changed their basic approach to social security from one of simply providing financial assistance on the basis of need to one that makes such assistance conditional upon fulfilling work requirements. Accordingly, welfare recipients have to fulfil duties such as doing community work, attending training courses or accepting government-subsidised work. In other words, public benefits become conditional and welfare recipients have duties as well as rights. For example, the New Labour government (NLG) in the UK believes work is the best means to tackle social exclusion and promote claimants' dignity (Secretary of State for Social Security, 1998; Hirsch, 1999). Thus, the NLG imposes new demands on eligibility for unemployment benefits, guided by the principle of 'work for those who can, security for those who cannot' (DSS, 1998). In fact, welfare has been a focus of policy reform in America since the early 1990s. In 1996, the Clinton Administration passed the Personal Responsibility and Work Opportunity Act by introducing time limits and work rules for government assistance. Accordingly, recipients of the Temporary Assistance for Needy Families (TANF) are eligible for federal assistance for a maximum of two years in a lifetime. Because states are granted the power to design the key elements of TANF, some states have established even stricter time limits and work requirements:

> Many states actually adopted shorter time limits and stricter work requirements than the federal law; some refused to treat new migrants to their state the same as long term residents; some instituted a family cap – no additional monies can go to a child born to a mother already receiving welfare … states that lower illegitimate births without increasing abortion will receive a monetary bonus. Teenagers have to live with parents, relatives, or in a designated facility and attend school. (Boris, quoted in Cochrane et al, 2001, p 140)

However, welfare-to-work programmes in the US have been rationalised in terms of human dignity. For example, the 'workfare' programme in Allen County (2004) of Indiana allows citizens to 'accept help while maintaining their dignity'. Similarly, the Hong Kong government launched a 'Support for Self-reliance Scheme' (SFS), under which unemployed benefit recipients have to meet welfare officers regularly about their job-search efforts and to do so-called voluntary work that is voluntary only in the sense of being unpaid. The Hong Kong government argues that this compulsory 'voluntary' work can enhance self-confidence and develop recipients' work habits (Social Welfare Department, 1999). Clearly, work has come to be associated with self-reliance and self-respect, which is basic to people's well-being. The positive effects of work become a justification for extending a government's power over citizens' behaviour. Workfare, therefore, is not just a welfare issue but also 'a fundamentally important issue for all working people and all those who care about the meaning of human dignity in society' (Welfare Watch, 1996). An issue of concern is whether workfare can truly enhance human dignity. As mentioned earlier, the concept of dignity is so vague that it can be easily manipulated by politicians to suppress the autonomy of the poor, forcing the needy out of benefit systems. There is an urgent need to develop effective criteria for assessing the impact of workfare on the dignity of welfare recipients.

A comparative study of the dignity of welfare recipients can enrich our understating of the relationship between welfare systems and the conditions of human dignity. Comparative welfare studies have become 'a central feature of most social policy studies' (Alcock, 2001, p 4). We can learn about the weaknesses and strengths of welfare systems by comparing them (Mabbett and Bolderson, 1999). We can learn better practices from other welfare systems, since 'new and potentially more effective social interventions can be discovered' by sharing knowledge internationally (Midgley, 1997, p 20). In this study we propose to evaluate the strengths and weaknesses of welfare systems by the extent to which they safeguard the dignity of welfare recipients.

Comparative studies can enhance our understanding of different welfare systems. The focus and criteria of existing comparative studies, however, seem to have been dominated by economic factors, especially the welfare expenditure of a country and the economic power of welfare recipients. Welfare expenditure and wealth distribution have always been a concern of academics. The earlier method of comparative welfare studies used macroeconomic outcomes such as welfare expenditure to measure the welfare efforts of a wide range of countries. Wilensky (1975, p 120), after comparing social security expenditure as a proportion of gross national product (GNP) in 64 states, concludes that 'economic level (GNP per capita) overwhelms regime type as a predictor of social security effort' over the long term. Based on this development, the level of welfare expenditure becomes one of the key criteria for evaluating a welfare regime. In short, the welfare achievement of a country is purely measured by its welfare expenditure regardless of its distribution among types of welfare services as well as the objectives and impact of social services on different social groups.

According to Cochrane, Clarke and Gewirtz (2001, p 14), 'Comparative social policy has continued to be dominated by approaches that centre on large-scale aggregate data that are mostly concerned with cash transfers and with issues of inequalities (and transfers) between socio-economic groups'. The main advantage of using existing and internationally aggregated data is to 'identify broad trends and draw equally broad conclusions' (2001, p 9). The key weakness of this approach is its inability to explain factors and processes that shape differences between countries. However, it is crucial to analyse what a state does rather than how much it has afforded (Esping-Andersen, 1990).

Since the publication of *The three worlds of welfare capitalism* (Esping-Andersen, 1990), comparative social policy has taken a new direction. It moves from 'ranking countries according to their welfare efforts to the recognition that there are different types of welfare states' (Kennett, 2001, p 77). Esping-Andersen's model is considered to be 'the most successful attempt thus far to develop a quantitative approach to a class analysis of comparative social policy' (Ginsburg, 1992, p 23). Esping-Andersen (1990) points out that there are three types of welfare regimes – liberal, conservative, and social democratic. The state, the family, voluntary organisations, and the market have different welfare roles in each type of regime. He uses the concepts of 'decommodification' and 'stratification' to compare the welfare impacts of a wide range of countries. Decommodification is 'the degree to which individuals, or families, can uphold a socially acceptable standard of living independent of market participation' (1990, p 37). Stratification is the degree to which the welfare state differentiates between different social classes. Following Esping-Andersen's approach, Kvist (2000, p 1) uses 'de-commodification of labour through easily accessible and relatively generous cash benefits' and 're-commodification of labour through conditioning of benefits and active labour market policies' to analyse the welfare experiences of Scandinavian welfare states. Esping-Andersen's model concerns the economic relationship between a person and the market, the social and economic status of social classes, and the welfare contributions of the state, the family, voluntary organisations, and the market. Again, economic factors play a dominant role in assessing people's financial conditions (decommodification) and their economic position in relation to their fellow citizens (stratification) in three types of welfare regimes.

The main criticisms of Esping-Andersen's approach are its over-generalisation of types of welfare state based on limited cases using a particular policy area (Alcock, 2001), 'the gender blind concept of decommodification, the unawareness of the role of women and the family in the provision of welfare, and the lack of consideration given to gender as a form of social stratification' (Bambra, 2004, p 202). As noticed by Cochrane et al (2001, p 17), there are new challenges to comparative policy studies:

> The demands for comparison that is attentive to differentiated populations (not just socio-economic hierarchies); to the interplay of unpaid work, paid work and welfare (not just work and welfare); and to the forms of domination and subordination, inclusion and exclusion that are constructed through welfare policy and practice (not just income inequality), are significant challenges to the comparative study of social policy.

In response to these weaknesses, researchers use the two dimensions of gender and race, examining the roles and positions of women and ethnic minorities in different welfare regimes. Ginsburg (1992, p 5), for example, uses the concept of 'institutional racism' to 'identify policy and administrative processes in the welfare state, which result in relatively adverse treatment of ethnic minorities'. Also, Dominelli (1991) argues that black people have been excluded from access to positive welfare resources, are low earners and are over-represented as subjects of the state's punitive measures. By analysing the British welfare state from a feminist and anti-racist perspective, Williams (1989) even describes the UK as a racially and patriarchally structured capitalism.

As the above discussion reveals, the main focuses of comparative social policy have been people's economic power and their financial relationships with other social institutions and racial groups. In Ginsburg's (1992, p 23) words, Esping-Andersen's approach is 'a quantitative approach to a class analysis of comparative social policy'. Its stress on the importance of economic power makes the levels of unemployment benefits and public assistance the main components of human well-being, while the key solutions to human problems are wealth redistribution and economic empowerment, through which a person can be liberated from financial constraints and gain freedom of choice in the market. As a result of this approach, people's social and psychological well-being has been marginalised or treated as a by-product of economic empowerment. Given the domination of economic factors, the economic relationships between various social institutions (the family, voluntary organisations, and government) also become the main concern of comparative welfare studies.

In addition to the dimensions of class, gender and race, a person's social and psychological condition in a welfare system should be studied, including human relationships, human learning and development, and social and political participation. These are the key elements of human dignity proposed by this study. We can better understand people's social and economic position in a welfare state through their interactions with various types of welfare services. Also, we can assess the performance of different welfare systems by comparing their services for welfare recipients. In short, the dignity of welfare recipients will be assessed from an economic, social and psychological perspective, while the performance of a welfare system will be evaluated by the impact of its provisions on key elements of human dignity.

Evidence shows that the different criteria used for comparing welfare systems lead to different conclusions. For example, the Swedish model has been regarded as the most effective system in meeting human needs (Doyal and Gough, 1991), as well as the classic example of a social democratic welfare regime. On the other hand, by assessing the Swedish government's active labour policy based on economic criteria such as the productivity of job seekers, the allocation of labour, direct displacement and wage pressure, Calmfors et al (2001, p 113) conclude that the labour market policy followed in Sweden in the 1990s was not efficient. They further stress that 'ALMPs [active labour market policies] should not be used as a means to renew unemployment benefit eligibility' (2001, p 61). Based on a focus on economic benefits, Holmlund (2003, p 45) makes similar comments: 'There is fairly clear evidence that subsidized employment has had large crowding-out effects....The experiences of youth programmes are largely negative: it has been difficult to find positive effects on earnings or employment'. Furthermore, Swedish unemployment insurance has been criticised for reducing unemployed workers' incentives to search for a new job and making them more reluctant to accept low-paid jobs. In addition, the International Monetary Fund even criticises Swedish welfare policies, such as the high level of taxation and high replacement ratios for social benefits, for discouraging work effort in the short term and lowering the effective supply of labour in the long term. It therefore suggests that 'A concerted effort to address these issues is necessary to raise sustainable long-term growth' (IMF, 2003).

The earlier studies evaluate the performance of Swedish welfare practices from a free-market perspective. Their results are one-sided and misleading because the Swedish government's social objectives for social protection, equality and full employment have been devalued. As Kvist (2001, p 9) points out: 'The Nordic activation strategy demonstrates that activation should not be related solely to economic factors such as increasing ordinary employment *per se*. It should also be linked to the broader goal of providing people with a meaning to their life through participation in daily activities'. Similarly, considering the impact of the UK's employment policy, Holmlund (1997, p 20) emphasises that policy prescriptions should recognise the objectives of unemployment insurance: 'Simply looking at changes in unemployment is not sufficient to gauge the welfare effects of UK policies'. Thus, a welfare system should be assessed by its impact on the social, economic and psychological well-being of welfare recipients. Based on this consideration, we use dignity as a framework for evaluating the welfare performance of four welfare systems. By doing so, we recognise that humans are social beings whose dignity can only be enhanced through positive social relationships, good opportunities for learning and development, and participation in social and political activities.

Apart from the domination of economic factors, Walker and Wong (1996) point out another weakness of current comparative social policy, namely, 'the Western construction of the welfare state'. This means that the welfare state has been defined as a capitalist–democratic project based on the experiences of western European countries, excluding countries with different social and economic institutions:

> Welfare states have been constructed as a capitalist–democratic project: they are commonly referred to as "welfare capitalist states" or "welfare capitalism". Those societies without either one or both of the supposed core institutions – a capitalist economy and a western parliamentary democracy – are effectively excluded from what is an exclusive club of mainly OECD members that are labelled, both popularly and scientifically, "welfare states". (Walker and Wong, 1996, p 69)

Thus, it is important to study the welfare experiences of non-European countries, analysing their welfare ideologies and practices. This type of study can enrich our understanding of other types of welfare systems. Against this background, the present study compares the recipients of unemployment benefit in four economies: two in Europe (the UK and Sweden) and two in Asia (China and Hong Kong).

To summarise: dignity has been widely viewed as the highest value of human society as well as the 'worthiest goal for a political and social movement' (Klein, 1998). The Universal Declaration of Human

Rights clearly states: 'All human beings are born free and equal in dignity and rights' (United Nations, 1948). As the meaning and context of human dignity have not been clearly defined, both supporters and opponents of 'workfare' have used it to justify their positions. Therefore, it is urgent to explore the concept of dignity so that it can be used to evaluate the actual impact of 'welfare-to-work' programmes in various welfare systems. As Miguel (2002) points out, 'the recognition of the concept of human dignity is useful in order to permit a civilised way of life'. In short, based on a clear concept of human dignity, the welfare actions of a country can be judged by the extent to which the dignity of the poor is safeguarded. Apart from this, dignity can be an alternative framework for classifying welfare systems, which are currently mainly assessed from the perspectives of class, gender and race. By using dignity as an alternative approach to welfare evaluation, welfare recipients will be treated from a holistic perspective, and their physical, social and psychological conditions in a welfare system will be taken into account. In addition, by comparing the effects on dignity of different welfare systems, we are able to identify which welfare initiatives have most enhanced or suppressed the dignity of welfare recipients. This provides a direction for future social policies that can enhance human dignity.

This present study consists of three parts. Part One (Chapters One to Three) introduces the background and rationale of the study, examining the concept of human dignity and developing key areas for assessing the dignity of unemployed persons. Part Two (Chapters Four to Seven) deals with the cases of China, Hong Kong, the UK and Sweden, investigating their welfare measures in relation to human dignity. Part Three (Chapters Eight and Nine) compares the dignity of unemployment benefit recipients in the four welfare systems. Finally, an alternative method of classifying welfare systems centred on human dignity is proposed, and the relationship between human dignity and welfare arrangements discussed.

TWO

Rationality, sociability and human dignity

As illustrated in Chapter One, since the concept of human dignity is vague it is hard to judge whether some welfare practices enhance or suppress the dignity of welfare recipients. Yet some governments cite dignity as a moral justification for regulating the behaviour of unemployed persons. Thus it is essential to explore the concept of dignity in order to assess the impact of current welfare measures on recipients. The exploration of human dignity should start from human nature. As Muzaffar asks, 'How can one talk of the rights of the human being without a more profound understanding of the human being him [her] self?' (quoted in Goolam, 2001). After an examination of the interaction between cognitive capacities and the social world, it is suggested that our worth as human beings resides in our possession of rational and social capacities striving for autonomy and mutuality. In meeting the needs of citizens, a society has to provide them with the necessary conditions for facilitating their autonomy and for developing their social relationships.

Human rationality and sociability

Dignity reflects the worth of human beings (Margalit, 1996). It is from this that we derive our capacity for autonomy and mutuality. Belief in human worth is shared by both western and eastern systems of thought. In Judaeo-Christian thought, the value of humans is derived from their being uniquely created in the divine image. Liberty is intrinsic to human dignity (Novak, 1998). A person has 'a capacity for insight and choice and an independent existence as a locus of responsibility' (1998). Moreover, Thomas Aquinas claimed that human beings have a capacity for and an orientation to a metaphysical knowledge of reality (Farrelly, 2003). In China, Confucius saw 'human nature as tending toward goodness' (Fu, 1991). 'Jen', the highest moral standard of humans, is a 'man's inner tendency and that is within man's ability to practice "jen"' (Fu, 1991). Mencius, an influential follower of Confucianism, further argued that human nature (hsing) comes from 'birth' or 'to be born with' (sheing). 'Hsing' consists of four innate and proper human aspirations: inter-human affection, righteousness, propriety and discernment of right and wrong (Hang, 1994). Thus, the Confucian school sees people as possessing inner capacities that allow them to make judgements and to pursue a moral life. Compared with other species, humans have 'unique neural capacities' that are expressed in their body structure:

> Human consciousness involves both the extended capacity of the modern neo-cortex in particular as well as profoundly developed pro-typical structures of the brain stem. But the human brain is unique, in part, because it has a million billion synaptic connections, making it one of the most densely connected network systems among natural and fabricated systems found on earth. (Word I.Q. Com, 2004)

This special physical design is associated with the operation of human rationality. Human beings can develop critical thinking, including the 'manipulation of information, as when we form concepts, engage in problem solving, reason and make decisions' (Word I.Q. Com, 2004). Because they possess 'purpose and agency, self-consciousness and will', humans are 'both objects of nature and subjects that can, to some extent at least, shape our own fate' (Malik, 2002a). In short, as rational beings, humans can make decisions and exercise choice to pursue personal or social objectives. Kant (1964, p 64) stresses the importance of rational capacities to the direction of our life: 'reason has been imparted to us as a practical power – that is, as one which is to have influence on the *will*; its true function must be to produce a *will* which is good, not as a means to some further end, but in itself; and for this function reason was absolutely necessary in a world where nature, in distributing her aptitudes, has everywhere else gone to world in a purposive manner'.

Humans' inner capacities also form the basis of social interactions. The ability to remember faces is essential to communication and to the establishment of social relationships, especially the attachment between children and parents. Researchers have found that humans can recognise patterns and images 'so much better than computers'. This is because the human brain and its neurons 'employ oscillatory memory systems, systems where the individual components can oscillate or freely change between states. In contrast, digital computer memories operate on a binary number system (1 or 0)' (Medical.Net, 2004).

Moreover, humans possess capacities for symbolic communication. After studying the behaviour of chimpanzees, Jacobs (2004) points out:

> We have the cognitive capacity to realize that communication can alter the behaviour of others at an age before we can utter one word sentences.... In humans the capacity for symbolic communication has evolved to surpass the level of this capacity in our ape cousins. Our reasons for and use of symbolic communication is far greater and more diverse than in the apes, to the best of our knowledge.

However, an individual's possession of social and rational capacities, together with a physical body, is not enough for a truly human life. This is because only through a process of socialisation can we find identities and be stimulated to further develop our innate capacities. The interdependence between a person's development and his or her society was stressed by Confucianism more than two thousand years ago. Both Confucius and Mencius said that we are built for helping others to attain their perfect state. Confucius pointed out, 'A benevolent man helps others to take their stand insofar as he himself wishes to take his stand, and gets others there insofar as he himself wishes to get there' (Fu, 1991). He further claimed that every human being was potentially our teacher from whom we learned both positive and negative examples: 'Even when walking in the company of two others, I am bound to be able to learn from them. The good points of the one I copy; the bad points of the other I correct in myself' (Tu, 1993, p 41). Modern psychologists also agree that people need to be stimulated by their environment. From Piaget's and Vygotsky's point of view, human knowledge is produced 'only through active, dynamic engagement with the environment' (Richardson, 2000, p 201). In short, human autonomy is associated with social interaction, which is 'a long, gradual process involving multiple changes and interactions' (Richardson, 2000, p 10).

The importance of human relationships to the development of a person's intrinsic rational and social capacities has been evident from studies in various disciplines.

Development and interactive systems

From the perspective of psychology, adults are necessary for infants' communicative development. Richardson (2000, p 206) explains:

If humans did not have the perceptual capability to extract social information in addition to perceiving the physicality of events there would be no such thing as socialisation through internalisation or negotiation. But it would be a mistake to focus on the abilities of the child alone ... socialisation requires sensitive contingent support, guidance and collaboration on joint enterprises, that is, context-controlled scaffolding, and this depends upon the ability of the scaffolder to extract social information from the invariances specifying the developmental status that the child brings to each situation. Thus it is necessary that components, adult and child, in the interactive system by which education, development and socialisation occur are capable of extracting invariances related to the mental and social capacities of each other.

The inborn ability to extract information is just a condition for human development; it is only through the involvement of significant others in the form of continual support and feedback that human development can actually be achieved.

Reasoning power and nurture

Studies from behavioural genetics show that human beings' reasoning power is based on 'nature and nurture':

Heritability of much behaviour is in the range of 30 percent (beliefs, schizophrenia), 40 percent (specific cognitive abilities, personality, delinquency), and occasionally 50 percent (IQ). This means that one-third to one-half of the variance for most behaviour is due to genetic differences among individuals. The same results thus indicate that the majority of the variance for most behaviour is due to non-genetic factors, the environment. (Plomin, 1990, pp 116–17)

As Plomin (1990, p 144) concludes, 'behavioural genetic research clearly demonstrates that both nature and nurture are important in human development'. This means that rational capacities are not static; they can be enhanced or constrained by the conditions of the social world.

Attachment and psychological well-being

The psychological health of humans is shaped by the quality of care and support they receive. Bowlby (1953, p 13) pointed out that the development of the character and mental health of children is influenced by the nature of their interactions with their mothers. What is believed to be essential for mental health is that an infant and young child should experience a warm, intimate, and continuous relationship with its mother (or permanent mother-substitute – one person who steadily 'mothers' a child) in which both find satisfaction and enjoyment.

A child who does not have such a relationship is called 'maternally deprived'. The ill effects of deprivation are associated with various types of behavioural and psychological problems. First, the consequences of maternal deprivation in an infant from six to twelve months old are withdrawal from strangers, backwardness in activities, lack of sleep and appetite, weight loss and susceptibility to infection. Second, with prolonged deprivation in the second year, a child's ability to form and maintain close and mutually satisfying affectional ties will be impaired. Third, prolonged and severe deprivation from the first year to the third will lead to 'very adverse effects of both intellectual and personality functioning' (Bowlby, 1953, p 224). As he observed (1953, p 39), 'Such children appear emotionally withdrawn and isolated. They fail to develop loving ties with other children or with adults and consequently have no friendships worth the name.' Further, he used Dr Goldfarb's study of 14,000 neglected and delinquent children in Barcelona to illustrate the close relationship between maternal deprivation and the level of intelligence. He noticed

> feeble and difficult attention due to [a child's] great instability; very slight sense of objective realities, overflowing imagination and absolute lack of critical ability; incapacity for strict abstraction and logical reasoning; noteworthy backwardness in the development of language.... (quoted in Bowlby, 1953, p 52)

The future adult lives of children are also affected by their relationships with parents:

> A young child's experience of an encouraging, supportive and co-operative mother, and a little later father, gives him a sense of worth, a belief in the helpfulness of others, and a

favourable model on which to build future relationships. Furthermore, by enabling him to explore his environment with confidence and to deal with it effectively, such experience also promotes his sense of competence. Thenceforward, provided family relationships continue favourable, not only do these early patterns of thought, feeling and behaviour persist, but personality becomes increasingly structured to operate in moderately controlled and resilient ways, and increasingly capable of continuing so despite adverse circumstances. (Bowlby, 1969, p 378)

The attachment theory clearly shows that the essence of a healthy social environment is intimate and warm relationships, which are the basis of humans' social and intellectual development. Again, it is confirmed that a person's intrinsic capacities can be realised only in interactive and supportive social processes. On the other hand, a person's reasoning power will be suppressed and his psychological health will suffer in an adverse social world with few personal contacts and without a sense of security. In short, attachment to significant others is a human need, and interdependent relationships are fundamental to our social and psychological health.

To summarise, humans are physically designed to be communicative and to develop a social life. Moreover, external stimulations and social support are the foundation of our self-identities and psychological health. Social interaction is also essential to the exploration of our rational ability.

Thus, our unique rationality and sociability are intrinsic to our humanity. Philosophers from both East and West have long observed these human qualities. Some people, however, are sceptical about the existence of these inner capacities. Farrelly (2003) points out that the use of philosophical foundations for moral education and character development may encounter serious objections because there is 'scepticism regarding our capacity to know with any degree of assurance reality as it is'. After analysing the studies of developmental psychologist Jean Piaget and other American psychologists on cognitive development, he concludes:

Those who, in accordance with the analytic-synthetic distinction, deny any knowledge of necessity in nature that is objectively based cannot account for the child's development into the concrete operatory period, nor, for that matter, for science itself. And those who deny man's knowledge of reality as being, in continuity with Thomas's understanding of this, cannot explain the pre-adolescent's enlargement of knowledge or the distinctive structure of his knowledge, shown both in his or her primitive scientific approach and in his or her value orientation and knowledge. The development of these insights can help show the human orientation to, and capacity for, knowledge of being on which metaphysics is based. (Farrelly, 2003)

Thus, modern scientific research findings have confirmed philosophical arguments on the nature of human beings made by eastern and western philosophers more than one thousand years ago. The human capacity for autonomy and mutuality implies that welfare policies should take account of these characteristics so that the social, psychological and cognitive development of human beings can be truly realised.

The uniqueness of social nature

Kant believed that the possession of autonomy is 'the ground of the dignity of human nature and of every rational nature' (Kant, 1964, p 103). Because of Kant's argument, autonomy has now been widely recognised as a fundamental capacity. For example, by exploring a theory of human need, Doyal and Gough (1991, p 54) argue that physical survival and personal autonomy are basic human needs so that they 'must be satisfied to some degree before actors can effectively participate in their form of life to achieve any other valued goods'. As Malik (2002b) points out, 'The unique character of human universals arises out of the existence of humans as rational, social beings with the power to act as political subjects – with the power, in other words, to transform themselves and their societies through reasoned dialogue and activity'.

The main focus of this account of human dignity is on the person as a self-directed entity with an autonomous capacity to develop his or her life following his or her reasons and motives. Little has been mentioned about a person's innate capacities for socialisation, and the interaction between human relationships and the development of rationality. Although he stressed our duty towards other persons, Kant did not consider human relationships essential to a person's dignity. However, Confucianism holds that humans should be understood 'within the context of a totality constituted of relations between human beings imbued with a sense of orderly beauty or a sense of harmony' (Shen, 2003). Confucius put human relations at the highest position of morality, believing that the harmonisation of relationships brought self-respect and the full development of one's abilities:

> A man who can carry out five virtues leads a life of jen.... They are earnestness, consideration for others, trustworthiness, diligence and generosity. If you are earnest, you will never meet with want of respect. If you are considerate to others, you will win the heart of the people. If you are diligent, you will be successful in your undertakings. If you are generous, you will find plenty of men who are willing to serve you. (Confucius, quoted in Shen, 2003)

Clearly, to achieve 'jen', the ultimate goal of being human, a person has to use his or her rationality to maintain a positive social relationship. Good human relationships are the basis of psychological well-being as well as the foundation for fulfilling one's personal objectives. As the argument earlier shows, the development of rational capacity has to go through a process of human interactions. Thus it is hard for autonomy to exist in a social vacuum. According to Mead, 'What goes to make up the organised self is the organisation of the attitudes which are common to the group. A person is a personality because he belongs to a community, because he takes over the institutions of that community into his own conduct' (quoted in Post, 2000, p 11). In short, human nature is sociability and we are born into the world in the relational contexts with our parents and the social world (Shen, 2003).

Human beings' social nature is the basis of their mutuality and autonomy. A person has special relationships with his social networks and the wider human society.

Long-term caring relationships

Unlike some animals which are able to take care of themselves with inborn survival capacities, children need a long and intensive period of care from significant others. As illustrated earlier, through intimate caring relationships children can develop self-identities, learn social skills, get basic materials for survival and maintain social support for maintaining psychological health. The caring relationship is also reciprocal. Very often, older people need to receive social and financial support from significant others, especially from their children. Thus the life cycle of human beings is a cycle of caring through which humans can survive and maintain social and psychological well-being.

Lifelong learning

Like caring, learning is a lifelong process involving both formal and informal education. Through socialisation, people obtain the social skills they need to lead a social and cultural life. In economically developed societies, formal education is the key to the professional knowledge and technical skills necessary for pursuing a career. In short, our rational capacity can be developed and social life enhanced through learning.

Interpersonal and institutional relationships

As social beings, people need to establish social ties with both informal and formal networks in order to obtain psychological support and goods and services for meeting physical needs. To Confucius, the sum of relationships and each relationship contributed to 'the development and overall constitution of the self' (Tu, 1982). Within informal networks, people are engaged in reciprocity. They have to take care of family members and provide support for significant others such as parents, children and friends. Within formal institutions, they have to fulfil civil and legal obligations by paying tax and participating in elections. Because of the interdependent relationship between the individual and society, people have rights as well as duties. Argyle (1991, p 147) argues that 'human nature is cooperative . . . culturally universal, partly innate, the result of evolution'. The interrelationship between individuals and social institutions not only meets our basic human needs but also enriches our social and cultural life. It is through these social relationships that humans can achieve development, create culture and advance civilisation.

Thus, the value of human beings also centres on our interdependency and reciprocity. According to Mendes (2000), the core of human dignity is 'the ability of human kind to *collectively* understand compassion and *collectively* understand the need for justice to remedy unnecessary suffering'. This means that humans have the intrinsic capacity to live collectively, pursuing a just society. To Confucius, the foundation of '*jen*' was love, which entails at the very least establishing 'reasonable, harmonious interactions with others' (Lin, 1988, p 122). In short, humans' communicative power and their reliance on the social world for psychological security, for developing identity, and for exploring rational capacity, all form a basis for pursuing a common life and for developing interdependent human relationships. In this study, by 'mutuality' we mean the interdependent and supportive relationship of humans through which we satisfy our physical and psychological needs and also develop our rational capacities.

Conclusion

This chapter argues that the dignity of humans resides in our possession of intrinsic capacities which strive for autonomy and mutuality. Mencius stressed that human nature is the combination of basic 'humanness' and 'The dignity of humans will be suppressed if such capacities cannot be developed in the social world through interdependent and supportive human relationships.' As Confucius pointed out, an interrelationship exists in all levels of society, from the individual, through the family and state, to the whole world. A person's humanity is achieved only with and through others (Chung, 2004). Human striving for autonomy and mutuality implies that a favourable environment should be created to achieve human dignity. To Kant, respect was the most appropriate response to the rationality of humans. This means that we should not treat other people as a means but as an end, so that they can develop their potential. Also, our social nature should be realised through 'social participation'. Social participation is about the fulfilment of one's caring duties and the enhancement of our social relationships. To be human is to utilise innate human capacities for achieving autonomy and mutuality. The suppression of human autonomy degrades people to the status of 'a normal animal' or even 'things'. The elimination of mutuality blocks the development of rationality and damages self-identity. Because of the intrinsic capacities of humans, it is the duty of our social world (including ourselves and social institutions) to provide a supportive environment to meet humans' developmental needs. The achievements of a welfare state should be fundamentally judged from this perspective.

THREE

Respect, social participation and four welfare states

In Chapter Two it was argued that human dignity derives from the innate human capacity for autonomy and mutuality. This raises the question: 'What should be done in order to promote autonomy and mutuality?' As far as the rationality of humans is concerned, Kant's answer – respect – is an appropriate response. As for the sociability of humans, social participation is the means to establish relationships with significant others and to be integrated into social and political life. This chapter first discusses the key factors by reference to which the extent of respect and social participation in a society can be effectively assessed. It then goes on to justify the choice of China, Hong Kong, the UK and Sweden as case studies in which the dignity of unemployed workers is compared.

Respect and social participation

Respect and social participation are crucial to promoting human autonomy and mutuality. Downie and Telfer (1969, p 16) emphasise that we have to respect a person for 'those features which make him what he is as a person and which, when developed, constitute his flourishing'. For Kant, respect is specifically associated with the rationality of humans. He (1964, p 105) points out that 'The principle "So act in relation to every rational being (both to yourself and to others) that he may at the same time count in your maxim as an end in himself" is thus at the bottom the same as the principle'. According to Sullivan (1989, p 78), for Kant '[r]espect is an attitude due equally to every person, simply because each is a person, a rational being capable of self-determination, regardless of social position, occupational role, learning, wealth, or any other special qualities he or she may or may not possess'. In other words, a person should be treated as an equal and a capable individual. Also, we should not pursue our own interests at the expense of others. Instead, it is our duty to help develop the rational capacity of other people. Thus, equal treatment and rational development are the logical working out of this notion of respect.

Social participation is a means to develop the social capacity of humans. It is a process through which people utilise their sociability to fulfil social roles, and establish essential relationships with significant others as well as social and political institutions, being sufficiently integrated into the social world. In short, social participation recognises the interdependence of human beings, especially a person's need for recognition and support for one's social and psychological well-being. That is, people make themselves appropriate to their environment; and their environment in turn contributes to their self-attainment or self-accomplishment. This is the highest degree of social integration, which is close to Confucius's ideas on 'da tong' (the Great Harmony):

> ... the elders having a happy ending, the youths having enough businesses to do, the young children having been well nurtured, and all the old men without wives, old women without husbands, old people without children, young children without parents having been taken good care of. (Wang, 1998)

The 'da tong' society, which provides a satisfying life for all members, needs contributions and commitment from individuals and all types of social and political institutions. Nevertheless, the state with legislative power should play a key role in making appropriate policies and promoting a supportive culture that can effectively create the conditions for human autonomy and mutuality. Thus, a welfare state should be evaluated for its contributions to the 'respect' and 'social participation' enjoyed by citizens. 'Respect' and 'social participation' provide benchmarks by which the promotion of human dignity in a society can be judged.

It is suggested that several factors can reflect the degree of respect in which a person is held and the extent of social participation in a welfare system.

Health for actions

To have good physical and psychological health is essential for a person to act rationally and to participate actively in the social world. Poor physical health will be a serious barrier to maximising a person's social life and learning. Also, people with poor mental health have difficulty in coping with their family and work duties. Thus, health is a crucial condition for people to be active in the social world and to maximise their potential.

As for social security provision, this implies that welfare recipients should be provided with sufficient resources to have a healthy diet and adequate psychological support to overcome worries, anxieties, low self-esteem, and depression. All of these psychological problems are barriers to a person acting rationally and leading a satisfying social life.

Fulfilling duties

For Kant, a person respects others by helping them to develop their rationality. As he stresses, 'the happiness of others is an end that is also a duty' (quoted in Long, 2004). To Confucius, the self comes to be what it is only in the context of family and society (Klemme, 1999). The self is also associated with duties that one has to fulfil. As Confucius put it, 'You yourself desire rank and standing; then help others get rank and standing. You want to turn your own merits to account, then help others turn theirs to account' (Lin, 1988, p 124). A person needs to fulfil 'his obligations and responsibilities as a member of the human community' in order to achieve the highest moral excellence (*sage*, a person who possesses the highest moral standards) proposed by Confucianism (Tu, 1993, p 43). An important task is 'the regulation of family' (Tu, 1993, p 40). This means that a person has to take care of one's family members at different stages of their lives. Confucius stressed that 'the ability to regulate relations within the family is founded on an individual's prior ability to cultivate his own life' (Lin, 1988, p 126). The fulfilment of family duties is practised not by the Chinese people but also by parents in the UK. A study by Kempson (1996, p 1) that examines 31 studies of the lives of poor families found that 'Parents are determined to provide the best food and clothing that they can for their children, even when it means going without themselves'. Another study (Farrell and O'Connor, 2004, p 4) investigating the impact of work on the lives of welfare recipients reported: 'Some parents used to go without a meal so that their child had more to eat.' It further points out, 'Children consistently remained every household's main priority both prior to, and following, the move into work'. Parents' caring commitments towards their children may be associated with a sense of meaning and pride which is essential to their psychological well-being. In this study, we are mainly concerned with whether unemployed parents have been provided with the conditions that enable them to meet their children's physical, social and educational needs.

Promoting social integration

As was illustrated in Chapter Two, human beings need attachment that provides them with a sense of belonging and security. With reference to social security provision, a recipient needs adequate resources in order to have some degree of social interaction with the social world, to lead a normal social life.

Like financial assistance, a positive social atmosphere directly affects the quality of social interactions. A positive image of welfare recipients can enhance social acceptance and maintain normal socialisation between unemployed persons and their fellow citizens. By contrast, negative welfare images produce suspicion and distrust. Thus, a welfare system's performance in promoting human integration can be assessed from both the levels of financial support provided and the image of welfare recipients presented.

Respecting humans as rational beings

In response to the rational nature of humans, it is the duty of a society to develop people's critical thinking, enhancing their knowledge and opportunities for self-determination.

Human learning

According to Kant, people have to develop their potential. 'It is a duty to cultivate the crude capacities of our nature, since it is by that cultivation that the animal is raised to man.' Education is the key to this goal: 'A human being can become human only through education' (Kant, quoted in Wood, 2003, p 40). Similarly, Confucianism holds that the life goal of human beings is the 'endless process of cultivating one's inborn nature' (Lin, 1988, p 125). In short, the dignity of human beings is advanced through a process of cultivation through education. Kant further explains:

> It is a duty of man to cultivate his natural powers (of the spirit, of the mind, and of the body) as means to all kinds of possible ends. Man owes it to himself (as an intelligence) not to let his natural predispositions and capacities (which his reason can use someday) remain unused, and not to leave them, as it were, to rust.… It is a command of morally-practical reason and a duty of man to himself to build up his capacities (one more than another according to the

variety of his ends), and to be a man fit (in a pragmatic
sense) for the end of his existence.... (Long, 2004)

In response to the development of human rationality, a welfare state
has to develop effective measures to enrich recipients' knowledge and
enhance their skills.

Self-determination

The direction of human rationality is towards autonomy. Autonomy
is characterised as 'a sense of competence, control and achievement'
(Granerud and Severinsson, 2003, p 610). According to Kant (2004),
'pure reason constitutes the act of free will', and 'only the act of choice
in the voluntary process can be called free'. In other words, freedom is
'independence of the compulsory will of another' (Long, 2004). Kant's
concept of freedom recognises the rights and ability of critical persons
to manage their lives. In short, freedom gives people a sense of control
over their lives. This also imposes restrictions on other humans and
social institutions attempting to suppress people's freedom for the
benefits of particular social groups. In response to the need for learning
and for exercising freedom of choice, social institutions have to provide
sound justifications for controlling behaviour. To respect people's
autonomy is to grant them 'at least the opportunity to make their
crucial life-affecting choices in a rational manner' (Hill, 1991, p 48).
This means that any control over people's behaviour should be based
on benefits to them, in order to enhance their rationality and mutuality.
  In the light of human self-determination, a welfare system needs to
provide opportunities for welfare recipients to manage their own lives.
This is to maximise their rationality. As Hill (1991, p 47) stresses, a
person should have 'a right to make certain decisions for himself or
herself without undue interference from others'. This is fundamental
to humans as 'purposive moral agents'. That is, human beings undertake
actions that are based on sound and substantive reasons. By contrast,
humans will be dehumanised if they are reduced to 'mere choosers of
options, individuals and isolated pursuers of wants and desires often
uncritically construed as needs' (Stetson, 1998, p 14). According to
Post (2000, p 7), democracy requires a social and institutional structure
that empowers us 'to choose our destiny, to decide our fate, to make
ourselves into what we wish to be. That is what self-determination
means'. In short, a welfare system needs to maximise the freedom of
welfare recipients by providing them with opportunities to participate
in welfare polices and by empowering them to manage their lives.

Equal value

All human beings are equal because of the possession of intrinsic capacities leading to autonomy and mutuality. Human dignity is therefore a justification for equal treatment. As Kant (2004) points out, people can judge themselves equal to others. Equal value is also the 'basis of the equal moral rights that all persons have' (Kapor-Stanulovic, 2003, p 4). In short, equality is the recognition of our human capacities that entitle us to 'respect' and to 'social participation' regardless of gender, class and race. The equal status of human beings also imposes restrictions on the power of a government as well as providing it with a clear direction in the treatment of poor citizens. This means that a welfare system has to treat welfare recipients and non-recipients, disabled clients and healthy clients with dignity and respect. Acceptance should also be promoted as a facet of a welfare system; otherwise, human beings will be devalued by stigma, which 'deprives people of their dignity and interferes with their full participation in society' (Granerud and Severinsson, 2003, p 603). The consequences of branding are rejection, de-individualisation and devaluation of self-esteem (Granerud and Severinsson, 2003). Margalit (1996, p 1) points out that 'A decent society is one whose institutions do not humiliate people'. Humiliation is 'the rejection of a person from the human commonwealth and the loss of basic control' (1996, p 3). Therefore, a welfare system has to make social integration its objective, which is built in a society with trust and acceptance.

Assessing human dignity

In recognition of the human quest for autonomy and mutuality, a government has to provide welfare recipients with opportunities and resources that promote 'respect' and 'social participation' in society. It is suggested that the following items are essential to enhancing human dignity; they also form the basis for evaluating and comparing the extent of human dignity in different welfare systems.

As Table 3.1 shows, the achievement of a welfare state can be assessed in terms of its commitment to human dignity. The performance of welfare systems in enhancing 'autonomy' and 'mutuality' reveals whether our rational and social nature has been respected and developed. This is about human development. The extent of equal treatment indicates the position of deprived groups in a society. This is about equality among different human groups. With the interactions of economic and social factors, the study of human beings can show us a country's

Table 3.1: Key areas for achieving autonomy and mutuality

Policy objectives	Areas of comparison	Achieving autonomy	Mutuality
Physical and psychological well-being	Financial assistance for buying daily necessities for maintaining physical health.		
	Health care for physical functioning.		
	Psychological support for mental health.		
	Training of welfare workers and the administration of a welfare system which deals with the psychological needs of recipients.		
Fulfilling caring duties	Support for parents to fulfil duties of care in health, education and social activities.		
Social integration	Support for recipients to participate in social and cultural life.		
	Welfare images of recipients presented by the state.		
Human learning	Government's ideas about human learning.		
	Support and opportunities for recipients' learning and developing skills.		
Self-determination	Opportunities and extent to which recipients are able to participate in policy making.		
	The extent to which receiving benefits promotes self-determination.		
Equal value	Government's attitudes towards the value of different social groups.		
	Special programmes for meeting special needs of disadvantaged groups.		
	Equal treatment in terms of age, gender, race or class.		

construction of, and basic attitudes towards, human dignity. Thus, the study of welfare states helps illustrate the conditions and development of human dignity in different socio-economic systems. Finally, factors which enhance or suppress human dignity can be identified. This can provide a clear direction for establishing a welfare state focusing on human dignity.

Human dignity and four welfare systems

As Chapter One illustrates, welfare-to-work is a key current focus of social policy, and many governments argue that their welfare programmes can enhance the dignity of unemployed persons. Against this background, this study examines this argument by comparing the dignity of unemployed persons in four welfare systems: China, Hong Kong, the UK, and Sweden. Because unemployed persons are economically weak citizens, social policies towards unemployed persons can reveal whether a welfare system is truly serving the needs of different social groups. As the traditional concept of the welfare state is derived solely from the welfare experiences of western European countries, the study of Asian welfare systems can enrich our knowledge of social welfare. Therefore, the case studies of this project include two Asian and two European welfare systems with different socio-economic characteristics.

China

China describes its socio-economic system as 'socialism with a specifically Chinese character'. Since 1978 the forces of capitalism have been harnessed to accelerate its economic development and create wealth. From 1979 to 2003, China's annual gross national product (GNP) grew from ¥362.4 billion (£23.4 billion) to ¥11.69 trillion (£756 billion). Also, the average annual growth rate in household consumption was 7% in this period. Dietmar Nissen, the East Asian president of BASF, a huge chemical company, declared that 'the speed and scale of growth in China over the past 12 years is a miracle' (*Economist*, 2004). Wen Jiabao, the prime minister of China, says: 'The Chinese people have, on the whole, begun to lead a life of moderate prosperity' (*Xinhua News Agency*, 2004a). The adaptation of a market economy to Chinese socialism was pioneered by the former leader Deng Xiaoping (1984), who stressed that the Chinese economy needed foreign investment:

> The experience of the past thirty years has demonstrated that a closed door policy would hinder construction and inhibit development ... we have to invigorate the domestic economy and open it up to the outside world ... we can use [foreign investment] to accelerate our development.

This move also implies that China has moved from her socialist welfare system to a pro-market welfare state. Prior to the open-door policy, the Chinese Communist Party (CCP) had established socialism in China in 1949. As a consequence, the central government could decide what to produce, how to produce it and how to distribute welfare.

However, China's economic structure has changed rapidly following the open-door policy of 1978. Ideologically, the private market has been confirmed as the key to the future development of Chinese socialism. In 1992, the 'socialist market economic system' was clearly proclaimed as the national goal at the Fourteenth National Congress (NC). The market has become a key element in allocating resources under state macro control. In 2004, the NC even amended the constitution to protect private ownership by adding 'lawful private property is inviolable' (Chan, 2004). As Laurence Brahm comments (quoted in Chan, 2004), 'One interpretation is that China is no longer communist'. Thus, China is no longer a planned economy but a mixed economy under the administration of a highly centralised state.

Structurally, the private sector has been playing an important economic role. In 2003, there were 2.97 million private enterprises with a total capital of ¥336.07 billion (£21.7 billion). They contributed to half of China's annual economic growth. More importantly, the Chinese government has radically reformed the state-owned enterprises (SOEs) in order to make them more competitive. This is 'the single most important issue upon which China's economic future hinges' (Steinfeld, 1998, p 3). Previously, the SOEs were the 'commanding heights' of the planned economy, providing employment and social welfare benefits like housing, health care, childcare, retirement benefits, and disability insurance for the vast majority of urban workers. As a result of the reconstruction of SOEs, the number of laid-off and unemployed people has increased rapidly. The official *Social Blue Book 2002* reported that a total of 48.07 million workers were laid off between 1995 and 2000 (J. Chan, 2003a). The Chinese government has noticed that 'the old labour and social security system had become unadaptable to the requirements of economic and social development'. As a result, the Chinese government has made 'every effort to establish a sound social security system that corresponds with the socialist market economic system' (Information Office of the State Council, 2002). Against this background, the study of the Chinese government's welfare policies in response to large-scale unemployment can enhance our understanding of the nature of social policy in a new type of welfare system: the 'socialist-market welfare state'.

Hong Kong

Hong Kong has always been regarded as a paradise for capitalists (Woronoff, 1980) as well as the best example of the free market economy in the world (Friedman, 1982). It was ranked as the freest economy in the world for the eleventh successive year by the Heritage Foundation. As the Heritage Foundation (2005) explains, Hong Kong is 'a free port with no barriers to trade. It has simple procedures for starting enterprises, free entry of foreign capital and repatriation of earnings, and transparency, and operates under the rule of law'. After tremendous economic growth in the 1970s and 1980s, however, Hong Kong has had to face an increasing number of unemployed people because of the decline of her manufacturing industries. In response to this challenge, the Hong Kong government has reduced welfare benefits and introduced welfare-to-work measures. Accordingly, unemployed claimants must regularly meet with their welfare officers, do 'voluntary work', and participate in job training in order to be eligible for public assistance (Social Welfare Department, 1998). Thus, Hong Kong represents the welfare development of the world's freest economic system in response to economic recession and unemployment pressures.

The United Kingdom

The UK's welfare state, although one of the first in Europe, has been greatly reshaped by the NLG. Based on the ideology of the 'Third Way', Tony Blair, the British prime minister, called his government a 'welfare-to-work government', which has sought to 'attack unemployment and break the spiral of escalating spending on social security' (quoted in Finn, 1998, p 105). The NLG has based its welfare policies on four principles: 'an active, preventive welfare state; the centrality of work; the distribution of opportunities rather than income; and the balancing of rights and responsibilities' (Powell, 1999, p 15). Such welfare principles were clearly set out in the 1998 social security White Paper, *A new contract for welfare*, which states: 'The new welfare state should help and encourage people of working age to work where they are capable of doing so. The Government's aim is to rebuild the welfare state around work' (Department of Social Security, 1998, p 23). Accordingly, several 'New Deal' programmes were introduced to target different categories of welfare recipients. Unemployed young people are forced to take a subsidised job or receive training on pain of losing their entitlement to benefits. The study of the UK's welfare measures can reveal whether a work-oriented welfare state can safeguard the dignity of unemployed persons.

Sweden

Sweden has been described as a model for capitalist societies as well as the best example of a welfare state. Its welfare achievements were evident from studies measuring the level of social security assistance, the extent of coverage, the degree of decommodification (Esping-Andersen, 1990), and the extent to which human needs are satisfied (Doyal and Gough, 1991). The Swedish government has emphasised the use of government power to regulate business and labour policies in order to achieve full employment and equality. However, Sweden has faced 'the most severe macro-economic crisis since the 1930s' (Palme et al, 2002, p 329). As a result, it has experienced two important changes: a shift away from progressive tax rates – the main basis for income redistribution – and the abandonment of full employment as the primary goal of economic policy (Wennerberg, 1995). What Palme (2002) described as 'the tax reform of the century' occurred in the 1990s. Also, there were changes in the provision of social security, including a reduction in the level of benefits, the imposition of greater restrictions on applications procedures, the setting of higher criteria for claimants, and an increase in checks. Many municipalities aim to get claimants back into the labour market (Swedish National Board of Health and Welfare, 1999). As a result of these changes, the Swedish welfare state 'does not seem fully capable of protecting the most vulnerable groups in society' (Bernhardt, 2004, p 5). The impact of recent Swedish welfare policies on the dignity of unemployed recipients can be examined against the background of these welfare developments.

To conclude, the welfare policies of different welfare systems will have a variable impact on the dignity of welfare recipients. The four selected welfare systems have their unique social, political, and economic conditions. China has a mixed economy ruled by an authoritarian regime; Hong Kong has a free economy supervised by a government with a largely administrative function; the UK has an increasingly work-oriented welfare system run by a parliamentary democracy and currently ruled by the NLG; and Sweden has a collective welfare system dominated by the Swedish Social Democratic Party (SDP). By comparing these four welfare systems, we are able to understand the dignity of welfare recipients in different social, economic and political environments.

Part Two:
Case studies

FOUR

Hong Kong and human dignity

With a population of 6.81 million, Hong Kong is one of the most developed societies as well as the world's freest economy. As a former British colony and now as a special administrative region of China, Hong Kong has had a government that has consistently followed the principles of the free market. David Wilson (1987, p 13), a former colonial governor, claims that Hong Kong was 'the prime example of a free-trade economy'; while Tung Chee Hwa, the first Chief Executive (CE) of the Hong Kong Special Administrative Region (HKSAR), confirmed that 'we remain firmly committed to upholding our system of free enterprise and will adhere steadfastly to the philosophy of small government with prudent fiscal management' (Tung, 2000, p 16). Hong Kong's economic development is associated with its free market policies. The former Financial Secretary of the HKSAR points out: 'a free market will lead to optimal distribution of resources, promote economic growth and create employment opportunities' (Leung, 2003, para. 24). Hong Kong has experienced rapid economic growth since the 1970s; its average annual GDP growth rate was 5% between 1989 and 1997 (Abacci Atlas, 2004). The Hong Kong government has imposed several financial restrictions to minimise its role in the market and maximise the freedom of its economy. First, public expenditure is limited to 20% of Hong Kong's GDP. Second, the government aims to maintain a balanced budget. Third, the HKSAR has to accumulate fiscal reserves equal to 12 months' expenditure. Fourth, a low-rate and simple tax system has long been considered the key to Hong Kong's economic success.

Because of the above fiscal measures, social welfare development in Hong Kong has been restricted. In keeping with free market philosophy, Hong Kong workers have limited labour protection. Hong Kong is one of the few developed economies without a minimum wage. It was not until 2002 that a Mandatory Provident Fund was set up to provide some form of retirement benefits. The scheme 'has consolidated the foundation of Hong Kong's capitalism by socializing and incorporating the whole working population in the market economy but has provided little protection for their old age' (C.K. Chan, 2003, p 123).

In recent years, Hong Kong has experienced an economic crisis as a result of the decline of its manufacturing industry, the Asian economic crisis, and the outbreak of the severe acute respiratory syndrome (SARS). Consequently, Hong Kong's unemployment rate reached a record high of 8.7% in 2003 (Labour Department, 2003). The former CE of HKSAR stressed that 'Unemployment is a prime concern of the community' (Tung, 2003, p 4). By using Hong Kong as a case study, this chapter explores how a free market economy responds to unemployment pressures, and assesses the impact of government policies on the dignity of unemployed workers.

The Hong Kong government's responses to unemployment

Unemployment has been the focus of Hong Kong government policies since the mid-1990s. Previously, Hong Kong experienced its golden age in the 1970s and 1980s, during which its unemployment rate was as low as 2% and its average annual GDP growth rate was as high as 5%. In addition, Hong Kong was ranked the world's eighth-largest trading entity; it also had the second highest per capita GDP in Asia, just below Japan's. However, Hong Kong's manufacturing industry declined rapidly following the open-door policy of China and increasing competition from other Asian countries such as Thailand, Singapore and Malaysia. From 1982 to 1994 Hong Kong's manufacturing workforce halved. The contribution of industry to Hong Kong's GDP also fell from 20% to 11% (Boulton, 1997).

In addition to the decline of manufacturing industry, Hong Kong's economy was hit by the Asian economic crisis in 1998. The former Financial Secretary pointed out:

> The impact of the Asian financial crisis is much more widespread and protracted for the whole region than anyone could have expected ... we are going through a painful economic adjustment period brought on largely by external factors. The high unemployment rate might remain with us for some time. Things are likely to get worse before they get better. We have to face up to this unpleasant reality. (Tsang, 1998)

Because of this negative economic environment, Hong Kong's GDP annual growth rate fell dramatically, from over 10% in 2000 to negative figures in 2001 (see Figure 4.1).

Figure 4.1: Hong Kong's gross domestic product 2000–04 (at constant 2000 market prices)

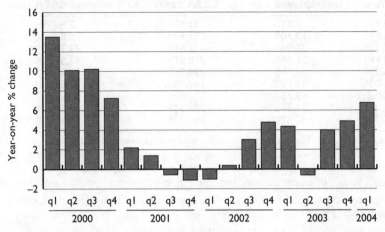

Note: Figures are the latest data released on 28 May 2004.
Source: Census and Statistics Department (2004a)

Facing economic uncertainties, some employers further downsized their workforce. As a consequence, Hong Kong's unemployment rate has risen rapidly. The unemployment rate in 2003 was 7.9%, the highest in the past two decades (Census and Statistics Department, 2004b).

Unlike in many developed economies which have unemployment insurance schemes, unemployed workers in Hong Kong can seek financial support only in the form of public assistance – the Comprehensive Social Security Assistance (CSSA) Scheme. CSSA is a means-tested and non-contributory scheme which is treated by the HKSAR as 'a temporary measure to assist recipients to tide over a period of financial hardship' (Social Welfare Department, 2004b, p 4).

Table 4.1: Unemployment and underemployment rate, 1995–2004

	Unemployment rate (%)	Underemployment rate (%)
1995	3.2	2.1
1996	2.8	1.6
1997	2.2	1.1
1998	4.7	2.5
1999	6.2	2.9
2000	4.9	2.8
2001	5.1	2.5
2002	7.3	3.0
2003	7.9	3.5
2004	6.9	3.5

Source: Financial Services and the Treasury Bureau (2004)

Table 4.2: Number of unemployed CSSA cases, 1992–June 2004

Year	Number of unemployed cases	Total CSSA cases	Unemployed cases as % of total CSSA cases
1992	2,957	81,975	3.6
1997	19,108	195,645	9.8
1998	31,942	232,819	13.7
1999	26,185	228,015	11.5
2000	23,250	228,263	10.2
2001	31,602	247,192	12.8
2002	43,237	271,893	15.9
2003	51,372	288,648	17.8
2004	47,821	293,306	16.3

Sources: Census and Statistics Department (2003); Social Welfare Department (2004c)

As a result of the poor employment market since 1998, the number of 'unemployed CSSA recipients' increased by 150%, from 19,108 in 1997 to 47,821 in June 2004.

In the past, the Hong Kong government believed that its main duties were to create a favourable business environment so that more jobs could be created. In keeping with this approach, the Hong Kong government showed little interest in 'active labour market policies'. However, in the late 1980s the previous colonial government responded to the restructuring of industry by establishing the Employee Retraining Board (ERB) in 1992 to help unemployed people aged over 30 to 'acquire new skills or enhance their employability to find alternative employment or re-enter the labour market' (Education and Manpower Bureau, 2004). Following the Asian economic crisis and the outbreak of SARS, and faced with the challenge of a large-scale and long-term unemployment trend, the Hong Kong government adopted 'a pro-active and pragmatic approach' to unemployment (Labour Department, 2003). Several strategies have been adopted to tackle unemployment. The first strategy, based on the Initiatives for Wider Economic Participation (IWEP), is to create temporary jobs in government departments such as the Agriculture, Fisheries and Conservation Department, the Food and Environmental Hygiene Department, and the Hospital Authority (LegCo Panel on Manpower, 2004). The second strategy is to provide training and assistance for vulnerable groups such as young people – for example, Youth Pre-employment Training Programme (YPTP), Youth Work Experience and Training Scheme (YWETS), and Youth Self-employment Support Scheme (YSSS) – and for middle-aged low-skilled workers – for example, Re-employment Training Programme for the Middle-Aged (RETPMA) and Incentive Allowance Scheme for Local Domestic Helpers (LDHs) (Economic and Employment Council, 2004). The third strategy is to strengthen the employment services of the Labour Department (details of these strategies are given in the following sections).

Despite rising demands for unemployment services, the Hong Kong government has to control public expenditure because revenues from land sales and corporate and personal taxation are declining. As well, the Hong Kong government always tries to maintain work incentives and suppress the dependency culture. Against this background, the HKSAR, following the examples of the US and Canada, adopted workfare as a new approach to social security provision. According to one senior government official, 'Our objective is to provide assistance to the vulnerable groups to enable, in the longer term, each individual and family to strive for self-reliance and self-improvement, and contribute positively to the development of the community' (Lau, 2000). As a result, actively seeking jobs and doing voluntary (that is, unpaid) work became the conditions for receiving CSSA. Also, the levels of CSSA benefits were reduced so that welfare recipients' living standards were expected to be lower than those of the working poor (Social Welfare Department, 1998). Against the background of these changes, this chapter examines the impact of the HKSAR policies on the dignity of unemployed persons.

The dignity of unemployed recipients

Meeting physical needs

Hong Kong does not have an official poverty line, and the levels of CSSA reflect a corresponding attitude on the part of the HKSAR towards the financial needs of citizens. In the absence of an unemployment insurance scheme, Hong Kong unemployed workers have to apply for CSSA. The key objective of Hong Kong's social security was 'to help those who are least able to help themselves' (Hong Kong Government, 1977, p 1) and CSSA is designed mainly for meeting people's basic needs. However, the levels of public assistance are always too low to provide recipients with a decent living. In the early 1980s, Chow (1982) suggested that Hong Kong's poverty line should be HK$400–499 (£27.38–34.15) a month for a single person and HK$2,000–2,199 (£136.89–159.51) a month for a family. But the government welfare benefits for a single person and a family of four were HK$350 (£23.96) and HK$965 (£66.05) respectively, only about half Chow's suggested level. C.K. Chan (1996) also reported that the average amount of public assistance for a four-member family from 1985 to 1990 was below 40% of a factory worker's monthly salary. After analysing the lifestyles of CSSA recipients, MacPherson (1994, p 9) concluded that 'the present rates of CSSA are inadequate for the maintenance of a decent minimum standard of living'. A respondent of the *Far Eastern Economic Review* (1995) also said that his welfare payment 'is not enough, not even for food'. Similarly, over 60% of unemployed CSSA recipients in Wong and Chua's (1998) study felt that the levels of benefits were too low to ensure a decent living.

Despite research studies in the 1980s and 1990s that consistently pointed out that the levels of public assistance were too low to meet basic needs, the HKSAR cut welfare payments at the end of the 1990s and again in the early 2000s. As a result, current levels of CSSA have already sunk below the 'basic needs approach (BNA)'. The BNA was established in 1996 by the British colonial administration in response to persistent pressures from political parties, community organisations and academics for a poverty line. The BNA is 'the amount of money given as financial assistance which enables a person to sustain a standard of living where that person's basic needs can be met' (Social Welfare Department, 1996, p 9). In 1998 the Hong Kong government claimed that, as the levels of CSSA were higher than the earnings of the poorest 25% of the workforce, a welfare cut was reasonable and necessary. According to the 1998 CSSA review, 'the levels of benefit should be kept down so that they are more in line with market wages for low-end jobs' (Social Welfare Department, 1998, p 23). As a result, the standard rates for single persons and four-member families were reduced. Moreover, special benefits for able-bodied recipients and their families, such as for removal expenses, spectacles, and long-term supplements for buying durable household items and clothes, were cancelled. Obviously, the HKSAR has scrapped the BNA as an objective measurement of the basic needs of recipients and has instead adopted a comparative approach based on the incomes of low-paid workers. This means that the basic survival needs of poor Hong Kong citizens cannot be guaranteed by the government.

Recently the Hong Kong government has cut the levels of CSSA benefits further, arguing that a fall in Social Security Assistance Index, a mechanism for annual adjustment of CSSA standard rates, prices because of deflation justified cutting CSSA payments by 11.1%. The cut has further pushed CSSA recipients towards a harsher life. After studying the life quality of CSSA recipients, the Hong Kong Caritas Community Development Service concludes that the recent cut in CSSA payments 'is negatively affecting the diets, health, social life and self-image of Hong Kong's elderly'. For example, one respondent of the study said, 'When I have no money, I live on congee (rice gruel) and salty fish that my neighbours give to me.' Another respondent even stressed, 'I eat two meals a day' and 'seldom cook rice because you need other dishes to go with it' (Catholic.org.hk, 2004).

As for medical care, CSSA recipients are exempted from medical costs at government clinics and hospitals. However, they cannot claim travelling expenses for treatment, nor could they obtain financial assistance for purchasing spectacles before 2005. The Hong Kong government completely ignored the importance of spectacles to health, especially for children, who badly need them to improve their eyesight for studies and social activities (C.K. Chan, 2002). Although the government, under the pressure of Legislative Council members and voluntary organisations, has promised to pay for glasses, payments are still subject to the discretion of welfare workers. This means that spectacles are still provided conditionally and recipients may have to undergo a complicated process in order to obtain them. The above evidence shows that the levels of Hong Kong's CSSA cannot provide the financial assistance poor unemployed persons need to maintain their health.

Meeting psychological needs

The Hong Kong government does not stress professional skills in handling CSSA cases. Staff members who are responsible for managing public assistance applications are not trained social workers or counselling professionals, but are required only to have completed secondary school and attended a four-day induction programme and a ten-day basic course (Social Welfare Department, 1996). In fact, the Hong Kong Social Welfare Department had already stated in the 1970s that 'professional expertise is not essential' in public assistance (Hong Kong Government 1979, p 21). Against this background, the staff of CSSA might not have adequate knowledge and sufficient skills for tackling applicants' problems. In this way, the needs of applicants 'are likely to be treated as financial needs only' (C.K. Chan, 1998, p 283). The Hong Kong Polytechnic University's study (1995) of the users of CSSA special grants reported that 7 out of 17 older people and 20 out of 29 families complained of the poor attitudes of their caseworkers. One of the respondents admitted that 'My impression was that the worker was unwilling to help me. It was like begging' (Hong Kong Polytechnic University, 1995, p 39). Also, home visits are a requirement of CSSA. A respondent pointed out that unexpected home visits not only threatened him but also put a lot of pressures on his family (Hong Kong Polytechnic University, 1995, p 39). Similarly, of 176 respondents of another study, 62% said the staff of the Social Welfare Department did not take any initiative in explaining to them the details of CSSA; 48% stressed the poor working attitudes of the staff concerned (*Ming Pao*, 2001b). The inadequate training and poor working attitudes of welfare staff have created a strongly stigmatising welfare system that has effectively deterred the needy from seeking public assistance. A 40-year-old unemployed man did not apply for CSSA and stole three pieces of bread from a restaurant. After being arrested, he said: 'Hong Kong people should be self-reliant, not live on CSSA' (*Ming Pao*, 2004e). Similarly, a 31-year-old unemployed man stole money from supermarkets because of poverty. According to the police, the man's self-esteem prevented him from seeking CSSA. His motivation in committing the crime was to make a living (*Ming Pao*, 2003a). More seriously, poor people were reported to prefer committing suicide to living on CSSA (*Ming Pao*, 2003d, 2004d). For example, Mr Lee pointed out that his wife strongly resisted seeking CSSA. She wanted to be self-reliant even though the whole family suffered starvation (*Ming Pao*, 2004d). Further, official figures showed that of a total of 1,025 cases of suicide in 2002, 48.7% were of unemployed persons (*Ming Pao*, 2003c). Hong Kong's suicide rate in 2003 was 17.6 deaths per 100,000 people, which is higher than that of the US in the same year (11 per 100, 000) (*Standard*, 2004). In short, Hong Kong's strongly stigmatising CSSA is associated with unemployed persons' crimes and suicides. Psychological pressures on human beings are being manipulated to reduce the pressure on public assistance.

Apart from assessing CSSA applications, staff of the Social Welfare Department now have to provide career counselling and enhance the employability of unemployed recipients based on the requirements of the Support for Self-reliance Scheme (SFS). However, without any professional qualifications in career guidance, it is unlikely that staff of the social security field units can effectively offer employment assistance. As nearly 90% of unemployed respondents agreed, 'unemployment is a very worrying issue to me' (Wong and Chua, 1998, p 19). Social security officers need social work and careers guidance training if they are to succeed in helping recipients to achieve self-reliance. Yet existing staff from both the Social Welfare Department and the Labour Department are 'unable to provide total care to the jobseekers, especially on their psychological needs' (Hong Kong Council of Social Service, 2001b). Wong and Chua (1998, p 32) suggest that the Hong Kong Social Welfare Department 'should consider the possibility of opening social work posts in social security field units for assessing the needs of CSSA recipients'.

To summarise, by changing the principle of CSSA from a 'basic needs' approach to one based on a 'comparison to market wages', the HKSAR has completely ignored basic necessities, which are essential to maintaining a healthy life. It no longer holds to the welfare principle of providing 'a baseline below which the standard rates should not be allowed to fall' (Social Welfare Department, 1996, p 9). That is evident from the exclusion of essential items such as long-term supplements, removal expenses, and rent deposits from CSSA, and making spectacles a discretionary item. In short, in setting the levels of welfare benefits the Hong Kong government's main concerns are the elimination of welfare dependency and the reduction in the number of CSSA recipients; it takes no account of the physical health of unemployed citizens. As a result, recipients, as reported in the studies earlier, cannot have adequate resources to buy enough food. In addition, staff with limited training in counselling and careers guidance are unable to address the psychological needs of unemployed recipients. More seriously, the stigma of CSSA is associated with crime and suicide. In spite of the Social Welfare Department's stress on a personalised service for recipients, the lack of professional qualifications of welfare staff and the strict requirements for job search and doing voluntary work create tension or even conflict between recipients and their caseworkers (see below). Therefore, the social and psychological needs of Hong Kong's unemployed persons have been institutionally suppressed by existing social security arrangements.

Fulfilling caring duties

Although Hong Kong provides nine years of free and universal basic education for children aged six to ten, unemployed parents receiving CSSA still find it difficult to fulfil their caring duties. After cancelling the long-term supplement, parents do not have the resources to buy clothes, shoes and furniture for their children. Also, they cannot give their children extra resources to participate in school activities or to lead a normal school life (MacPherson, 1994). A welfare organisation found that, among 81 CSSA children, 64% could not afford extra-curricular activities (Ming Pao, 2004a). More seriously, 40% of them even suffered from hunger as a result of inadequate resources. In response to the living conditions of these children, the Social Welfare Department claimed that CSSA provides only for the basic needs of recipients; social activities should be paid for by parents' savings, school arrangements and charity (Ming Pao, 2004a). The poor attitudes of welfare officers further discourage or even prevent recipients from obtaining necessary services, especially discretionary items such as spectacles. For example, Mrs Fung, a CSSA recipient, applied for money to send her son to kindergarten, but the worker told her, 'a full day is not approved but half-day'. Later, when she needed money to buy two school uniforms, the same worker said, 'Perhaps two uniforms will not be approved, but one' (Hong Kong Polytechnic University, 1995). Obviously, the welfare rights of recipients are conditional, 'regulated by the administrative procedures, the quality of welfare workers, the relationships between recipients and welfare staff, and the welfare expectations and behaviours of recipients themselves' (C. K. Chan, 1998, p 287). With limited resources, some parents may use illegal means to meet their children's needs. It was reported that an unemployed man planned to commit burglary in order to have the money to buy a New Year's present for his three-year-old son. However, he was arrested and jailed for 16 months (Ming Pao, 2004b). The case reveals the importance of a welfare system to provide adequate resources to help parents to meet the social needs of children. Unfortunately, the existing CSSA fails to help parents to fulfil their caring duties. As a result, poor children are suffering from a shortage of food and are deprived of a normal social life.

Social integration

The present CSSA unemployment benefit does not take applicants' social needs into account. After examining the expenditure patterns of CSSA recipients, MacPherson (1994, p 3) points out, 'In order to pay for food, households cut back on clothing, transport, household goods and social activity of all kinds'. Following benefit cuts in 1999 and 2003, unemployed recipients find it more difficult to spread meagre benefits to cover social gatherings or to buy special food to celebrate important festivals. For example, one respondent from a previously mentioned study said, 'It costs to visit relatives'. Another respondent explained, 'You are supposed to buy at least some fruit when you visit. I do not have money so I do not visit anymore' (Catholic.org.hk, 2004). It is evident that, because of financial constraints, unemployed recipients are unable to have normal social contact, but are excluded from social and cultural life.

In Hong Kong, the poor image of CSSA forms another barrier to recipients leading a normal community life. To some extent, such negative images are related to the Hong Kong government's welfare policies. First, as recipients are required to do 'voluntary work', they are subject to state control, unlike other, normal citizens. In Hong Kong some offenders are also sentenced to do community service. The requirement to undertake 'voluntary work' can be perceived as a punishment inflicted on those dependent on public benefits. Second, the government has occasionally released the names of people suspected of welfare abuse to the mass media. For example, the Social Welfare Department disclosed details of two exceptional fraud cases to the mass media, including of one person who lived in a luxurious housing area and another with nearly HK$2 million (£136,892) savings (*Ming Post*, 1998). Even though only 57 such cases were found among over 200,000 recipients, the Hong Kong Social Welfare Department still claimed that welfare fraud was so serious that 120 extra welfare workers had been employed to investigate it. In addition, a hotline was set up to encourage the public to report cases of abuse. These actions might create the impression that welfare abuse is serious, and that the unemployed are the largest group living on public benefits. A survey conducted by the Hong Kong Policy Viewers (1998) reported that the plurality (largest group) of respondents (34.9%) believed most CSSA recipients were unemployed persons. Actually, older people form the largest group of CSSA cases (about 70%); the unemployed make up only just over 10%. The survey further showed that nearly 60% of respondents supported a low level of assistance for CSSA unemployed cases for fear of creating a culture of dependency. More seriously, 23.6% of respondents thought that CSSA unemployed recipients were lazy. As the study concluded, the respondents' attitudes towards CSSA unemployed recipients had been shaped by the government's political propaganda against the unemployed.

Thus, CSSA recipients have been presented as dependent, prone to abuse the system, and helpless. Such negative images are likely to create tremendous psychological pressures on recipients on the one hand, and become a barrier to social inclusion on the other. One respondent of the above-mentioned study stressed, 'I fear they will look down on me and think I am after their money' (Catholic.org.hk, 2004). Similarly, Wong and Chua's study (1998) reported that 65% of respondents did not want others to know that they were receiving CSSA. Nearly 60% of their respondents believed people would look down on families receiving public money. The above studies suggest that two groups of citizens have been produced as a result of the Hong Kong government's policies: the self-reliant and hard-working on the one hand, and the dependent and lazy on the other. The former might be influenced by the government's discourse on welfare recipients and develop a bitter feeling towards the latter. The latter, being made dependent and helpless, will be associated with an inferior social role, separating themselves from the rest of the community. Such a divided social relationship was revealed by a CSSA respondent who declared, 'I am apathetic. No money, no passion. This is not my world; it is the world of those who have money' (Catholic.org.hk, 2004). Thus, the Hong Kong government's social security measures can hardly promote social integration and mutual acceptance between CSSA recipients and the general public. On the contrary, the measures create bitter feelings, suspicion, and distrust between recipients and non-recipients.

Human learning and development

The promotion of self-reliance, the enhancement of employability, and the tackling of youth unemployment have dominated Hong Kong's employment policies. For the unemployed on CSSA, the objectives of welfare reform are to avoid the 'emergence of a dependency culture' (Social Welfare Department, 1998, p 6) and to 'encourage and help those of working age on CSSA to re-enter the labour market and move towards self-reliance' (1998, p 9). The Hong Kong government has therefore adopted a new welfare-to-work approach to social security provision. As the Director of Social Welfare stresses, 'we are committed to build a caring community so that people can develop their potential and thereby to enable them to take responsibilities for themselves and to participate and contribute to our economic and social life without over-reliance on the provisions of the Government' (Social Welfare Department, 1998, p 2). Accordingly, unemployed recipients have to 'enroll in the SFS [Support for Self-reliance] Scheme as a condition of receiving assistance' (Social Welfare Department, 2004b, p 2). They also have to sign 'a Job Seeker's Undertaking to indicate that they fully understand their obligations to comply with all the requirements under the SFS Scheme' (2004b, p 3).

The SFS consists of three components: the Active Employment Assistance Programme, the Community Work Programme, and Disregarded Earnings.

The Active Employment Assistance (AEA) Programme

The AEA mainly provides information on job vacancies and career guidance for unemployed recipients. Recipients are also required to (Social Welfare Department, 2004a, p 7):

- apply for at least two jobs per fortnight;
- be present at the social security field unit every fortnight to develop and review action plans to find employment with the assistance of the staff;
- attend job interviews as and when arranged by the Social Welfare Department; and
- participate in the employment assistance programmes as and when arranged by the Social Welfare Department to enhance their employability.

The Community Work (CW) Programme (Social Welfare Department, 2004b)

A recipient has to do community work for a maximum of three days or 24 hours a week. The objectives of the CW are to help unemployed recipients to:

- develop a work habit;
- improve their employability;
- widen their social network;
- enhance their self-esteem;
- pave the way for, eventually, gainful employment; and
- contribute to society, in parallel with their job searching.

Disregarded Earnings (DE)

CSSA recipients can continue receiving assistance throughout their first month back in work. They are subsided to the level of CSSA assistance if their wages are too low to meet basic needs.

Apart from the above measures, the Social Welfare Department also uses non-governmental organisations (NGOs) to carry out employment related services. The contracted NGOs provide unemployed persons with individualised employment assistance services to 'enhance their employability as well as their ability to sustain employment' (Social Welfare Department, 2004d). It is expected that 27,000 unemployed people can be served over a four-year period. Details of these initiatives are as follows (LegCo Panel on Welfare Services, 2002):

The Special Job Attachment Programme (SJAP)

The SJAP is a two-year programme contracted out to 13 NGOs. The NGOs provide CSSA unemployed recipients and other non-CSSA unemployed persons with information on job searching, counselling, job attachment and follow-up support. During the job attachment period, participants can receive a monthly allowance of HK$1,805 (£123.55) for a maximum of six months. The SJAP was started in January 2001 and was extended for a further year in 2003.

The Intensive Employment Assistance Fund (IEAF)

The IEAF is a three-year programme launched in 2001. Unlike the SJAP, the IEAF does not have a job attachment period. IEAF projects provide services such as intensive counselling, work motivation training, job matching and placement as well as post-placement support.

The Ending Exclusion Project (EEP)

Started in March 2002, the EEP targets CSSA single-parent families whose youngest child is under 15 years old. The EEP consists of a voluntary employment assistance programme, childcare support and intensive counselling.

The Hong Kong Government has taken special initiatives to tackle the serious problem of youth unemployment:

Youth Pre-employment Training Programme (YPTP)

The YPTP targets young school leavers aged 15–19 with the aim of developing their 'job skills, working experience, and credentials, and to enhance their employability and competitiveness' (Labour Department, 2004a). The YPTP consists of two elements, 'modular training' and 'workplace attachment training'. Modular training aims at providing young people with essential basic vocational and interpersonal skills. It consists of courses such as 'Job Search and Interpersonal Skills Training', 'Leadership, Discipline and Team Building Training', 'Computer Application Training' and 'Job-Specific Skills Training'. 'Workplace Attachment Training' is provided for participants following the modular training. The duration of workplace attachment is one month, during which participants can receive a monthly training allowance of HK$4,000 (£273.78), while the employers who offer the placement receive a subsidy of HK$2,000 (£136.89) per trainee per month (Labour Department, 2003).

Youth Work Experience and Training Scheme (YWETS)

The target group of YWETS is young people aged 15–24. The aims of YWETS are to 'enhance the employability of young people, including work experience and job skills, and brighten their employment prospects, through the provision of on-the-job training' (Labour Department, 2004a).

YWETS has three parts. The *induction course* is a 40-hour course in which participants learn skills and knowledge of job search and interview, communication, work attitude, discipline and team building. In *case management services* social workers act as 'case managers' by providing personalised career counselling and support services such as pre-employment assessment, formulation of career plan, job matching, on-the-job support, and so on. With *on-the-job training* participants are employed as 'trainees' for between 6 and 12 months. If they attend vocational training courses on a part-time basis, HK$4,000 (£273.78) can be reimbursed for expenses related to course and examination fees.

More than 57,000 young people have participated in this scheme since 1999 (Labour Department, 2004c). Participants can get a monthly allowance of HK$4,000 (£273.78), while the employers offering the placement receive a subsidy of HK$2,000 (£136.89) per trainee per month (Labour Department, 2003).

Youth Self-employment Support Scheme (YSSS)

The main objective of YSSS is to provide young people aged 18–24 with the necessary skills to start a business. Participants have to attend courses in vocational skills and basic skills in self-employment such as market research, promotion strategy, sales techniques and financial management. Then, service providers of YSSS act as 'business managers' to help participants to develop their business plans, providing the necessary equipment and facilities and offering administrative support for them (Labour Department, 2004d).

The Graduate Employment Training Scheme (GETS)

Under GETS, fresh university graduates are placed in training posts. Employers who provide the posts and also offer on-the-job training for participants can receive a monthly subsidy of HK$2,000 (£136.89) for six months. In 2003 1,100 graduates benefited from the scheme.

With the decline of manufacturing industry, many middle-aged workers with low educational attainments are unable to find suitable jobs in the open market. In order to solve the pressure of unemployment on this group of workers, 11,000 temporary jobs offered by various government departments were extended for one year (Tung, 2004). Moreover, special employment initiatives have been launched to improve the skills and enhance the employability of middle-aged workers.

The Employee Retraining Board (ERB)

The ERB offers a wide range of courses such as job-search skills courses, job-specific skills courses, general skills courses, courses for the elderly, courses for people with disabilities, self-employment courses and tailor-made courses (Education and Manpower Bureau, 2004). The ERB provides full-time courses with a placement, lasting from one week to three months. Courses that seem to be suitable mainly for those with low educational attainment and skills include domestic helpers training, security and property management training and personal care-worker training.

Courses offered by the ERB are classified into five types (Education and Manpower Bureau, 2004):

- core course on job search skills;
- job-specific skills courses;
- general skills, language and computer courses;
- tailor-made courses for employers; and
- self-employment programmes.

All full-time courses are free. Participants who attend courses that last for one week and with an attendance rate of over 80% can receive a retraining allowance of HK$153.8 (£10.53) a day. The maximum monthly allowance is HK$4,000 (£273.78). Full-time graduate trainees also can get job market information, job counselling and placement services.

Re-employment Training Programme for the Middle-Aged (RETPMA)

In order to encourage employers to recruit workers aged over 40 and also offer them on-the-job training, the government provides a three-month training allowance of HK$1,500 (£102.67) a month (Labour Department, 2004b). There were 2,048 placements in 2003 (Labour Department, 2004d).

Special Incentive Allowance Scheme for Local Domestic Helpers

An incentive allowance has been provided for local domestic helpers who are willing to travel to work unsocial hours or outside their own districts. Successful applicants can receive an allowance of HK$50 (£3.42) a day for a maximum of 24 days a month or 144 days a year. A total of 99 applicants received this allowance (Labour Department, 2003).

Although Hong Kong is widely regarded as the freest economy in the world, the HKSAR is now playing an active role by offering temporary jobs for low-skilled workers and by providing employment training for secondary-school leavers, university graduates, and middle-aged unemployed workers. Clearly, the Hong Kong government is intervening in the operation of the labour market and putting more public expenditure into job creation and work-placement allowances. Such practices seem to contradict Hong Kong's non-interventionist ideology. However, further exploration shows that the present labour policies mainly aim at safeguarding the long-term interests of Hong Kong's market system. This is because the labour market initiatives are temporary, age-biased and market-oriented. First, jobs offered by government departments are low-paid and short-term. This means that the government can end its commitment whenever the employment market becomes stable or there is a need to finance other services. Second, the Hong Kong Jockey Club Charities Trust and the Lotteries Fund, a non-government source of revenue, were used to finance employment programmes for CSSA recipients. For example, HK$200 million (£13.69 million) was used to finance 100 Intensive Employment Assistance Projects launched by voluntary organisations (Social Welfare Department, 2004d). These programmes are not permanent but last for only two to three years. Third, more generous allowances and systematic programmes have been provided for young formal-education leavers than for middle-aged and older unemployed workers. It is understood that the Hong Kong government is facing tremendous pressure from youth employment; one in four unemployed persons is aged 15 to 19 (Table 4.3). This, however, cannot justify the existing unfair employment measures for middle-aged and older unemployed workers, who account for 21.1% of the unemployed population, especially since most of them are main breadwinners and have to bear a heavy caring burden (Table 4.3). Such unfair treatment

Table 4.3: Unemployment rate by age

Period	15–19	20–29	30–39	40–49	50–59	60+	Overall
			Age group				
2001	23.4	6.2	3.5	4.6	5.4	2.7	5.1
2002	30.7	8.2	5.4	6.7	8.2	5.0	7.3
2003	30.2	8.8	6.0	7.3	9.4	4.5	7.9
2004	26.2	6.9	4.9	6.5	8.7	5.9	6.9

Source: Census and Statistics Department (2005)

is revealed by the maximum period of job placement for middle-aged participants of SJAP, which is six months, with a monthly allowance of HK$1,805 (£123.55). By contrast, the training period for the YWETS can be up to 12 months. Young participants also can obtain a higher monthly allowance of HK$2,000 (£136.89).

In fact, the Social Welfare Department has noticed that unemployed recipients of CSSA are characterised by low educational attainment (65% had no more than primary education), older age (69% in the 40–59 age group), and limited skills (over 50% without special occupational skills). Similar findings were reported by Wong and Chua (1998), who found that 77% of unemployed respondents were over 40 years old; of those, 38% were over 50 years old. More than half (51%) of the unemployed recipients who had stopped getting CSSA were receiving benefits again. Thus, more long-term and intensive training courses are required to build up the confidence, and enhance the skills and knowledge, of CSSA recipients. However, the existing training courses do little to improve general educational attainment; nor can recipients upgrade their employment skills. A study examining the employment situation of middle-aged workers showed that some respondents were unable to attend some training programmes because their educational qualifications did not meet the basic requirement. As well, the courses 'could not meet the needs of the current labour market' (Hong Kong Council of Social Service, 2001a). As a result, middle-aged workers can find only low-skill, low-wage, temporary jobs, and so find it hard to earn the stable, reasonable income they need to be self-reliant. This explains why nearly half (47.9%) of the 265 respondents who stopped receiving CSSA in the past were receiving it again (Wong and Chua, 1998). In addition, the government provides limited support for mature students who are striving to improve their basic education. For example, the tuition fee for evening sixth-form courses was increased by 505%, from HK$1,620 (£110.88) to HK$9,800 (£670.77). Students in such courses, however, are mostly low-income earners or unemployed workers, who find it difficult to afford such a high tuition fee (*Ming Pao*, 2001a). This means that those who missed formal education opportunities in the past find it hard to escape from their current low-paid and insecure employment.

It should be stressed that the training allowance provided by the government is in line with its priorities for education, especially improving the quality of human resources. As C.H. Tung, the former Chief Executive of HKSAR (2003, p 9), stresses:

> Our people are our most valuable resource and the key to the development of a knowledge-based economy. One crucial means of promoting economic restructuring is by investing in education. Only by developing our own local human resources and providing opportunities for continuing education for people of all walks of life can we prepare ourselves for the changes in the marketplace. This is of utmost importance to the well being of our people and the long-term development of Hong Kong.

The Financial Secretary (Tong, 2004, p 6) also emphasises that human resources are 'our single most precious asset' and 'Through training and retraining of our workforce, we will help them to help themselves by enhancing their knowledge and skills'. The content of retraining programmes shows that the Hong Kong government depends on young people to develop the future economy, which is why more benefits and better training courses are being offered to young unemployed persons. On the other hand, with limited financial and employment support, it is hard for middle-aged unemployed workers to change their career paths, nor can they be equipped with adequate skills to cope with a changing labour market.

Self-determination

As illustrated earlier, unemployed CSSA recipients have to meet conditions in order to be eligible for public assistance, including applying for at least two jobs per fortnight, developing and updating an individual work plan, writing job-seeking diaries, attending regular work-plan interviews, doing community work, and participating in employment training arranged by the Social Welfare Department. If a CSSA recipient fails to comply with these requirements, the Social Welfare Department will reduce or even terminate his or her benefits. For example, when a chronically ill recipient failed to attend a day's 'voluntary work', his family's CSSA entitlement was reduced by 14 days, nearly half the family's benefits for a month (*Ming Pao*, 2004c). The government always stresses that personalised support will be provided for recipients to enhance their employability. However, as illustrated earlier, since welfare staff are not trained in social work, counselling or careers guidance, their effectiveness in helping recipients to form a personalised plan and to give psychological support is in doubt. It was reported that welfare officers of the SFS Scheme did not understand unemployed recipients' training needs and the employment barriers they face, nor could they provide them with up-to-date job information. In addition, the requirement of applying for a certain number of jobs in a fixed period has put a lot of pressure on recipients, who have to face continuous frustration in searching for jobs (Hong Kong Council of Social Service, 2001b).

Also, CSSA recipients are not free to choose the type of work they want to do. The Social Welfare Department (1998, p 15) puts it clearly: 'The messages that we aim to get across are "Any job is better than no job", "Low pay is better than no pay", and "CSSA is a safety net and a last resort".' Because Hong Kong does not have a minimum wage, CSSA recipients have to accept low-paid jobs with poor working environments. As a result, they still need to live on CSSA even if they are in employment. For example, of 559 CSSA recipients who got jobs after participating in the SJAP, 26% (146) changed only from the 'unemployment' to the 'low earnings' category. Just 21% (116) of them were able to dispense with CSSA (LegCo Panel on Welfare Services, 2002). The evidence shows that unemployed recipients have been pushed by harsh welfare requirements to take up jobs that do not provide them with the level of income they need to be self-reliant.

Because of the Hong Kong government's increasing control over welfare recipients' behaviour, some recipients may choose to stop receiving public benefits or do 'low-paid jobs' in order to safeguard their freedom. It is evident that, among those who had already left the CSSA, only 25% had got a job (Hong Kong Council of Social Service, 2001a). Also, 25% of unemployed respondents stopped receiving CSSA even though their incomes were less than their CSSA payments (Wong and Chua, 1998). The requirements of active job-seeking and 'voluntary work' leave unemployed benefit recipients with little control over their time and activities. Nor do they have a choice over the type of jobs they do. Thus, the autonomy and unique needs of an unemployed person have been systematically suppressed in the interests of removing them rapidly from the benefit system.

The autonomy of Hong Kong's CSSA unemployed persons is further limited by the few opportunities they have to participate in decision-making. Hong Kong became a Special Administrative Region (SAR) of the People's Republic of China (PRC) after 1997. During the British administration, Hong Kong was a bureaucratic-capitalist state (C.K. Chan, 1996), in which most political power was in the hands of senior government officials and representatives of business and professional bodies. Since 1997, however, there has been little change in the unequal distribution of political power between the working class and the business community. The former CE of Hong Kong, Tung Chee Hwa, was elected by an 800-person selection committee derived mainly from the social and economic elite. He is assisted by an Executive Council, whose members are appointed by him. As a result, members of the Executive Council are mainly politicians of pro-China political parties and organisations, professionals and businessmen. Meanwhile, the Legislative Council (LC) is composed of 30 directly elected members representing geographic districts, and 30 indirectly elected members representing functional (occupational) constituencies. Since many members of the LC are representatives of industries or professional bodies including banks, insurance companies, lawyers, doctors, teachers, and so on, their interests may be contrary to those of unemployed people. Also, since the directly elected members do not constitute a majority, they are too weak to challenge the government's policies.

Following the political strategy of the previous colonial regime, the HKSAR uses more than 500 consultative bodies to gather community views on its policies. In practice, these bodies are taken mainly from the social and economic elite. For example, members of the Social Welfare Advisory Committee and the Social Security Appeal Board are mainly drawn from academics, leaders of voluntary organisations, the business community, and professional bodies. As the CE appoints all members, the government can select members whose welfare ideologies are close to its own.

Moreover, the working committee reviewing the level of CSSA benefits included only representatives from various government departments, chaired by the Director of Social Welfare (Social Welfare Department, 1998). In other words, the quality of life of unemployed CSSA recipients is mainly determined by senior government officials and Hong Kong's social and economic elite in the Executive and Legislative Councils. The poor have been institutionally excluded from the decision-making process.

To summarise, Hong Kong's CSSA recipients are politically weak, and such weakness has been transferred to the welfare sphere in which they are subject to control and domination. As illustrated earlier, unemployed recipients have to do community work and to be regularly checked in order to be eligible for financial assistance. Welfare recipients have become subject to the control of welfare bureaucrats and required to work for their benefits. Unfortunately, welfare recipients have found it difficult to secure access to the promised individualised services and skills needed for self-reliance due to the lack of systematic and longer training courses for the neediest groups such as middle-aged and older workers, and due to the inadequate qualifications of welfare workers. If the state fails to deliver the promised services for unemployed recipients, its control over welfare claimants seems to be difficult to justify, since this type of control treats CSSA recipients only as objects or even criminals, disregarding their feelings, needs and, fundamentally, their autonomous capacities. A study mentioned earlier found that over 60% of respondents were actively seeking jobs even before the SRS was launched (Wong and Chua, 1998). On the other hand, nearly 60% of CSSA unemployed respondents felt subject to age discrimination that excludes them from the job market (Wong and Chua, 1998). Clearly, the existing control over recipients' behaviour has ignored the underlying unemployment difficulties of CSSA recipients. The control only forces unemployed workers to accept any pay and working conditions on offer, and does little to promote their self-reliance or their long-term career development. In short, the existing control over unemployed workers seems to be an additional punishment imposed on the victims of a market economy.

Equal value

By virtue of possessing the capacities for autonomy and mutuality, all human beings have the same worth regardless of social class, ethnic group or gender. However, the Hong Kong government sets an example by discriminating against unemployment benefit recipients. The Social Welfare Department (1998, p 15) openly declares:

> We should aim to change the attitudes of the unemployed recipients who are less motivated by placing emphasis on their 'social responsibilities' and the need to re-establish self-reliance, and helping them understand how employment contributes to the well-being of an individual, the family and the whole community.

Similar views of the unemployed are also expressed in other official welfare documents. For example, one Social Welfare Department pamphlet stresses that a CSSA recipient 'has the obligation to work and support himself/his family through assistance offered to him to reduce his/his family's dependence on public funds' (Social Welfare Department, 2004b, p 4). The authority has impugned the morality of the poor, portraying them as 'irresponsible citizens'. Such a negative image of the poor, as illustrated above, has been further enhanced by exaggerating the problem of welfare abuse even though only a small percentage of fraud cases were found. It is clear that a 'moral panic' concerning unemployed persons has been created in Hong Kong society, and the 'deviant' image of unemployed citizens helps justify the government's control over their daily lives. Such a negative image further stigmatises the existing public assistance scheme, deterring the needy from living on public welfare. This helps explain why the general public is unwilling to seek government financial support and why some recipients have very low self-esteem. In order to maintain equal social status with other citizens, the poor, as is evident from the above studies, try to escape from CSSA even if their incomes are lower than public benefit levels.

In addition, the Hong Kong government's workfare approach is associated with age-biased training policies. As illustrated earlier, middle-aged and old unemployed persons can attend only short training courses and obtain fewer training allowances than their young counterparts. The Hong Kong Council of Social Service (2001a) criticises the Hong Kong government's measures for tackling unemployment as they 'merely focused on young persons' and lacked 'a comprehensive employment policy which can coincide with the economic policy for the middle and old aged persons'. Because of the weaknesses of the existing policies, middle-aged and older workers can find only low-paid and low-skilled jobs in the market. They will continue to face the problems of job and income insecurity.

Apart from being class-biased, the HKSAR also discriminates against adult and able-bodied CSSA recipients. Under CSSA regulations, disabled and older CSSA recipients can apply for supplements and special grants to meet special needs. However, able-bodied adults or children are not entitled to the long-term supplement, which provides extra resources for recipients living on CSSA for more than 12 months for buying household and durable goods, and paying for dental treatment (dentures, crowns, bridges, scaling, fillings and root-canal treatment) (Social Welfare Department, 2004a). Obviously, these measures ignore the daily and health needs of able-bodied recipients. It seems that the underlying assumption of this policy is that healthy recipients can find a job in the labour market if they want to.

Another issue is the exclusion of recent immigrants from CSSA benefits. Under financial pressure caused by the reduction of revenues from taxation and land sales, the HKSAR changed the CSSA residency requirement from one year to seven years. As the Social Welfare Department (2004a, p 3) states, the CSSA beneficiary 'must have been a Hong Kong resident for at least seven years'. In other words, new immigrants have to work for more years in order to be entitled to unemployment assistance. This implies that a large number of immigrants have to accept extremely low wages in order to survive. Their rights to unemployment assistance are denied and politically suppressed for the first seven years. The Society for Community Organisations criticises this policy for creating more hardship for new immigrants and also for depriving children of the right to assistance (*Standard*, 2003). Thus, new immigrants in Hong Kong have been treated as 'the most inferior people' among the stigmatised unemployed citizens.

This section shows that the weak and the most disadvantaged groups have not been provided with an equal opportunity to participate in policy-making. Their politically weak situation has been transformed into social welfare disadvantages. As illustrated above, older unemployed workers can attend only very short-term training courses, receiving less financial support than their young counterparts. Also, the right of new immigrants to unemployment assistance has been suppressed. All in all, unequal treatment makes the welfare system unattractive to poor unemployed persons, and new immigrants have little choice but to accept any jobs and salaries to meet survival needs.

Conclusion

Hong Kong has been widely recognised as the finest example of a free market economy in the world; as discussed above, it is also a good case study of a capitalist welfare system's attitudes towards the dignity of economically weak citizens. Human dignity in Hong Kong seems to be narrowly defined as 'labour market participation' and 'contribution to society'. The objective of the social security measures around workfare is to 'change the attitude of the unemployed recipients who are less motivated' (Social Welfare Department, 1998, p 15). At the family level, work is an expression of being a good parent. The Social Welfare Department (2004b, p 2) claims: 'Participation in paid employment can help people build better lives and provide their children with an active, valuable role model.' At the societal level, the Hong Kong government stresses that compulsory community work will 'improve the recipient's self-esteem and confidence' and help them to 'gain a better understanding of the community' (Social Welfare Department, 1998, p 20). According to the Director of Social Welfare (K. W. Tang, 2004, p 6), the focus of Hong Kong's welfare policies is to help welfare recipients to be 'productive, participative and contributive members of our society'.

After treating the unemployed as unmotivated, dishonest persons with few family and social responsibilities, the Hong Kong government has justified its control over the daily lives of those living on public benefits. Accordingly, unemployed recipients are required to take action to change their 'negative life styles' by actively seeking jobs and making contributions to society through compulsory community work. In short, the unemployed have been construed as 'inferior citizens' and the welfare system has become a rehabilitative institution for improving their characters.

The Hong Kong government has boasted of the success of its welfare reforms by announcing a significant decrease in the number of CSSA recipients:

> The results of the AEA programme have been encouraging. Since implementation of the programme in June 1999, more than 16,000 CSSA recipients have joined the programme and 1,400 of them have found jobs. The unemployment caseload has decreased by 21% since June 1999 to about 25,500 in April 2000. (Lau, 2000)

However, the objective of self-reliance stressed by the Hong Kong government has been implemented without qualified welfare staff; well-designed employment training programmes (especially for middle-aged and older unemployed workers) are lacking, as is adequate labour protection. As shown earlier, staff of the Social Welfare Department have failed to tackle the psychological needs and actual employment barriers of unemployed recipients. Without adequate educational qualifications and technical skills, middle-aged unemployed persons find it difficult to compete with their young counterparts in the labour market. Without minimum wage legislation, a significant number of recipients have moved from the 'unemployed' to the 'low-earning' category. For example, the number of low-earning CSSA recipients increased by 218%, from 4,714 to 14,995 between 1995 and 2004 (Social Welfare Department, 2004c). This also explains why over half the unemployed persons who had left CSSA in the past were receiving it again (Wong and Chua, 1998). As pointed out by Peck and Theodore

(2000, p 131), 'workfarist logic dictates that targeted social groups are driven into the labour market, where they are expected to remain, notwithstanding systemic problems of under employment, low pay and exploitative work relations'.

It is evident that Hong Kong's workfare practices have forced a large number of poor citizens out of the public welfare system without giving them adequate financial support. Over 50% of social security enquirers did not apply for assistance after knowing more about the requirements of CSSA. And only one in four unemployed persons who gave up CSSA actually got a job (Hong Kong Council of Social Service, 2001b). Together with the implementation of short-term employment programmes for participants, the above evidence suggests that the Hong Kong government's self-reliance measures are half-hearted and short-sighted; it does not have a long-term and comprehensive service to equip the unemployed with better educational attainments and advanced skills to enhance their employability.

The weaknesses of the Hong Kong government's self-reliance measures further suggest that 'workfare' has been deliberately used to exclude the increasing number of unemployed recipients. The CE had explained the financial pressure of Hong Kong in its Policy Address:

> Public expenditure still continued to grow at an average annual rate of 5%. Having public spending consistently exceeding the rate of economic growth is a departure from the principle of small government we have always promoted. If expenditure continues to grow unchecked, we will have no alternative but to keep on raising taxes and increasing fees, thus channeling more and more resources to the Government. Such a move will only result in less efficient use of community resources and a deteriorating business environment. None of us would like to see this happen. (Tung, 2003, p 17)

Facing such tremendous fiscal pressure, the Hong Kong government's strategies are to adhere to its traditional 'small government' and 'big market' principles by reducing public expenditure so that a low-taxation regime can be preserved. As the present Financial Secretary emphasises:

> I am committed to upholding the important principles stipulated in the Basic Law to manage public finances prudently: keep expenditures within the limits of revenues

and strive to achieve a fiscal balance. I am also committed
to keeping a simple and low tax regime and maintaining
the stability and integrity of the monetary system. (Tong,
2004, p 19)

In response to the economic downturn since the mid-1990s, Hong
Kong's free market welfare system attempts to safeguard its low-tax
and limited labour protection system by reinvigorating the work ethic
and enhancing personal and family responsibilities. As a result, the
self-esteem and social respect of CSSA recipients have been
undermined. To preserve their dignity, some recipients stop claiming
CSSA; some give up benefits to live on even lower private incomes.
All in all, Hong Kong recipients are finding ways to emancipate
themselves from an undignified welfare system based on the slogans
of 'self-reliance' and 'self-betterment'.

FIVE

China and human dignity

China has experienced dramatic social and economic changes since adopting an open-door policy in 1978. Before that, the Chinese government mainly followed the principles of socialism, according to which the needs of workers and their family members, such as medical care, housing, education and retirement, were met by state-owned enterprises (SOEs). This is because all means of production were in the hands of the Chinese Communist Party (CCP); full employment had been achieved at the expense of surplus labour in state enterprises. Under the work unit welfare system, public welfare was restricted to the 'three no's' – people with no income, no family support and no working ability. In other words, only marginalised groups such as disabled persons, widows and older people without any family support and with limited working ability would receive social assistance. Under this type of welfare system, there was no room for unemployment services; public welfare in the form of social assistance was also less developed, being restricted to certain deprived groups.

However, economic changes under the open-door policy have generated tremendous welfare pressure on the Chinese government. Economically, China is no longer a planned economy but a mixed economy. The Chinese government has recognised the importance of free market forces to economic growth. *The Economist* (2004) rightly points out that 'China's leaders still call themselves communists, but they have become capitalists in practice'. As a result of local and foreign investments, China's gross domestic product (GDP) increased by nearly seven times between 1983 and 2003, from US$227.4 billion to US$1,412.3 billion (World Bank Group, 2005). Its annual GDP growth rate was as high as 8.6% from 1993 to 2003 (World Bank Group, 2005). China has received the second largest amount of foreign direct investment after the USA, being the world's sixth largest economy. As Jiabao Wen, the Chinese prime minister, points out: 'The Chinese people have, on the whole, begun to lead a life of moderate prosperity' (*People's Daily*, 2004d).

In order to enhance the cost-effectiveness and efficiency of SOEs, a large number of surplus workers in the SOEs have been laid off. A total of 25.5 million workers were laid off from 1998 to 2001 (Xinhua

News Agency, 2002). As a result of these economic changes, the previous 'work unit' welfare arrangement has been under severe attack. Laid-off workers from SOEs have lost welfare benefits previously provided by their employers. In order to prevent economic problems leading to social crisis, the Chinese government has carried out a series of welfare reforms, tackling the financial, health and retirement needs of the poor. As the latest Social Security White Paper (Information Office of the State Council, 2004) stresses, the social security system is 'an important guarantee for the social stability and the long-term political stability of a country'. Accordingly, new welfare measures such as old-age insurance, medical insurance, and the minimum living standard guarantee (MLSG) have been established in recent years. In 2004, nearly 6% (22.04 million) of China's urban population lived on the MLSG (*China Daily*, 2004c). Clearly, the Chinese government has been attempting to reconstruct its welfare system in response to social demands caused by the expansion of the private market and the contraction of public enterprises.

In this chapter, Shanghai is used as a case study to illustrate the impact of both central government and local government policies on the dignity of unemployed workers. Shanghai is the most economically developed province in China, and has successfully attracted a great deal of foreign investment. As Deng Xiaoping, the most influential figure in modern Chinese history, pointed out, China needs Shanghai to 'acquire international status in finance' (Deng, 1991). Shanghai is the 'Head of the Dragon', the most economically developed region in China. The central government's objective is to build Shanghai as the financial centre of Asia. As a result of economic growth, the average household income of Shanghai residents increased by more than four times, from ¥2,182 (£141.14) to ¥8,773 (£567.46), between 1990 and 1998. Shanghai is also the 'leader' in welfare reform. The MLSG was established in Shanghai in 1993 and has now became China's 'most basic form of government social assistance' (*China Daily*, 2003). Actually, Shanghai was the first province to establish three social protection measures: the MLSG for urban residents; a minimum wage for workers; and basic unemployment compensation for laid-off employees along with a guarantee of salaries. Thus, the case of Shanghai directly reflects current and future Chinese welfare policies.

Central government and Shanghai municipal government unemployment policies

The development of China's welfare policies over the past two decades is a response to the changing employment relationship between the state and its workers as well as the emergence of new employment relationships in the private market. Following the introduction of the market economy, the Chinese government no longer upholds the socialist ideology of full employment but a 'market-oriented employment mechanism' (Information Office of the State Council, 2002). As a result of this change, new workers cannot enjoy the work unit welfare system in a planned economy, while old workers' benefits have dramatically fallen as a result of the financial difficulties of SOEs due to restructuring. This fundamental change of employment relations has obliged the Chinese government to establish 'a social security system independent of the enterprise with multiple financial resources' (China Internet Information Centre, 2002a).

One of the most difficult issues that the CCP has to handle is the elimination of the old type of socialist working relationship between SOEs and their workers in a safe and acceptable manner. To achieve economic efficiency and reduce the government's financial burden, the number of SOEs was dramatically reduced from 262,000 in 1997 to 159,000 in 2003. The Chinese government established re-employment service centres (RSCs) to help the large number of redundant workers from SOEs. Of 1.96 million redundant workers in June 2004, 1.22 million entered the RSCs (Ministry of Labour and Social Security, 2004a). Laid-off workers in the RSCs maintain 'a special type of employment relationship' with their SOEs. They are issued with a 'laid-off worker certificate' and stay with RSCs for a maximum of three years, where they receive a basic living allowance. The SOEs also pay their old age, health, and unemployment insurance premiums (*People's Daily,* 2002a). The allowances the RSCs pay to laid-off workers are worth more than unemployment insurance benefits. In addition, the RSCs provide laid-off workers with job-search advice, free job training, and information on job vacancies (Xinhua News Agency, 2002). The RSCs are transitional units, which help SOEs to reduce the costs of production and provide short-term financial assistance as well as a minimal protection for laid-off workers. In this way, the resistance of workers can be minimised and social stability maintained.

However, not all laid-off workers have been properly cared for by their SOEs. Also, the Chinese welfare system does not provide adequate services for unemployed workers in the free market. Social and economic pressures such as 'the loss made in numerous SOEs, bankruptcy of inefficient enterprises, massive laid-off workers, unemployment, population in poverty, and also vulnerable groups in the transitional process' (Ma, 2001) have directly threatened China's stability. The Hong Kong Centre for Human Rights and Democracy recorded over 120,000 protests and demonstrations in China in 2000 (Conachy, 2001). Against this background, the central government issued the 'Unemployment Insurance Ordinance' in 1999 in order to 'safeguard the basic living of unemployed workers and also promote re-employment' (State Council, 1999). Under the ordinance, employers have to pay 2% of their wage bill, while employees pay 1% of their salaries as contributions. In addition, unemployed persons have to meet several basic conditions in order to be eligible for unemployment benefits (Shanghai Municipal Government, 1999): their unemployment must be involuntary; they must be urban resident of Shanghai; they must have made contributions to the unemployment insurance fund for at least 12 months before being unemployed; and they must have registered as unemployed and be actively seeking employment.

The duration of the unemployment benefits depends on the duration of contributions. A person who has contributed for more than one year but less than two receives benefits for only two months. The maximum benefit period for a person who has contributed for less than five years is 12 months. For those who have contributed for less than ten years but more than five, the maximum benefit period is 24 months. The level of unemployment benefit is set in relation to other types of benefits. It is higher than the minimum living allowance (MLA) but lower than the minimum wage. In addition, those on unemployment benefits for more than 13 months receive a reduced rate, about 80% of the first 12 months. Clearly, unemployment insurance provides a basis for SOEs to further their modernisation. After establishing unemployment insurance, 'the basic livelihood guarantee system for people made redundant from state-owned enterprises is being gradually orbited into this system' (Information Office of the State Council, 2002). In June 2004, 4.54 million workers received unemployment benefits (Ministry of Labour and Social Security, 2004b).

The RSCs provide a minimal level of support for SOEs' laid-off workers, while unemployment insurance gives basic protection to workers in open employment. However, some marginal groups cannot receive these benefits, such as disabled people, older people and families that cannot find sufficient resources to care for their members. In response to this gap, the Chinese government introduced its social assistance system following the publication of the *Regulations on Urban*

Residents' Minimum Standard of Living in 1999. The political and economic importance of this system is clearly revealed in a statement made by the State Council (1997):

> In recent years, one of the important tasks of the Chinese Government is to improve traditional social welfare by establishing a comprehensive social security system. The establishment and implementation of social security fully reveals the strengths of the socialist system, showing China's Communist Party and the Chinese Government are full heartedly serving the public. This helps maintain social stability and promote economic reforms. All levels of government institutions should pay serious attention to this work by using effective measures to tackle it.

The MLSG mainly targets three groups of people:

- people who are without income, working abilities, or relatives;
- those who are unemployed or are receiving unemployment benefits but whose family incomes are below the level of the MLA; and
- those who are earning the national minimum wage or retired workers who are receiving retirement benefits, but whose family incomes are lower than the MLA.

With the RSCs, the unemployment insurance scheme and the MLSG, the Chinese government has established a 'social security system with Chinese characteristics' based on 'Three Security Lines' (China Internet Information Centre, 2002a):

> The first security line is the basic living guarantee system for the laid-offs from the SOEs, which is aimed to guarantee the basic living standard, pay social insurance contributions and promote re-employment. The second security line refers to the unemployment insurance system targeted at the unemployed, which provides the unemployed with unemployment benefit and actively promotes their re-employment since the 1990s.... The third security line refers to the minimum living standard guarantee system of urban residents covering all urban residents whose family income per capita is lower than the prescribed level.... The 'Three Security Lines' are well integrated and have effectively guaranteed the basic living of the laid-off workers, the

> unemployed and the low-income residents, serving as an
> effective social safety net.

Clearly, the 'Three Security Lines' are a response to the expansion of the market economy and the deterioration of the old worker–work unit welfare system. Also, the main objectives of these measures are to provide a basic living for poor people in order to maintain social stability and to facilitate economic development. In other words, China has transformed its communist welfare system into a residual welfare regime. Such a development has fundamentally changed its ideology, from the pursuit of equality and social justice to the maintenance of work motivation and self-reliance.

Shanghai takes a leading role in social welfare reform in China. It was the first local authority to introduce the MLSG in 1993 to 'provide a basic living for individuals or families to overcome their difficulties, maintaining social stability and promoting social development' (Shanghai Ministry of Civil Affairs, 1996). In 1997, the central government urged other provinces to follow Shanghai's example by setting up a minimum income level in their regions. By the end of 1999, the central government had required all provinces to establish an MLSG. Under this measure, urban residents have a welfare right to financial assistance. The State Council (1999) declares, 'Household members who are living together where the average income of family members is lower than that of the minimum standard of living allowance in their areas are entitled to basic assistance.'

At first, the cost of the MLSG was mainly the responsibility of local authorities. As a consequence, levels of assistance in some provinces were too low to meet even the survival needs of people. Later, the central government provided extra financial support for local authorities and now meets about 40% of the costs of the MLSG. As a result of this change, total expenditure on the MLSG increased dramatically between 1996 and 2002, from ¥3 million (£194,049) to ¥104 million (£6.73 million). The total number of recipients also increased from 0.85 million to 1.93 million in this period (Tang, 2003, p 7); most of them were laid-off or unemployed workers and their dependants (Table 5.1). In 2004, 22.6 million residents in cities and 3.67 million people in rural areas were receiving the MLSG (Ministry of Civil Affairs, 2004a).

Both local and central governments' documents clearly show the importance of social welfare for social stability. The Shanghai municipal government (1996) states that the objectives of the MLSG are to protect the basic living of urban residents as well as to maintain social stability and promote social progress. In 2003, 445,900 people from 215,000

Table 5.1: Categories of recipients of Minimum Living Standard Guarantee (MLSG), 2002

Categories of recipients	Number	%
Laid-off workers	6,970,000	36.1
Unemployed workers	2,990,000	15.5
Dependants of laid-off or unemployed workers and others	5,540,000	28.7
Currently employed	1,910,000	9.9
Three NOs	970,000	5.0
Retirees	930,000	4.8
Total	19,310,000	100

Source: Douji et al (2002), cited in Shang and Wu (2004, p 269)

households were receiving the MLA, which was about 4.5% of Shanghai's urban population. Among them, 175,700 people came from unemployed families. Since local government decides the level of MLA, there is wide variation in benefit levels. Shanghai is one of the regions that have a higher rate of MLA.

Apart from providing financial assistance for the unemployed, the Chinese government emphasises education and retraining. According to a White Paper on education, titled *China's employment situation and policies*, the government aims to raise the education levels and vocational skills of workers, especially to enhance the employability of laid-off workers through retraining (*China Daily*, 2004f). A total of 15.3 million laid-off workers undertook re-employment training between 2001 and 2003 (*People's Daily*, 2004a). Thus, in response to the expansion of market economy, the Chinese government now adopts an active labour policy by doing 'everything possible to enlarge the scale of employment' (Information Office of the State Council, 2002).

To summarise, China has experienced rapid social and economic change over the past two decades. With the planned economy transformed into a mixed economy with a large volume of SOEs, the Chinese government has to tackle the negative consequences of the contraction of state welfare and the expansion of the market economy, especially unemployment and low wages. Three social security schemes – the RSCs, the unemployment insurance scheme, and the MLSG – have been set up to meet pressing social demands. Shanghai plays a key role in piloting these welfare measures, providing practical experiences for the whole country. Unlike under its previous welfare measures, the Chinese government now stresses market participation as an effective means to tackle poverty. It tries to provide unemployed workers with new skills to re-enter the labour market. The State Council points out, 'The major goals of China's labour and social security efforts at the beginning of the new century are promoting employment, protecting employees' rights and interests, coordinating labour relations, raising people's incomes and improving social security' (Information Office of the State Council, 2002). Based on the welfare experiences of Shanghai, the following section investigates whether the dignity of unemployed persons can be safeguarded in a new type of mixed economy – socialism with Chinese characteristics.

The dignity of unemployed recipients

Physical needs

Unemployed workers in Shanghai can apply for unemployment benefits and the MLSG if they meet the requirements for contributions and residence. However, the two programmes provide different levels of assistance. The central government states that the level of unemployment insurance benefit should be below the minimum wage but higher than the MLA. Very often, unemployment benefit is set between 70% and 85% of the minimum wage. The minimum wage policy was implemented in Shanghai in 1993 and the monthly minimum wage was ¥635 (£41.07) in 2004 (Shanghai Municipal Government, 2004a), while the monthly MLA allowance was ¥290 (£18.76) per person (*China Daily*, 2005).

The national objective of the MLSG is to provide a minimal level of assistance to meet the basic needs of poor people. The guidelines of the State Council (1999) state: 'The level of MLA for urban residents should meet the needs of their basic daily necessities such as food, clothing, and housing. Expenses such as water, gas, electricity, and education for children should also be considered.' As 'the lowest level of financial support in the social security system' (*People's Daily*, 2002b), the MLA is also described as the basic line as well as the survival line. The MLA rate, which in Shanghai has always put the city among the most generous group of provinces, is set with regard to the following criteria:

* the living standard of each person;
* expenses for maintaining a basic living;
* the inflation rate; and
* the economic development and financial conditions of the Shanghai municipal government.

In 2005, the monthly rate of MLA in Shanghai was ¥290 (£18.76) (*China Daily*, 2005). The total number of recipients was 417,400 in

2004. The recipients of the MLSG, however, were reported to be unable
to lead a decent life. A study conducted by the Social Policy Research
Centre of the Chinese Academy of Social Sciences (J. Tang, 2003)
reported that most recipients could buy only the cheapest food
regardless of its nutritional value. Over half the recipients were unable
to eat meat weekly. Similar problems were reported in three other
cities, where unemployed respondents claimed (Cook and Jolly, 2000,
pp 18–19):

- no good clothes to wear
- family has poor equipment
- difficulty getting food and clothes
- no money to pay heating, rent
- no ability to pay back loans, don't dare borrow
- cramped living space.

Thus, because of the low level of assistance, recipients of the MLSG
do not have adequate resources to pay for daily necessities, especially
for buying an acceptable amount of food of the quality to maintain
physical health.

The biggest problem for poor people in China is the cost of health
care. Less than 10% of the Chinese population is protected by medical
insurance (Central Television International, 2004). By June 2004, only
116.28 million of China's 1.3 billion people participated in the basic
national health insurance scheme (Ministry of Labour and Social
Security, 2004a). Wang Daming, a member of the National Committee
of the Chinese People Political Consultative Conference (CPPCC),
the top advisory body in China, observed that poor families have
'three types of worries' – illness, children dropping out of schools, and
lack of money for celebrating festivals (*People's Daily*, 2002c). Unlike
their counterparts in the UK and Sweden, who are members of a free
national health service, poor people in Shanghai can obtain only
temporary and selective medical assistance. This means that poor citizens
cannot get regular medical care, and medical treatment is limited to
certain special diseases such as AIDS and cancer. In 2003, the Shanghai
municipal government issued 2,000 'health help cards' for poor
chronically ill patients who regularly need medicine and to consult
outpatient services. A total of ¥69.5 million (£4.5 million) was paid
towards poor people's medical costs.

Even workers who make contributions to unemployment insurance
get only limited assistance for health care. They can obtain ¥10–20
(£0.65–1.30) a month for outpatient services and receive only 50–

70% of hospital treatment costs (*People's Daily*, 2002c). Although the central government has urged hospitals and related health services to grant concessions to the poor (State Council, 1999), it has set out no clear guidelines and administrative procedures to cover medical care of the poor.

Although Shanghai is a prosperous region, the municipal government has imposed several restrictions on medical care assistance (Shanghai Ministry of Civil Affairs et al, 2003):

- Eligible applicants are limited to certain groups: (a) those who lose their ability to work or who get no support from family members; (b) older people and children from families receiving the MLA; and (c) patients with special diseases such as mental illness and cancer.
- Some applicants have to pay at least ¥1,000 (£64.68) to be eligible for government assistance.
- Poor people can apply for medical assistance only once a month.
- Temporary medical assistance for unemployed workers and for families living on the MLSG has been granted recently. However, the poor can apply only once.
- Unemployed workers can visit only hospitals that are designated by the Unemployment Insurance Office in their region. It is only after the approval of the relevant unemployment offices that unemployed patients can be treated at other hospitals. And only 70% of the medical subsidy will be provided for the unemployed who have their treatment at the designated medical institutions (Shanghai Labour and Security Bureau, 2004a).
- Unemployed workers' eligibility for medical assistance is further restricted by their behaviour. Pregnant workers whose children exceed the number designated by the national birth control policy, or workers whose physical problems are caused by fighting or other illegal activities, cannot apply for any medical assistance (Shanghai Municipal Government, 1999).

Clearly, the unemployed are unable to get adequate medical protection. The existing temporary and partial medical subsidies mean that unemployed patients are expected to use extra resources such as family savings or financial support from friends, relatives or charities to cope with medical expenses. Unemployed benefit recipients suffering from chronic illness find it especially difficult to bear the medical costs because government assistance is time-limited. The existing policies cannot cope with the long-term medical needs of poor patients (Shanghai Ministry of Civil Affairs et al, 2003).

The exclusion of poor people from health services was reported also in three other big cities, namely, Beijing, Ya'an, and Changchun. Laid-off workers in a study stressed (Cook and Jolly, 2000, pp 18–19):

* can't afford to see the doctor
* when sick don't go to see the doctor
* no medical insurance, can't afford to see a doctor.

Two recent studies consistently show the seriousness of the health care problem. The Chinese Social Science Academy found that 50% of respondents said that they would not go to hospital when they were sick (J. Tang, 2003). A national study conducted by the health ministry reported 36% of patients in cities and 39% in rural areas did not visit doctors because of financial difficulties. More seriously, 28% of patients even left hospital before the completion of treatment due to financial constraints (BBC News, 2004).

The above evidence reveals that current medical measures in China can provide only short-term and meagre support for unemployed persons. Because of financial difficulties, many patients are suffering from delays in treatment, incomplete treatment or even no treatment. To tackle the medical needs of poor people, the Chinese government is piloting a national 'Urban Health and Poverty Project' to provide medical assistance for poor unemployed and immigrant workers in the four cities of Shenyang, Chengdu, Xining, and Yinchuan (Xinhua News Agency, 2004a). Since the project covers only a few cities and a small population, most poor people in China are still unable to afford basic health care. In short, poor medical care has excluded poor unemployed people from realising the basic right of survival, undermining China's recent economic achievement.

Psychological needs

The Chinese government uses traditional neighbourhood organisations to implement the MLSG. The central government has granted street committees (SCs) and resident associations (RAs) the power to manage the MLSG (State Council, 1999). However, staff from these two social organisations are not social welfare professionals but front-line officials who chiefly deal with community issues. Some of them are even volunteers who support the services of local authorities. Apart from dealing with MLA applications, the staff of these organisations have to work on other health and community issues. To assess the eligibility of applicants, local authorities can use home visits, interview neighbours and send official letters to relevant private and public organisations seeking information (State Council, 1999). Since staff of both SCs and RAs have close contact with applicants because of their local nature, they might have a better understanding of the employment and financial situations of poor families. They can also help applicants to solve non-material problems (J. Tang, 2002). The main weaknesses of this type of management are 'the lack of professional quality and inconsistencies' (J. Tang, 2002). Most responsible officers do not have higher education qualifications, nor do they have a clear understanding of the concepts of unemployment and social assistance. Some of them even misunderstand the objectives of the MLSG, and display traditional charitable attitudes towards recipients. Some consider recipients to be lazy and hopeless. However, they think that they are doing something good for the applicants. Because of these limitations, the quality of services provided by the staff of SCs and RAs is variable.

In fact, being laid off and becoming unemployed is a painful experience to many people. Laid-off workers feel 'loss of face, nothing to live on, fed up, can't sleep, hollow, empty, lonely, isolated, no-one to talk to, couldn't accept it, now resigned to it, initially optimistic, now discouraged' to express their social and psychological conditions (Cook and Jolly, 2000, p 13). Thus, it is urgent to 'raise the education level of the staff of RAs, enhancing their professional skills' (J. Tang, 2002) so that they are capable of helping welfare recipients to overcome difficulties. In addition, China suffers a serious shortage of psychologists. With a population of 17 million, Shanghai only has 100 therapists (*China Daily*, 2004a). Clearly, no specific counselling programmes are designed for tackling the social and mental problems of unemployed persons, whose psychological needs are neglected in the present welfare system.

Apart from the quality of welfare workers, the administrative procedures of the MLSG pose a barrier to the needy. Under central government guidelines, the names of recipients should be made public. The general public is also encouraged to report any suspected welfare fraud to the authority. This reveals the unbalanced power relationship between the state and the general public as well as government distrust of poor people. MLSG administrative arrangements have two implications. First, the existing grass-root administrative units are being used to deal with a new social security scheme. This means that the traditional political function of neighbourhood organisations has become mixed with their social welfare function. Under this mixture, grass-roots organisations' political role may dominate their caring role. Second, since most SC and RA staff are not professionals but have low educational qualifications, recipients' problems are likely to be treated simply as financial problems. In this way, the underlying needs of unemployed applicants in terms of education, interpersonal relationships and mental health cannot be effectively tackled.

Both the central and the Shanghai municipal governments are aware of the poor quality of the existing welfare administration. The Ministry of Labour and Social Security, therefore, focuses on three directions for future welfare management: institutionalisation, professionalisation and socialisation. One of its objectives is to implement a human-centred service that can improve the quality of welfare services (*People's Daily*, 2004c). After reviewing the structure and human resources of front-line social security offices, the Shanghai municipal government (2004b) tried to raise the quality of Employment Support Workers (ESWs) in 2004. There are 3,500 ESWs in Shanghai. Most are former staff of SOEs, the majority of whom also experienced the problems of retraining and unemployment. Starting from April 2004, new ESWs have to pass an examination. On-the-job training courses are also provided for old ESWs in order to enrich their knowledge of employment services, making them more professional (*People's Daily*, 2004c). It should be stressed that in November 2003 Shanghai became the first province in China to grant social workers professional and official status (*People's Daily*, 2003f). Aspiring social workers have to pass a comprehensive examination organised by the Civil Affairs Administration (Xinhua News Agency, 2004b).

To summarise, the management of the MLSG further reveals that social assistance in China has been mixed with the political practices of the CCP. Administratively, SCs and RAs were made front-line welfare units for managing new social demands in a mixed economy. In addition, the release of recipients' names to the public shows the absolute power of government authority over her people because welfare recipients have little right over their privacy. All these arrangements also assume that financial needs are the key concern of applicants and that, so long as the financial needs of applicants have been met, social stability can be maintained. But in reality recipients' complex psychological and employment problems might not have been adequately tackled. Nevertheless, the Shanghai municipal government is starting to improve the quality of its social assistance and employment services by enhancing the training and professional skills of relevant workers. This will be a key step towards meeting the psychological needs of unemployed workers in the future.

Fulfilling caring duties

The introduction of a free market and the restructuring of SOEs have shifted the caring burden from the state to the family, with parents becoming main carers of children. But the contraction of public enterprises directly weakens the caring capacities of laid-off workers, who are mainly aged 35–50 and still have to take care of elderly parents and children (Xinhua News Agency, 2002). Unemployed parents find it difficult to fulfil their caring duties as a result of the low level of the MLSG and unemployment benefits. In addition, application procedures are complicated. First, families living on the MLSG have to apply to schools in order to obtain tuition fee concessions or exemptions. After the schools have accepted the applications and signed the application forms, parents have to take the forms to the Social Assistance Management Offices or RAs (Shanghai Ministry of Civil Affairs and Shanghai Municipal Education Committee, 2001). In practice, the success of recipients' applications depends on the attitudes of school administrators as well as the financial circumstances of the schools. As the education rights of poor children have not been clearly set out in the MLSG, the educational opportunities of the poor are uncertain. Second, Chinese people put much emphasis on 'face'. Some parents are unwilling to disclose their financial circumstances to schools for fear of creating a negative image of their children. Because of these welfare barriers, some parents find it difficult to pay for their children's educational expenses. Some parents have even considered stopping their children's studies for financial reasons. As J. Tang (2003) shows, 77% of poor respondents are unable to pay for school expenses; 7% even said that they would stop children from going to school because of the financial burden. Similarly, an official study reported that one of the biggest worries of unemployed families in Shanghai is children's tuition fees, especially at high school (*China Daily*, 2004d). The Shanghai Jiulong Model Middle School is the only school which provides free education in Shanghai (Shanghai Municipal Government, 2003). A respondent of another study complained, 'the tuition fees are too high to pay for' and the state 'should take appropriate care of children of laid-off workers' (Cook and Jolly, 2000, p 27).

Although the Chinese government introduced a policy of providing nine years of compulsory education in 1986, only 87.3% of young people study in junior secondary schools (Ministry of Education, 2004). The national gross enrolment in senior high schools was only 42.8% (China Internet Information Centre, 2004). A survey conducted by the Central Committee of China Association for Promoting

Democracy reported a dropout rate in rural junior high schools of nearly 40% (Xinhua News Agency, 2005). In a country that traditionally emphasises the value of education, some children are deprived of educational opportunities because of poverty. It has been estimated that the privatisation of public services has kept 20 million children out of school, and about half the population are unable to afford medicine or hospital fees (J. Chan, 2003). The above evidence illustrates that poor unemployed parents are unable to meet their children's educational needs, not to mention other social needs that are essential to their social development.

Unlike under the planned economy, patients now have to pay medical expenses from their own savings or through medical insurance. Unfortunately, less than one quarter of the population is covered by medical plans or insurance. Because of high medical costs, many parents are forced to 'delay obtaining treatment for their sick children or even to give up altogether' (*Shanghai Star,* 2004). For example, Mr To had already paid ¥80,000 (£5,175) for treating his one-year-old baby, who was suffering from pneumonia, a congenital heart disease and septicaemia. Despite having used all his savings, he still had to get more for the treatment. He worriedly pointed out, 'I feel so frustrated every day. Without money, we have to leave and the only thing we can do is to wait for our baby to die' (*Shanghai Star,* 2004). Although the Shanghai Children's Medical Care Fund was set up in 1996 to help those under 18 to cover medical costs, its financial conditions are strained because the annual membership fee of ¥40 (£2.59) is too low to cover total expenses.

It should be stressed that the financial capacities of unemployed women workers to care for newborn children have been enhanced by a three-month birth supplement. However, in order to be eligible for the supplement, pregnant women have to meet the requirements of the national birth control policy, which limits women to one child only. Again, the welfare right is conditional on whether recipients have followed the central government's population policy.

After the reconstruction of welfare provision in China, the caring burden has been substantially transferred from the state to the family. However, with low levels of MLSG and unemployment benefits, poor parents find it difficult to fulfil their caring duties. Apart from meeting survival needs, unemployed parents have no extra resources to pay for education-related costs, not to mention the expense of children's social and cultural activities. Also, unemployment benefits have been linked to a person's commitment to the state's family policy. Thus, the new social security scheme that has emerged from the market economy is still linked to the central government's population policy.

Social integration

According to the guidelines of the State Council (1999), the MLSG is designed mainly to meet the basic necessities of the poor. In practice, recipients of the MLSG, as illustrated earlier, have inadequate resources to buy nutritious food. Also, recipients of unemployment insurance have to pay part of their medical fees. This shows that poor unemployed people find it difficult to meet their physical needs. It is therefore not surprising that they do not have the extra resources to lead a normal social life. J. Tang (2003) has found that 39% of respondents did not visit friends and relatives in the Chinese New Year and other festivals. In Chinese society, exchanging gifts and eating out are popular social activities for celebrating festivals. Married adults have to give red-pocket money (a traditional practice according to which married persons give money to unmarried persons) to children during the Chinese New Year. However, poor unemployed workers had 'no money to get together with relatives and friends' and 'can't have everyday entertainment (watch ball games, go to concerts)' (Cook and Jolly, 2000, pp 18–19), and they tried to 'avoid social interactions' such as weddings and New Year engagements (2000, p 35). Obviously, poor unemployed people cannot fulfil common social expectations; they are socially excluded from the rest of society.

The most stigmatising practice of the MLSG is the use of public notice as a requirement of application. Under this practice, the applicant's name, age, number of family members, address and the amount of support are made public. Also, comments from the public are part of the process of assessment. Applicants in Sichuan province even have their details published three times before any entitlement is approved (Shang and Wu, 2004). It is argued that this reduces the abuse of public welfare because China does not have an effective system to accurately assess the income of recipients. Thus the involvement of the public, especially recipients' neighbours, can be an effective strategy in tackling welfare fraud. However, the most problematic issue is the intrusion into privacy, especially since Chinese society puts much emphasis on 'face'. As a result, this is a barrier to the poor realising their welfare rights. Senior government officials, in fact, notice that 'some families refuse to apply for assistance for fear of their children suffering discrimination at school' (*People's Daily*, 2002c). The existing practice is a strong social stigma which institutionally discourages the poor from seeking public support.

On the other hand, the central government understands the political implications of unemployment and has attempted to mobilise government departments and the community to support laid-off workers. Local government officials were asked to express concerns for laid-off workers. It is hoped that a culture of supporting the re-employment of the unemployed can be created in society (*People's Daily*, 2003a). The State Council (1997) emphasises:

> We should express our traditional Chinese noble values of respect for older people, caring for children, and mutual help. We should widely mobilise collective resources by organising activities to bring 'warmth and support' for the poor. We should stress mutual help for the family.

Apart from government officials, societal resources in terms of private donations and financial contributions from trade unions and labour organisations have been encouraged to help fight poverty. As stated in the *Shanghai social assistance measures*, 'Government promotes and encourages enterprises, units, social organizations and individuals to make donations to support social assistance' (Shanghai Municipal Government, 1996). Labour organisations are also called to help workers who are still in financial difficulties even after receiving the MLA. The State Council (1999) points out, 'The MLSG is based on the principle of providing a basic living for urban residents. It also stresses the combination of state assistance and supplementary resources from society. The direction is the promotion of self-help in terms of labour market participation.' Based on these principles, senior officials of the Shanghai municipal government have mobilised community resources and organised 'heart-warming activities'. For example, 225,300 visits were arranged for poor people and a total of ¥6.42 million (£415,265) was provided for the poor (Shanghai Municipal Government, 2004c). The central government hopes that such official activities can create a spirit of mutual help in society (State Council, 2001). At the national level, a total of ¥18.11 billion (£1,171 million) was raised from 'heart-warming activities' between 1994 and 2004. Also, government and non-government organisations have paid 55.778 million visits to poor families (Information Office of the State Council, 2004).

The above policies reveal that the Chinese government is adopting two approaches towards the unemployed workers. On the one hand, poor unemployed benefit recipients have to face extremely stigmatising pressure by having their names released to the public. On the other hand, government officials actively express their concern towards the poor through home visits and collective activities. Undoubtedly, collective concerns for unemployed families can enhance a spirit of mutual help and promote communication between the poor and the general public. However, the publication of recipients' names in Chinese society is an extremely stigmatising practice. The evidence earlier clearly shows that complicated application procedures and the release of the identity of recipients have deterred the needy from seeking state assistance. This is an area that future reforms of China's social assistance should tackle. Otherwise, recipients will find it difficult to lead a normal social life, which is an essential part of social integration.

Human learning and development

After stopping job allocations, the Chinese government has adopted 'active employment service measures' (Information Office of the State Council, 2002). China has to tackle tremendous pressure on employment. The decreasing number of public enterprises poses a direct challenge to the relationship between hundreds of thousands of workers and the CCP. It is a great challenge to the Chinese government to equip laid-off workers with skills essential for obtaining jobs in the open market in order to establish a new type of relationship between previous state workers and China's unique socialist market system. The central government emphasises the duty of all levels of government departments to create jobs or to enhance the employability of laid-off workers. Jintao Hu, Chairman of the Chinese government (similar to the Prime Minister in the UK), stresses that doing good work on employment and retraining is related to the basic interest of the public as well as to the stability of China's reforms (*People's Daily*, 2003c). Jiabao Wen also asked leaders of local authorities to be directly involved in managing employment issues, committing sufficient resources and developing effective administration for this task (*People's Daily*, 2003d).

The RSCs represent the most typical combination of providing benefits and facilitating training. The Chinese government insists that 'all relevant employment and social security departments should work together, keeping closer contacts with the grass-roots, and studying their difficulties and problems. Also, policies which are relevant to the re-employment of laid-off workers should be fully implemented' (Ministry of Labour and Social Security, 1998). Against this background, a wide range of programmes have been launched to improve the skills or create business opportunities for unemployed workers.

'Jobs beneficial to the community' and the '40–50 Project'

In recent years, the Shanghai municipal government has put much emphasis on the so-called 40–50 Project ('40' means unemployed female workers aged over 40, while '50' represents unemployed male workers aged over 50). Studies reveal that the majority of unemployed workers are over 40 years old but with low qualifications. They find it more difficult to get jobs in the open market. In order to increase their employment opportunities, the central government asked government organisations to employ older laid-off workers and those who have been unemployed for more than one year for doing 'jobs beneficial to the community'. These jobs are mainly community services such as cleaning, planting, public security and the maintenance of public facilities (*People's Daily*, 2003a). Apart from providing additional financial assistance, the government also pays the social insurance premiums of those working in jobs beneficial to the community.

The Shanghai municipal government has created more than 60,000 jobs a year for unemployed people to work in services such as 'environmental protection', 'city environment', 'transportation', 'helping disabled persons and older people in the community', and 'hygiene and cleaning'. The Shanghai Federation of Trade Unions also launched a scheme called 'Hundred Enterprises with Thousands of Jobs for Community'. According to the scheme, business associations organise public enterprises to offer jobs that need few skills and with flexible working hours for unemployed workers classified as being 'in employment difficulty'. It is expected that 10,000 jobs will be offered from 2004 to 2007 (Shanghai Municipal Government, 2004c).

Youth Placement Scheme

In face of increasing pressures on youth unemployment, the Shanghai municipal government has implemented a Youth Placement Scheme. Unemployed university graduates aged 16–25 (under special circumstances participants can be up to 30) are arranged to work in well-established local and international companies for three to six months. In some cases, the training period can be extended to 12 months. The government pays living costs for participants and training costs for the companies involved. In this way, unemployed young people can learn required skills and gain relevant working experience. Since 2003, a total of 27,000 university graduates have participated in this scheme. It is reported that as many as 60% of participants obtained jobs upon completing their placements (Shanghai Labour and Security Bureau, 2004b).

Subsidies for vocational training

The Shanghai Labour and Security Bureau (2003) pays for all or half of the training fees of those attending designated vocational training courses. Unemployed workers, surplus labour from rural areas and graduates of higher education institutions can attend courses preparing them to work in the catering industry or to be domestic workers or gardeners.

In 2004, the Shanghai municipal government changed its policy on subsidising vocational training. After obtaining a Certificate on Training Subsidy from Employment Training and Guidance Centres, unemployed workers can choose any training programmes that help enhance their employment opportunities (Shanghai Municipal Government, 2004d).

Concession and training for self-employment

Laid-off workers setting up their own businesses are entitled to the following benefits (Ministry of Labour and Social Security, 2001):

- *Tax exemption*: unemployed workers who run 'community service businesses' are exempted from paying business tax, personal income tax, city maintenance tax and education additional tax.
- *Business registration measures.* They also do not need to pay commercial administrative fees. Those who start 'community service businesses' are exempt from commercial administrative fees for three years.
- *Administrative charges.* Unemployed people are exempt from paying administrative charges for three years if they run 'community services businesses'. Those who set up other private businesses do not need to pay administrative charges for one year.
- *Loan policy.* State banks are ordered to actively help those who need financial assistance for running businesses.

According to the State Taxation Administration, community service businesses are services or activities for the convenience of local residents. These businesses include (Ministry of Labour and Social Security, 2004b):

- household cleaning and hygiene services
- primary health services
- childcare and education services
- care for disabled children and educational training services
- care of older people
- patients' care and after-school care for children
- family planning counselling
- good child guidance.

Recently, the Chinese government has launched a training course in 14 cities (including Shanghai) for people intending to set up small businesses. The course was developed by the International Labour Organisation (*Wen Wei Po*, 2004). The Shanghai Labour and Security Bureau has also introduced a training course called 'Touching Net'. The course teaches people to set up businesses through the internet and unemployed participants are exempt from tuition fees (*Evening News Post*, 2004).

Following the central government's policy, Chinese banks provide small loans for unemployed people to set up businesses. A 'business and loan' programme will provide loans for unemployed persons who have completed business training courses (*People's Daily*, 2004b).

In Shanghai, unemployed persons who plan to run businesses without sufficient deposits can get support from the local government. The Shanghai municipal government has specific loans for promoting employment. Under the scheme, a loan guarantee is provided for those taking out loans for less than three years (Shanghai Municipal Government, 2004e).

Unemployed persons who start businesses while receiving unemployment benefits are allowed to continue receiving their benefits. This is to support their business ventures in the earlier stages of operation (Shanghai Municipal Government, 1999). It is estimated that unemployed persons in Shanghai have set up 10,000 community stores, restaurants and small enterprises, which have generated more than 140,000 jobs.

Incentives for employing laid-off workers

Financial incentives are used to increase the employment opportunities of laid-off workers. If companies offer contracts of at least three years for laid-off workers and the total number of such workers is over 30% of its workforce, they can be exempt from corporation tax, city maintenance and construction taxes, and education supplementary tax (*People's Daily*, 2003e).

The above programmes clearly show that the Chinese government has attempted to combine welfare and training by providing unemployed persons with the required skills to get jobs in the open market or to start their own businesses. In the earlier stages of establishing a national social assistance system, the central government was already urging that 'By implementing the MLSG, local governments have to encourage and support able-bodied applicants seeking jobs and being self-reliant. After receiving more income from the labour market, they can gradually improve their living conditions' (State Council, 1997). Following the central government's policy, the goal of Shanghai's social assistance has been to help recipients achieve self-reliance (Shanghai Municipal Government, 1996). The Ministry of Labour and Social Security reported that 20 million workers had attended retraining courses from 2000 to 2003, and their employment rate was over 60%. Also, among 310,000 people who had participated in self-employment training programmes, 64% started their own businesses or got a job (*People's Daily*, 2003d). After regarding the market economy as an essential part of China's unique socialism, the Chinese government sees the open labour market as the most effective long-term means to tackle poverty.

Self-determination

Under existing political and administrative arrangements, the unemployed have few opportunities to participate in the policy-making process. China is a one-party state in which all major policies are decided by the Chinese Communist Party (CCP). Although the constitution of the People's Republic of China states that the National People's Congress (NPC) is the highest decision-making body, the Standing Committee of the Political Bureau (SCPB) is actually the power centre that determines policy and controls all administrative, legal and executive appointments.

As for social assistance, 'The levels of the MLA are decided by local government' (State Council, 1997, para 29). In Shanghai, government officials may seek advice from experts, especially academics, in launching new policies. As Zheng Han, Mayor of Shanghai, emphasises, 'It's good practice to get comments and opinions from specialists to help the government design policies and we'll hold on to the tradition and improve it' (Shanghai Municipal Government, 2003). Thus, we were told by a researcher that the Shanghai municipal government consulted academics of a university on issues to do with the MLSG. However, this type of consultation mainly depends on the good will of government officials, and is not bound by any legal requirements. Because local government officials are key decision makers, the influence of academics on the levels and implementation of MLA is likely to be limited.

On the other hand, recipients of unemployment benefits and claimants of the MLSG are subjected to a certain degree of control over their behaviour. According to the Shanghai Unemployment Registration Measures published by the Shanghai Labour and Social Security Bureau, unemployment benefit recipients have to fulfil several duties, including reporting job-seeking actions, applying for jobs recommended by Employment Offices, and attending vocational training courses (Shanghai Municipal Government, 2004g). In applying for unemployment benefits, applicants have to sign an 'accepting employment services contract' at social security service centres. Those who meet the criteria of 'employment difficulty' are required to sign an 'employment mutual consensus contract' and register as 'unemployed'. It is the Shanghai municipal government's objective to offer jobs for those who are in 'employment difficulty' within three months. Those who are seeking jobs or are receiving employment training have to attend community services organised by resident organisations. Recipients who reject two job offers or fail twice to attend employment services or participate in community services have their benefits terminated (State Council, 1999).

Furthermore, unemployed recipients cannot obtain medical benefits if their health problems are caused by fighting or other illegal activities. Nor can their families obtain any funeral grants if their death is caused by fighting or any illegal activities. In addition, despite making contributions to unemployment insurance, unemployed workers have to renew their unemployment benefits every three months. Poor unemployed workers are also required to do community service. Such requirement is based on the guidelines of the State Council (1999) which states that 'Those who are of working age and are receiving the MLA should participate in community services organized by resident associations'. More importantly, as mentioned earlier, the names of recipients of the MLSG are released to the public. The measures earlier show that the rights to unemployment benefits are not based on purely financial contributions but depend also on whether recipients are good citizens, observing the laws of the Chinese government.

Despite having set up an authoritarian regime, the CCP has attempted to use administrative arrangements to encourage some degree of public participation. One strategy is to provide social security information to the public about such things as the level of benefits, application procedures and feedback channels, and the relevant legislation. According to the guidelines of the State Council (1997), 'By implementing the MLSG, the principles of openness, equality and democracy should be stressed'. Later, the State Council (2001) further urged local authorities to adopt more appropriate channels to encourage democratic participation and to provide more information to the public. The Ministry of Civil Affairs (2004b) has also asked local authorities to provide more opportunities for the public to monitor the MLSG: 'Let the public know the management of the MLSG in order to build an open system based on fairness and justice.' In Shanghai, the municipal government set up a hot line, encouraging the public to express views on the MLSG. Government officials are also required to answer public complaints within a certain period and to handle them properly. Those who are not satisfied with the administration can ask for 'administrative review' (Shanghai Labour and Security Bureau, 2004c). Thus, the Shanghai municipal government has encouraged some degree of participation, mainly through recipients' feedback on the existing administrative procedures and the service quality of staff.

Overall, under the present political structure unemployed recipients have little power to influence social security policies. As mentioned earlier, several administrative arrangements have been made to improve the communication between the government and welfare recipients by releasing information on social security schemes and encouraging public feedback and complaints. However, the extent of participation is rather limited, and it applies only to minor issues. Unemployed workers are unable to force the authorities to change policies. Policy making is in the hands of senior government officials, and the process of policy making is top-down, operating mainly from central to local government.

Equal value

Both the central government and the Shanghai municipal government have clearly recognised the negative impact of the restructuring of state enterprises on employment and on the living standard of laid-off workers. Thus, the central government has urged all local authorities to make employment their first priority, making every effort to help laid-off workers to meet their needs and creating more job opportunities. The slogan 'trying hard to help the deserving poor' has become one of the key features of public assistance. As the central government stresses, local authorities should 'provide assistance for eligible citizens'; all eligible poor people should be protected by the MLSG (State Council, 2001). As illustrated in the subsections earlier, special assistance has been made available to older workers and unemployed workers with 'special difficulties'. In Shanghai, the priority of employment policy is to help women over 40 and men over 50 to get jobs in the open market (China Internet Information Centre, 2002b). The Ministry of Civil Affairs (2004b) has further asked local government officials to help the poor though practical actions. Overall, both the central government and the Shanghai municipal government emphasise the potential of unemployed workers and their right to access basic services. The central government has deliberately constructed a culture of acceptance of unemployed workers. However, low levels of assistance and the publication of names have damaged the social status of the poor. One of the tasks of the Shanghai municipal government is to put social pressure on those who are lazy (Shanghai Municipal Government, 2004c). Clearly, the Chinese government's ambivalence towards the unemployed may reflect on the one hand its intention to placate the poor and on the other hand its concern about welfare dependency in a market economy.

More importantly, the needs of unemployed persons in rural areas have long been neglected. The MLSG was developed mainly in urban areas as a result of the contraction of state enterprises. Its targets are mainly urban residents (State Council, 1999). However, the unemployment problem is more serious in rural areas. The deregulation of agricultural prices and production has forced tens of millions off the land since the mid-1980s. According to the China Poverty Relief Fund, 30 million rural people lack adequate food and clothing, and another 60 million have an income of less than US$100 a year (J. Chan, 2004). However, only certain categories of poor people in rural areas can receive public assistance (Shanghai Ministry of Civil Affairs, 2004), such as:

- those without any relatives or whose relatives are unable to take care of them;
- those who lose the ability to work; and
- those without any sources of income.

Able-bodied adults are not regarded as deserving and have been excluded from public assistance. A representative of the National People's Congress criticised the existing social security arrangements for not including the protection of farmers. The existing social security measures benefit only workers in cities. The rights of farmers are being eroded, exposing a gap in the existing legislation (*China Labour and Protection Post*, 2004).

More and more rural workers move to work in urban areas as a result of rapid economic growth in the big cities. In 1984, restrictions on farmers seeking employment in cities were introduced. It was reported that there were 113.9 million migrant workers working in cities, accounting for 23.2% of the total rural labourers (Xinhua News Agency, 2004c). For example, there were 23 million migrant workers in Guangdong, 20% more than its registered population. However, they cannot apply for the MLA because they are not entitled under city laws and regulations to be registered as permanent urban residents (*China Daily*, 2004b). More seriously, as few as 15% of migrant workers' children in Qingdao province are receiving education (China Internet Information Centre, 2004). Nationally, of 19.8 million migrant workers under 18 years of age, nearly half do not go to school (*China Daily*, 2004d).

In addition, the rates of MLA which poor unemployed persons receive have been greatly affected by the different welfare measures of local authorities. Unemployed workers living in economically developed provinces can obtain higher social security benefits than those in less developed ones (Table 5.2). For example, in 2003 the level of MLA in Beijing was ¥233 (£15.07) per person, in Shanghai ¥139 (£8.99).

Table 5.2: Level of Minimum Living Standard Guarantee (MLSG) per person per month, 2001–02

Region	Level of MLSG (¥)	Region	Level of MLSG (¥)
National average	*152*		
Beijing	285	Jilin	136
Shanghai	280	Henan	136
Tianjin	241	Chongqing	134
Tibet	207	Hubei	131
Guangdong	182	Sichuan	130
Liaoning	172	Hunan	130
Shanxi	156	Guangxi	129
Jiangsu	156	Gansu	128
Shandong	154	Xinjiang	127
Qinghai	152	Inner Mongolia	118
Hebei	131	Heilongjiang	117
Fujian	151	Hainan	110
Yunnan	149	Shaanxi	108
Ningxia	144	Guizhou	104
Anhui	143	Jiangxi	96

Note: Exchange rate: £1.00 = 15.46 yuan.
Source: Douji et al (2002), cited in Shang and Wu (2004, p 269)

However, it was ¥81 (£5.24) in Jiangsu and even ¥36–43 (£2.33–2.78) in provinces such as Shanxi, Henan, Inner Mongolia Autonomous Region and Hebei (*China Daily,* 2003).

'The whole social security system lacks unity and coherence', and suffers from 'structural defects' (China Internet Information Centre, 2002a). New patterns of inequality are emerging in China, which is the most problematic issue in the transition from a socialist to a mixed economy.

The above figures clearly reveal that two types of welfare system have been created in China over the past two decades. The population of 1.3 billion is divided by social class, the nature of residency (temporary for migrant workers and permanent for urban dwellers), geographical location (rural versus urban), and the financial circumstances of local authorities. Unemployed persons are accessing different welfare systems, and are unequally treated under existing welfare arrangements. Lacking any welfare benefits, unemployed migrant workers and their children, however, are the poorest section of the population in cities.

Shanghai is one of the few cities that provide financial support for poor people in rural areas as well as extending the social insurance system to migrant workers. About 3.3% of the rural population (44,500 families or 104,600 people) are claiming the MLSG (Shanghai Municipal Government, 2004). The Shanghai municipal government (2004f) also sends employment support workers to rural areas, providing them with job information and career advice. However, the social security system is still mainly serving the needs of urban residents and was extended to small towns through the 'township social security plan' in 2003. The key objective of the extension is to boost industrial development in small towns in Shanghai suburbs. As pointed out by Zheng Han, Mayor of Shanghai (Shanghai Municipal Government, 2003): 'The city government hopes the new township scheme will help attract more rural population to move to small tows and thus boost more industrial parks there to replace the existing scattered industries in the rural areas.'

Accordingly, rural farmers have to move to towns and become residents in order to be eligible for social security benefits. Clearly, social security provision in Shanghai is not based on the concept of citizenship but on 'residence-ship'. Those who live in areas that have a lot of industrial or commercial activities or that are expected to enhance the future economic development of cities can obtain social security benefits.

The evidence earlier clearly shows that Chinese citizens living in different parts of China get different types and different levels of assistance as a result of the traditional division of residency between rural and city areas, as well as variations in the welfare ideologies and the financial circumstances of different local authorities. Thus, the welfare rights and the quality of life of unemployed recipients are not equal but differentiated by residency and geographical location. The central government also admitted that the development of social security in rural areas 'will still have a long way to go' (Information Office of the State Council, 2004). Thus, more work is needed to tackle the inequality of social welfare among Chinese citizens in different provinces as well as among cities, suburban areas and rural areas.

Conclusion

Several issues surround the dignity of unemployed persons in China. The first is the expansion of the free economy and the contraction of public enterprises. The second is the transitional welfare measures designed to tackle welfare needs. The third is the traditional political practices and the political domination of the CCP. As discussed in this chapter, new social protection is required to meet the financial needs of unemployed workers, who in the past were automatically offered jobs by the government. The objective of the central government is to set up a labour and social security system which corresponds to 'the development of China's productive forces as well as the needs of the socialist market economy' (Information Office of the State Council, 2004). However, with low levels of assistance, the new welfare system provides protection for the poor only in the form of unemployment insurance, the MLSG, and the basic livelihood guarantee system (BLGS) for laid-off workers. The local authorities are also urged to follow the principles of 'providing basic living and eliminating dependency' (State Council, 1997). It seems that the Chinese government is trying to reduce welfare dependency in a new welfare system. Following the direction of welfare policy, one of the focuses of Shanghai's MLSG is to apply social pressure on those who have working abilities but are lazy (Shanghai Municipal Government, 2004f). At present, the new welfare system can provide only financial assistance for meeting the survival needs of recipients, whose medical, psychological and social needs have been neglected. As J. Tang (2003) points out, 'The poor find it hard to meet health, education and social needs. Thus, they are far from having a good quality of life and human dignity.'

However, it should be stressed that the central government and the

Shanghai municipal government understand the underlying causes of unemployment and also recognise the potential of unemployed workers. Employment has been seen as the most effective way to improve the quality of life of the poor in a mixed economy. Thus, a wide range of training programmes and employment opportunities have been created for unemployed recipients. The new welfare system in China emphasises learning, targeting the most disadvantaged groups through such initiatives as the '40–50 Project' for older workers.

The case of Shanghai shows that China's welfare system is developing and improving. The Chinese government has attempted to base its social protection system on China's unique problems and the available resources. As the State Council points out, 'Through reforms and development, a national unified social security system will be put into practice step by step' (Information Office of the State Council, 2004). For example, by June 2004 116.28 million people were participating in basic national health insurance. Now, the central government is planning to extend health insurance to private companies and is also studying measures to solve the health problems of a worker's family members (Ministry of Labour and Social Security, 2004a). It was reported that China has achieved a remarkable reduction in poverty: from 1978 to 2004, the number of people in poverty fell from 250 million to 29 million (Xinhua News Agency, 2004c). The sums invested in poverty reduction increased from ¥9.8 billion (£634 million) in 1994 to about ¥30 billion (£1.94 billion) in 2003 (Xinhua News Agency, 2004d). However, a Chinese economist, Qinglian, estimated that the Gini coefficient in China had risen from 0.15 in 1978 to 0.59 in 1999 (Conachy, 2001), revealing that little work has been done to tackle inequality. Also, under the existing one-party politics, the poor participate little in the decision-making process. This is another aspect of dignity that the Chinese government needs to address.

As discussed earlier, Chinese society has been divided by residency and geographical location. This is apparent from differences in access to welfare between migrant workers and permanent urban residents, between poor regions and economically developed regions, and between rural areas and cities. It is understood that the central government is trying to tackle the differences, especially to protect the large numbers of migrant workers. For example, the Ministry of Labour and Social Security asked companies to abolish unreasonable charges on the employment of migrant workers, while local authorities were also ordered to draw up employment and education training plans for these workers (China Internet Information Centre, 2004).

Guangdong Province is also planning to introduce a unified unemployment insurance system for both urban residents and farmers (*China Daily*, 2004b); while the Shanghai municipal government allows migrant workers to apply for residence cards so that they are entitled to the same benefits as local residents (*Shanghai Daily* and China Internet Information Centre, 2004). The latest government White Paper on welfare policy also admits the inadequacy of the existing welfare system (Information Office of the State Council, 2004):

> China still has a long way to go to develop its social security services to a satisfactory level.... To press ahead with the improvement of the social security system is an important task for the Chinese Government in its efforts to build a moderately prosperous society in a comprehensive way.

In addition to these welfare inadequacies and inequalities, the dignity of unemployed persons has been suppressed by having their names released to the public and by linking their welfare entitlements to their behaviour. An unemployed worker's access to medical treatment is related to the causes of his health problems. Therefore, the new welfare system has become a means for the CCP to extend its control from the planned economy to a mixed economy. Regarding the welfare of workers, J. Chan (2003) ventured the criticism that 'China is more like a giant sweatshop for the world's major corporations'. After the introduction of the market economy, the political questions are whether the CCP is still controlled by the working class and whether it will safeguard the welfare of the working class in a mixed economy. The development of the Chinese welfare system reveals the changing nature of the ruling party as well as its relationship with Chinese workers.

SIX

The United Kingdom and human dignity

The New Labour government's (NLG) landslide victory in the 1997 general election opened a new chapter for the British welfare state. Unlike previous Labour governments, which had emphasised collective provision and wealth redistribution, the NLG attaches greater importance to the private market as an effective mechanism not only for wealth creation but also for welfare delivery. Also, the NLG stresses the distribution of opportunity through education and training rather than the redistribution of wealth through, for instance, raising benefit rates. Work, therefore, has been promoted as a means to tackle poverty and to improve the life quality of the poor. Against this background, the NLG has sought to reform the social security system based on welfare-to-work programmes aimed at enhancing the employability of unemployed people. In addition, 'work' has been considered as a means to enhance a person's self-esteem and life satisfaction. Therefore, a moral foundation has been laid to justify the state's control over the behaviour of claimants. One issue central to the debate about 'welfare to work' is 'compulsion'. Deacon (1997, p 35) has asked, 'Is it reasonable to withhold benefits from those who refuse to participate in such measures, and, if so, how should such a sanction be imposed and maintained?' This chapter attempts to examine the impact of New Labour's welfare initiatives on the dignity of the UK's unemployed persons.

The New Labour government's policies towards unemployment

The New Labour government is proud of its economic achievements. From the 1980s to the early 1990s, the UK experienced poor economic performance with an unemployment rate which at times exceeded 10%. Thereafter the economy gradually recovered. In August 2004 the unemployment rate in the UK was only 4.8% (1.44 million unemployed workers), while the labour participation rate was 74.6%, one of the highest among European countries (Human Resource Management, 2004). Against these economic achievements, Gordon

Brown, the Chancellor of the Exchequer, asserted at the Labour Party conference in 2004:

> No longer the most inflation prone economy, with New Labour, Britain today has the lowest inflation for thirty years.

> No longer the boom-bust economy, Britain has had the lowest interest rates for forty years.

> And no longer the stop-go economy, Britain is now enjoying the longest period of sustained economic growth for 200 years.

> And no longer the country of mass unemployment, Britain is now advancing further and faster towards full employment than at any time in our lives. (Brown, 2004)

He concluded, New Labour is 'today the only party trusted with the economy'.

The NLG's economic policies and welfare initiatives are interdependent. The government has attempted to build a new welfare regime around work. In fact, this welfare approach seems to follow in the footsteps of the previous Conservative government, which was described as having imposed a 'stricter benefit regime' (Finn, 1998, p 106). This is because, during the Conservative administration, the objectives of welfare policies were to 'reduce welfare dependency by restricting benefit eligibility, by improving and policing the job seeking behaviour of the unemployed, and by pricing claimants into work' (Finn, 1998, p 106). A White Paper, *Employment for the 1990s*, argued that unemployment 'could be considerably reduced and many vacant jobs filled if unemployed people looked more intensively and more effectively for work' (Department of Employment, 1988, p 57). Clearly, the causes of unemployment were linked to a person's motivations and job-seeking behaviour. Therefore, unemployed workers were expected to put more effort into solving their own problems. Based on this welfare approach, several initiatives were launched in order to improve the employability and work incentives of the unemployed. For example, young unemployed people aged 16–17 could no longer apply for Income Support; instead they were given a Youth Training guarantee. Those aged 18–25 who had declined a place in a scheme were required to attend a four week 'Workwise' course. If they failed to attend the course, they would lose 40% of their benefit for the week in question.

After New Labour's victory in the general election in 1997, the Secretary of State for Social Security announced that the overall aims of reform were to 'reduce poverty and welfare dependency and promote work incentives' (Harman, 1997). The core welfare ideologies of NLG come from the Third Way, under which work is held to be 'central to self-esteem and standard of living' and also 'one main content of opportunity' and 'involvement in public space' (Giddens, 2000, p 103). In the face of an ageing population and an increasing dependency ratio, Gordon Brown believes 'the most successful economies will be those who encourage the maximum number of people of working age into the labour market' (*Guardian*, 2004c). A greater supply of labour can also facilitate economic growth and avoid skill shortages and inflationary pressures. Thus, the focus of the NLG's employment policy is to provide employment opportunities for all; its objective is to have at least three quarters of the working age population in work by the end of the decade. Two strategies have been adopted to enhance the employability of unemployed persons and to protect the income of those working in the labour market. The first is the implementation of various types of 'New Deal' programmes for different unemployment claimants such as New Deal for Young People (NDYP), New Deal for 25 Plus, New Deal for Lone Parents, New Deal for 50 Plus, and New Deal for the Disabled. Based on this work-oriented welfare approach, the right of unemployed workers to Jobseeker's Allowance (JSA) has been linked to specific requirements of New Deal programmes. In short, welfare duties have been used to promote a work-oriented welfare policy.

In the UK, there are two types of JSA for unemployed persons: contribution-based and income-based. To be eligible to these two types of assistance, an unemployed person should be (Multiple Sclerosis Society, 2005):

- capable of work
- available for work
- actively seeking work
- under 65 (for men) or 60 (for women)
- not working, or working on average less than 16 hours a week
- not in full-time education (with limited exceptions)
- living in the UK (though it can be paid for short periods of temporary absence)
- have entered into a Jobseeker's Agreement.

There are also specific requirements for the two schemes. The contribution-based JSA is a non-means-tested personal fixed-rate benefit for those who have paid National Insurance contributions. The level of benefits may be reduced if the recipient works part-time or has an occupational pension. Eligible recipients can receive benefits for up to 26 weeks. The income-based JSA is a means-tested benefit for those who have an inadequate National Insurance contribution record or who have exhausted their entitlement to the contribution-based JSA. The amount of benefit depends on a person's age and the number and age of family members. Those who receive the income-based JSA can also access other benefits such as Housing Benefit and Council Tax Benefit.

The rates for both contribution-based and income-based JSA are presented in Table 6.1.

In order to enhance the employability of unemployed recipients, unemployed persons who make a new or repeat claim to the following benefits after April 2000 are required to attend a work-focused interview (WFI):

- JSA
- Income Support
- Incapacity Benefit
- Housing Benefit and Council Tax Benefit

Table 6.1: Weekly amounts of Jobseeker's Allowance (JSA), 2004–05

		£
Contribution-based JSA		
Aged 16–17		33.50
Aged 18–24		44.05
Aged 25+		55.65
Income-based JSA personal allowances		
Single people	aged 16–17	33.50
	aged 18–24	44.05
	aged 25+	55.65
Couples	both aged 16–17	33.50
	both aged 16–17, one disabled	44.05
	both aged 16–17, with responsibility for a child	66.50
	one aged 16–17, one 18–24	44.05
	one aged 16–17, one over 25	55.65
	both aged 18+	87.30
Lone parents	aged 16–17	33.50
	or depending on their circumstances	44.05
	aged 18+	55.65
Dependent children	from birth to the day before the 19th birthday	42.27

Source: Jobcentre Plus (2004a)

- Invalid Care Allowance
- Widow's Benefit.

Through the mandatory WFI, the NLG aims to tackle 'long-term reliance on social security benefits' by equipping recipients with skills for a changing labour market (Kelleher et al, 2002, p 2).

In contrast to these requirements, the NLG has introduced some basic income protection measures for those working in the labour market, through the National Minimum Wage and Tax Credits. The National Minimum Wage was introduced in April 1999, and has been described as 'an important cornerstone of Government strategy aimed at providing employees with decent minimum standards and fairness in the workplace' (DTI, 2004). The rate in 2004–5 for those aged 22 and over is £4.50 per hour, while for 18–21-year-olds the figure is £3.80 per hour. There are two types of tax credit: Child Tax Credit (CTC) and Working Tax Credit (WTC). CTC provides extra child care support for families with an annual income less than £50,000, while WTC is designed to help people on low incomes and can include support for qualifying childcare (Direct.gov.uk, 2005). In addition, the EU Working Time Directive was implemented in 1998, limiting the number of weekly working hours that an employer can require of most workers to 48. In short, additional financial support for working families and the improvement of working conditions have made people better-off in paid work than on public benefits. Thus, a rewarding labour participation system together with punitive welfare-to-work measures has been created for tackling poverty and unemployment. The following section attempts to examine the dignity of unemployed workers in the UK's work-centred welfare environment.

The dignity of unemployed persons

Meeting physical needs

A healthy body is a precondition for cognitive development and social interaction. Previous UK governments and the current NLG have rejected 'scientific methods or findings in the field of poverty research as valid for policy making' (Veit-Wilson, 2004). Instead, the concept of less eligibility has traditionally affected the UK government's policy towards financial assistance. Accordingly, the levels of social security benefits have been 'below the level of low wage rates' (Veit-Wilson, 1999, p 101). Several research studies show that benefit levels are inadequate to meet recipients' basic necessities. After analysing 31 studies of the living conditions of welfare claimants, Kempson (1996) concluded that social security recipients were unable to avoid real hardship, and they fell behind with basic household bills such as rent, mortgage, gas, electricity, water and Council Tax. As a respondent exclaimed, 'There's absolutely nothing I spend my money on except just surviving, you know, paying bills and buying food' (Kempson, 1996, p 4). Gordon et al (2000) found that, because of inadequate money, 4% of respondents could not afford 'meat, fish or vegetarian equivalent every other day' and a 'warm, waterproof coat'. Similarly, by studying the living standards of 37 families claiming Income Support or JSA, Farrell and O'Connor (2004, p 5) reported that it was only after securing jobs that respondents were able to afford healthy and balanced meals. A recent study (NCSR and DWP, 2004) also found that deprivation still existed in a significant number of households, especially lone parents: 10% of them could not afford 'meat/fish every other day'. Overall, 12% of respondent families (25% for lone parent families) were unable to buy 'new clothes when needed' (2004,).

The NLG defines poverty as 'household income below 60% of the median income'. On this measure, Income Support for a couple with two children under 11 would have provided only 71. 4% of what was needed in 2001–02 (Flaherty et al, 2004, p 62). Moreover, in the same year, there was found to be a 75% risk of poverty where the head of household was unemployed and 63% risk where that person was sick, disabled or a lone parent (Flaherty et al, 2004, p 39; see Table 6. 2). Of the UK population more widely, including households in work as well as those without work, 22% (12. 5 million people) were living on less than 60% of median income in 2001–02. Moreover, according to the study by Gordon et al (2000), 77% of unemployed people and 70% of Income Support recipients had a greater risk of poverty.

The research findings earlier show that poverty is still a serious problem in the UK. Unemployed recipients and lone parents suffer a higher risk of deprivation than other disadvantaged groups. Unemployed persons living on JSA are unable to maintain a balanced diet and struggle to pay bills. As pointed out by Flaherty et al (2004, p 66), 'The overall conclusion concerning poverty since 1997 is that there has been some considerable progress with regard to children, but very little progress with regard to poverty as a whole'. Thus, childless recipients of income-based JSA and income support are being left behind.

Accessing medical care is a right of all UK residents. The National Health Service (NHS) provides comprehensive preventive, curative and rehabilitative services for the general public, delivered largely free at the time of receipt and funded mainly from general taxation. Public spending on health care accounted for 6.7% of the UK's GDP in 2004, and has planned to rise to 7.2% per year in real terms between 2002/03 and 2007/08 (HM Treasury, 2004b). Unemployed people are even exempt from paying for prescription charges. In short, loss of income does not exclude unemployed families from receiving treatment as a result of the collective provision of health care.

Meeting psychological needs

Apart from physical health, the psychological well-being of unemployed persons is essential to their rational and social functioning. Very often, unemployed persons experience low self-esteem, lack a sense of self-worth and suffer from stress. After reviewing various studies of low-income households, Kempson (1996, p 3) pointed out that 'The stress and despair associated with life on a low income leads some to become deeply depressed and, in a few extreme cases, to suicide'. Some unemployed persons are worried about not having enough money to buy daily necessities; some feel helpless and their lives have little meaning. As a respondent of a study declared, 'Everything was grey, everything seemed grey before ... and there was nothing, no social time, no free time, no pleasure, nothing and it was horrible' (Farrell and O'Connor, 2004, p 45). Feelings of dependence, stigma and frustration are common experiences of unemployed persons. As a respondent of Perkins' (2001, p 85) study said:

> It's so depressing being at home day in and day out, your sleeping pattern changes, you've got nothing to do, you generally don't feel good about yourself. People talk and will say "well he's on the dole, he shouldn't be on the dole he should be getting work, get a job, lazy so and so".

Another respondent was disappointed with his financial dependency:

> I felt bad. Always fucking begging, well not begging because like it was me Mum, but that's how it seemed, always asking her for money.

Clearly, unemployment brings tremendous social and psychological pressures on the unemployed. Unemployed families, therefore, need not only financial assistance but also social and psychological support. As a study of the backgrounds of sanctioned JSA recipients revealed, most of them suffered significant problems (Saunders et al, 2001, pp 9–10), such as

- literacy problems
- learning difficulties
- confidence, nerves, psychological problems
- alcohol and drug addictions
- criminal records
- lacking in social skills
- tendency to violence
- living in 'vulnerable' housing (for example, temporary accommodation)
- health problems.

Thus, effective services and good quality welfare staff are required to tackle the complicated problems of JSA recipients.

In implementing the welfare-to-work strategy, the NLG introduced Personal Advisers (PAs) for New Deal participants. Accordingly, JSA applicants have to meet with their PAs, who are expected to assess the needs of unemployed persons, assisting them in overcoming employment barriers. In addition, the NLG developed the 'ONE' service, an integrated approach to benefits and employment advice. As mentioned earlier, all new or repeat claimants of some benefits are required to attend a work-focused interview (WFI). The main objectives of this policy are to 're-position them [welfare recipients] as potential workers and re-equip them for a changing labour market' (Kelleher et al, 2000, p 2). The PA of ONE

> should assess individual circumstances and needs in relation to employment. This was intended to be an holistic and integrated response which could identify and begin to address clients' difficulties by accessing services, support, advice and guidance to help people into or towards work. (Kelleher et al, 2002, p 10)

In fact, the Jobcentre Plus (JCP) has promised to provide high quality and personalised services for recipients. As stated in the JCP Customer's Charter (Jobcentre Plus, 2004b), it will

- treat you with respect
- be fair and helpful

- treat you as an individual by giving you the service you need
- behave professionally.

In addition to the services of JCP, young people aged 13–19 can access various types of services from Connexions Personal Advisers, including choosing subjects at schools and mapping out future career options. Connexions is a welfare programme which provides counselling and guidance for young people.

Unfortunately, the capacities of PAs to provide personalised services have been limited by their training. With the exception of those who work for the Connexions services for young people, PAs receive only a short period of on-the-job training. Newly recruited PAs can receive 'an average of 73 days' training, whereas existing personal advisers received an average of eight days' training' (House of Commons, 2002). Also, the contents of training are mainly policy procedures and benefit levels such as 'Employment Service training', 'Labour Market training', 'Jobseeker's Allowance procedures' and 'Benefits Agency-specific training'. By exploring the attitudes of PAs on training, Kelleher et al (2002, p 28) found that 'The majority of staff [PAs] felt that the training provided had been inadequate either in terms of content or timeliness'. PAs are poorly equipped even to conduct interviews. According to one PA, 'little attention' has been given to 'how to conduct a start-up or work-focused meeting with new clients' (Kelleher et al, 2002, p 27).

Findings of various research studies show that service quality is mixed and inconsistent. Some PAs were seen as 'friendly, helpful and approachable' (Millar, 2000). On the other hand, ineffective PAs 'treated people with a lack of respect and did not have enough of the right sort of information'. Similarly, after examining the experiences of recipients from WFIs, Costello et al (2002) reported both positive and negative views on PAs. Positively, respondents felt the WFI was 'more structured and proactive in finding them work' and their needs were addressed 'more empathetically than other Advisers had in the past' (2002, p 54). Negatively, some felt their long-term needs in terms of referral to relevant training courses with recognisable qualifications 'were often not addressed' (2002, p 55). Also, some said their PAs 'lacked sufficient knowledge of training provision available in the local areas' (2002, p 55) and also struggled to provide tailor-made and continued support for them.

The mixed experiences among recipients were also reported by Davies et al (2004) who investigated the services of JCP. Some respondents felt 'they engaged in a meaningful, relevant and substantive discussion' with their PAs (2004, p 9). On the other hand, some complained that 'the discussions were not tailored to their situation, were not sufficiently detailed, or did not tell the individual something they did not already know' (2004, p 9). They further reported that PAs did not have sufficient knowledge of JCP benefits, lacked sufficient time to provide services, and failed accurately to assess jobseekers' readiness to work or to help those who spoke little English.

By examining the effectiveness of ONE, Green et al (2001) found that the average length of the first meeting among lone parent respondents was 34 minutes, which was less than the recommended 45 minutes. Also, 23% of respondents said that the meeting (s) 'failed to provide all the help or assistance they required' (2001). Furthermore, 30% of respondents mentioned a negative aspect of ONE, such as:

- they had to repeat a lot of information;
- they disliked having to contact more then one office;
- the Personal Adviser's knowledge of benefits was poor; and
- they had not had enough time with their Personal Adviser.

Similar problems with ONE were reported by respondents on JSA: 32% cited a negative feature and 26% claimed the service failed to provide assistance for them (Green et al, 2001). After interviewing clients who had participated in a WFI, Osgood et al (2002) reported that most respondents could not get a clear explanation of the purpose of the initial meeting and the role of a Personal Adviser. As a result, 'many clients [were] unaware of their rights and responsibilities or indeed what ONE could offer them'. More importantly, some felt their PAs 'had lacked training or adequate knowledge of the benefit system' (2002).

In a national survey, Loumidis et al (2001) reported mixed feedback from participants in the 'New Deal for Disabled People Personal Adviser Service'. The PAs had a positive impact on participants including (2001, p 150):

- having a 'kick start';
- continuous contact with a PA;
- raised confidence, increased self-esteem;
- identifying a career path;
- attending a training course;
- experience of a work placement;
- direct financial help;
- information and advice about benefits, and financial support;
- being helped to look for jobs;

- receiving help with practical and financial aspects of starting a small business; and
- being told about a vacancy, which leads to employment.

However, a quarter of the 65% of respondents who left the service expressed dissatisfaction. Among those who still received the services, a third claimed the service 'Was unable to offer help and support you wanted'. The negative features of PAs were (2001, p 151):

- poor match between the client's interests and abilities and the options arranged (work-related activities, job interviews);
- inadequate information or advice about benefits and tax credits;
- slow pace or lack of response from the PA;
- breakdown in communication with the PA.

Because of inadequate training and a heavy workload, it is difficult for PAs to achieve the objective of an individualised, client-focused service:

> ... difficulties in sustaining individualised follow-up in the form of caseloading by Personal Advisers. Clients were not always able to see 'their' adviser for follow-up meetings since this continuity was often compromised in favour of meeting appointment scheduling targets. And, clients were not usually asked for their preference on these occasions. The service was not always, therefore, able to provide a smooth or a complete 'pathway' for clients. (Kelleher et al, 2002, p 4).

In the light of the varying backgrounds and complicated nature of clients' problems, Loumidis et al (2001, p 148) conclude that the service requires PAs to have 'highly developed competencies and skills, across a range of different kinds of expertise. If there is insufficient supply of such people there will be negative impact on clients'. The fact is that the requirement to deal with clients from various backgrounds 'lies beyond the capacity of welfare-to-work initiatives as currently envisaged' (Dean, 2003, p 442). The variety and complexity of client problems are such that training should include more detailed information on employment services and benefits and cover 'learning about dealing with different clients' (Kelleher et al, 2002, p 28). Kelleher et al (2002, p 5) also conclude that the Department for Work and Pensions (DWP) has to clarify the role of the PA, and develop 'a more sophisticated definition and understanding of, and approaches to the assessment of, work-readiness and the barriers to employment'.

The above evidence consistently shows that PAs find it hard to provide personalised services for unemployed persons because they lack sufficient knowledge of employment services and counselling skills for coping with various types of unemployed persons and their complicated problems. Therefore, more effective training and resources are required to enhance the capacities of PAs in order to conduct effective assessment and help overcome underlying barriers to employment.

Fulfilling caring duties

Unemployed parents' caring duties towards children have been helped by collective services in health and education. The British welfare state was established after the Second World War following the publication of the Beveridge Report in 1942, the Education Act of 1944 and the introduction of the NHS in 1948. Accordingly, free medical care and primary and secondary schooling have been provided for British citizens regardless of their class, gender or race. Unemployed parents, therefore, are able to fulfil their caring duties towards their children's health care and education even though they lose income.

However, unemployed parents have limited resources to provide children with a decent living. In the UK, by the late 1990s 3.8 million children (30% of the total) were living in poverty. After analysing data from the *Poverty and Social Exclusion in Britain* Survey (Gordon et al, 2000) and the *British Household Panel Survey*, Adelman et al (2003) found that 9% of children experienced persistent and severe poverty between 1991 and 1999. The Households Below Average Income data from the DWP (2003) reveal that between 1998 and 2001 16% of children lived in poverty for at least three out of the four years of this period. Lone parent families (Table 6.2) and families with 'Head or spouse unemployed' (Table 6.3) had a higher risk of being in poverty.

Table 6.2: The risk of income poverty by family status in 2001–02

Family status	Risk of income poverty (%)
Lone parent	53
Single without children	23
Couple with children	22
Single pensioner	22
Pensioner couple	22
Couple without children	11

Source: Flaherty et al (2004, p 40)

Table 6.3: Risk of income poverty by economic status in 2001–02 (defined as living in households with below 60% of median income after housing costs)

Economic status	% living in poverty
Head or spouse unemployed	75
Other inactive[a]	63
One or more in part-time work	33
Head or spouse aged 60+	26
Self-employed	22
One in full-time work and one not working	17
One in full-time work and one in part-time work	5
Single or couple, all in full-time work	3

Note: Poverty defined as living in households with below 60% of median income after housing costs.

[a] Other inactive = all those not included in previous groups, including the long-term sick, disabled people and non-working lone parents.

Source: Flaherty et al (2004, p 39)

Table 6.4: Percentage of children lacking certain basic necessities

	PSE		PSENI
	% lacking one	% lacking two	% who cannot afford item/activity
Three meals a day	(3)	(5)	(1)
Warm waterproof coat	6	11	(3)
School uniform	6	18	(1)
Celebrations	10	20	(1)
Hobby/leisure	5	(10)	4
Leisure equipment	9	17	8
Play group	(4)	(7)	(3)
Educational games	12	21	5

PSE: *Poverty and Social Exclusion in Britain* Survey, 1999 (Gordon et al, 2000)

PSENI: *Poverty and Social Exclusion in Northern Ireland* Surveys, 2002/03 (Hillyard et al, 2003)

Note: Figures in brackets indicate less than 20 weighted cases.

The PSE survey in 1999 defined a child as 'deprived' if lacking one or more necessities because her/his parents could not afford them. The PSENI used a similar list to determine which necessities children were lacking because their parents could not afford them.

Source: Flaherty et al (2004, p 148)

Because of financial constraints, children from poor families are unable to afford 'basic necessities' and participate in a normal social and school life. The *Poverty and Social Exclusion in Britain* Survey (Gordon et al, 2000) showed that 30% of poor children were unable to pay for celebrations and 26% lacked leisure equipment (Table 6.4). Indeed, the government's support for school uniforms is also inadequate. The local authority grant for a secondary school child's uniform on average was £51.20 a year, which was lower than the average annual cost of

£178 a year. The Citizens' Advice Bureau has criticised the Government for making 'many significant strides to meet its pledge to end child poverty, yet (failing) to help low-income families meet the extra, unavoidable costs associated with education' (*Guardian*, 2004b).

Similar findings on the lack of basic necessities were reported by other social scientists. Gordon et al (2000) estimated that 33% of British children go without at least one of the things needed, such as three meals a day, participation in out-of-school activities and adequate clothing. Another study conducted by the National Centre for Social Research (NCSR) and DWP found that 5% of lone parents could not afford a waterproof coat for each child and in 13% of cases two pairs of shoes for each child. Poor parents also do not have adequate resources to buy school uniforms. A further study (Morris and Ritchie, 1994, p 4), which interviewed 60 couples with dependent children in the early 1990s, revealed that some parents 'regularly go without food, have difficulty clothing children, and have to deny them recreational spending'. As the evidence earlier illustrates, poor parents have found it hard to cope with children's education-related costs and expenses for social activities.

It should be stressed that the NLG regards tackling child poverty as its top priority. Gordon Brown emphasises: 'Child poverty is a scourge on our society and eradicating it is a priority both for the Government and the devolved administrations' (HM Treasury, 2002). Given that child poverty is associated with a wide range of factors such as low income, worklessness, and poor health, education and housing, the NLG has adopted a multi-dimensional approach to alleviate it through initiatives like Sure Start and through financial help in the form of Child Tax Credit and the Working Tax Credit. Sure Start is a NLG's initiative on tackling child poverty in deprived areas through increasing childcare places, improving children's health development, and enhancing parents' childcare knowledge and skills. The overall objectives of the NLG are to:

- ensure a decent family income, with work for those who can and extra support for those who cannot;
- provide excellent public services – including a world class education system for all, ensuring that children from poor backgrounds have the skills and education they need to break the cycle of disadvantage; and
- target the neediest families through the Sure Start Programme and the Children's Fund, for those with additional needs and at key stages in life. (HM Treasury, 2004a, p 9)

Table 6.5: Value of the income support (IS) scales over time and comparison with the Family Budget Unit low cost but acceptable (LCA) budget

	Lone parent plus two children under 11			Couple plus two children under 11		
	IS per week	LCA budget per week	Difference	IS per week	LCA budget per week	Difference
January 1998	98.70	122.21	−23.51	121.75	154.04	−32.29
February 2001	119.95	126.37	−6.42	158.10	158.16	−0.06
April 2002	135.70	129.53	+6.17	166.40	162.11	+4.29

Source: Flaherty et al (2004, p 63)

With the objective of tackling child poverty, the NLG has increased the means-tested benefit rates for children under 11 as well as the levels of child benefit. By comparing differences between the levels of Income Support (IS) and the amount of the 'low cost but acceptable' budget standard from the Family Budget Unit of York University (Flaherty et al, 2004), it can be shown that the living standard of IS families has clearly improved (Table 6.5), to the point where IS levels for families with young children appear to have been adequate by this standard since 2002.

In summary, it is evident that poor unemployed families have had difficulties in meeting 'basic necessities' and the 'social and recreational needs' of children. In response to the serious problem of child poverty in the UK, the NLG has provided services and extra financial help for poor families. It is clear that the government's policies are centred on work-related benefits. As child poverty is related to a large number of workless families, economic rewards have been designed for those participating in the labour market. Moreover, further help has been offered to families living in the poorest areas through initiatives such as Sure Start. In short, a more solid foundation has been established to solve the financial and development needs of children by reducing the number of workless families and by providing preventive services.

Social integration

The social needs of unemployed persons have been limited by the NLG's work-oriented welfare approach. As 'work' has been presented as the most effective means to escape poverty, the level of financial support for those living on public benefits, while now adequate to meet basic requirements according to some measures, is still too low to fulfil social and cultural aspirations. It is reported (NCSR and DWP, 2004) that 9% of all respondent households (20% for lone parents) could not afford 'friends/relatives for a meal once a month', and 6% (14% for lone parents) were unable to have 'celebrations with presents at special occasions'. Gordon et al (2000) also found that 2% of respondents could not pay 'visits to friends or family'; 3% were unable to attend 'weddings, funerals' or to buy 'presents for friends/family once a year'. According to Perkins (2001, p 90), limited welfare benefits restricted respondents' social contacts, contributing to their low self-esteem:

> Say if you want to go to the pub you can't buy a round. You just feel cheap and you just don't want to go with them.

> I do feel somewhat guilty, whenever somebody buys me a drink … everything's waiting on this promise of when I get this job and I have some money.

Farrell and O'Connor (2004) also reveal that respondents could lunch out with a friend only after an increase in family income for paid work. It is also only after obtaining a job that the respondents felt they were 'fitting in more with peers and losing the stigma of claiming benefits' (2004, p 6). The above studies clearly show that people living on state benefits are unable to lead a normal social and cultural life, which becomes the privilege of people in the labour market.

Human learning and development

The NLG sees the British welfare state as an investment, and this is considered to be the most effective approach to tackling poverty and achieving social justice. As Tony Blair points out:

> We must give the unemployed youth the skills to find a job; give the single mother the childcare she needs to go out and work; give the middle-aged man on a disability benefit the support and confidence to go back into the office. Only in this way will we drive up social mobility, the great force for equality in dynamic market economies. (*Guardian*, 2002)

Against this welfare ideology, the key function of the NLG is to 'take action to open up work opportunities to those denied them', to 'carry employment opportunity to all' (Chancellor of the Exchequer Gordon Brown quoted in Finn, 1998, p 105). Education and training have now become core elements of the NLG's work-oriented welfare state. The key question, however, is whether effective training is being offered to welfare recipients whose behaviour has been regulated by welfare administrators. As already noted, the Conservative government in the 1990s already required jobseekers to actively seek employment or attend job training. The NLG has followed similar policies, introducing a wide range of New Deal programmes for different types of claimants. This subsection examines the contents and effectiveness of the NLG's training measures in enhancing human learning and development.

New Deal programmes attempt to target the employment needs of different social groups; their details are as follows.

New Deal for Young People (18–24)

All new claimants for JSA have to attend a 'New Jobseeker's Interview' at the local Jobcentre (JC) or Jobcentre Plus (JCP). After being unemployed for six months, claimants undergo a four-month 'Gateway' period of intensive employment preparation before being offered one of the following options:

- a subsidised job with a private sector employer for six months, including one day per week training;
- full-time further education for a recognised qualification for 12 months;
- work experience in the non-profit sector for six months;
- participation in an 'environmental taskforce' project for six months, again with one day per week training; or
- assistance in setting up one's own business for six months.

Jobseekers can get at least the same amount of JSA with each option. Those who work with a voluntary or environmental group can obtain a grant of £400. Also, financial support for books and relevant materials will be given to those who choose full-time education and training.

New Deal for 25 Plus

This programme targets unemployed people aged 25 or above who have been claiming JSA for at least 18 months. Recipients have to work with PAs for a 'Gateway' period of four months, during which employment services and career planning are provided. If the recipients cannot find jobs after four months, they need to enter an 'Intensive Activity Period' which lasts from a minimum of 13 weeks up to a maximum of 26 weeks. They are required to undertake 30 hours per week of programmes in this period. According to the government, the programmes are individually tailored activities such as education and training courses, work-focused training, work experience placements and help with motivation. Subsidised jobs are also provided for recipients. People who have been unemployed for more than two years can study a full-time employment-related course for up to a year or an Open University course, during which they can still receive JSA.

New Deal for 50 Plus

The programme targets unemployed persons aged over 50 who have been receiving benefits such as IS, JSA, and Incapacity Benefit for more than six months. New Deal PAs provide career guidance and necessary training for recipients. Extra financial assistance is provided for those working for at least 16 hours a week in the form of Working Tax Credit. Moreover, there is an in-work training grant of up to £1,500 for older employed workers.

New Deal for Lone Parents

This is a voluntary programme for lone parents whose youngest child is under 16 years old. However, lone parents on IS are now required to attend initial job advice interviews if their children are aged over five. New Deal PAs provide employment guidance and draw up a career plan with recipients, especially of childcare assistance. In order to assist those newly employed, and to help sustain the employment of those already employed, a new job grant of £250 as well as a four-week extension of housing benefit are provided for those moving to work. They are also offered a weekly bonus of £40 for a year (*Guardian*, 2004c).

New Deal for Disabled Persons

The New Deal for Disabled Persons was introduced nationally in 2001. It is available to claimants who satisfy the conditions for claiming Incapacity Benefit (IB) or other disability benefits and basically involves a voluntary work-focused interview and access to a job-brokering service appropriate to the particular needs of each disabled person. Between July 2001 and September 2002, 27,850 people had registered with job brokers; 6,099 (22%) of them had got jobs, and 1,400 had moved into sustained employment (26 out of 39 weeks from initial job entry). Job brokers discuss employment needs with disabled people, planning appropriate actions to overcome job barriers. Job brokers also continue to support their clients for the first six months in work.

New Deal – Self-employment

Jobseekers on New Deal for Young People or New Deal for 25 plus are allowed to 'test trade' for up to 26 weeks. They have to prepare a business plan which should be approved by the JCP. They can receive an allowance equivalent to JSA plus a top-up grant. New Deal PAs introduce necessary training to the unemployed for preparing their business, and continue to provide support for the recipients for up to two years after recipients are no longer claiming JSA.

New Deal for Partners

The programme is for the partners of those receiving JSA, IS, IB, and Carer's Allowance; they can obtain advice from PAs as well as receive financial assistance for childcare.

New Deal for Musicians

Jobseekers who want to make a career as musicians can choose this programme. They are referred to someone with music industry experience, who acts as a mentor, offering support and advice. Recipients can attend a modular open-learning course specially designed for musicians. The course lasts up to 26 weeks, covering musical and business skills.

From 1998 to 2004, over 2.3 million people participated in various New Deal programmes. Most of them were participants of two compulsory programmes (Table 6.6). For example, among 416,260 participants in 2004, 41.5% and 25.4% of them were from New Deal for Young People and New Deal for 25 Plus respectively.

Intermediate labour market programmes

The main objective of these programmes is to give those who are furthest removed from the labour market 'a bridge back to the world

Table 6.6: Number of jobseekers on each New Deal since 1998

New Deal programmes	1998	1999	2000	2001	2002	2003	Total
New Deal for Young People	212,930	192,300	174,970	163,170	165,450	172,870	1,081,680
New Deal 25 Plus	77,750	141,950	116,330	118,530	113,790	105,580	673,920
New Deal 50 Plus			24,830	35,080	31,830	6,300	98,040
New Deal for Lone Parents	6,620	69,080	71,190	80,080	109,870	97,880	434,720
New Deal for Disabled People				7,090	28,740	33,630	69,460
New Deal for Partners							7,480

Source: House of Commons (2004b)

of work by improving participants' general employability' (Marshall and Macfarlane, 2000). Jobseekers are offered temporary paid work, which can last up to 12 months, together with training and personal development and job-search activities. These programmes are financed by various sources, including New Deal, European Social Fund, local regeneration funds and project earnings. Marshall and Macfarlane reported 5,300 places or jobs in 65 operating intermediate labour market programmes, involving around 9,000 people per year. These programmes include environmental work, childcare, town centre guides, information technology services, sports and community work. Seven out of ten places are for people aged 18 to 25. Both vocational training (up to Level 2 and above) and basic skills training, together with childcare and benefits advice, have been provided for the participants. (In the UK, Level 2 refers to a standard equivalent to five GCSEs at A-C or a National Vocational Qualification (NVQ) at Level 2. Level 3 means a standard equivalent to two A levels or a NVQ at Level 3.)

Education Maintenance Allowance

Implemented in September 2004, the allowance provides financial assistance for those aged 16–19 in full-time post-16 education programmes. It is a means-tested benefit, and a weekly allowance of £10, £20 or £30 is paid to applicants according to their household income. Bonuses are also given to students who remain on their courses and make good progress with their learning.

Adult Learning Grants

The Adult Learning Grant is being piloted in 19 local Learning and Skills Council areas. It is a means-tested financial assistance scheme for young adults aged 19–30 to study up to Level 2. Adult learners who are studying at undergraduate levels 2 and 3 can apply for a means-tested learning grant. The grant provides financial support for two to three years for adult learners to study full-time. The maximum grant available is £30 per week (Learndirect, 2004).

Career Development Loan

This is a deferred-repayment bank loan that helps learners to pay for vocational learning or education. Learners can borrow from £300 to £8,000 to fund any full-time, part-time or distance-learning vocational course that lasts no more than two years, plus up to one year's practical experience if this is part of the course. The Department for Education and Skills pays the interest on the loan. Learners repay the loan to the bank over an agreed period at a fixed rate of interest.

The above welfare programmes and financial support schemes for unemployed persons have several features. First, compulsory requirements target mainly young unemployed as well as long-term unemployed persons. At the same time, voluntary participation is allowed for older people, disabled persons and lone parents. This shows that the NLG has special expectations of the younger generation, hoping their skills can be improved through basic and formal education. As a result, more resources have been provided for young people to tackle their employment, social and psychological problems.

Second, although the NLG always stresses the importance of enhancing the employability of unemployed workers, adult unemployed persons aged over 25 receive limited support for improving their skills and qualifications. Those who have been unemployed for less than two years can engage in full-time education for a maximum of only two weeks a year. Based on the existing JSA regulations, adult unemployed persons can study only part-time courses of less than 16 hours per week or courses from the Open University. However, they are required to start work immediately once jobs are available. As mentioned earlier, only those who have been unemployed for more than two years can take up full-time education for one year. However, longer periods of education and career training have been offered for unemployed young people. For example, participants of the New Deal for Young People can receive 12 months vocational training up to

Level 2. They can also receive financial assistance for travelling and course costs. On the other hand, only nine months of vocationally oriented programmes are offered to unemployed persons aged over 25.

Older unemployed workers also receive less support for full-time education and training than their younger counterparts. They can attend only some basic skills programmes. The Learning and Skills Development Agency (Macleod, 2003, p 9) has noticed the weaknesses of existing training policies for adult and older unemployed workers, and suggests:

> If we are to stimulate demand for learning among those who have not participated in the past and perhaps now have the greatest need of intensive participation in learning to help them back into the labour force on a sustainable basis, it would seem sensible to create measures that enable unemployed people to learn full-time.

Third, teenage parents have been provided with more support for study than other benefit groups. Under a financial and childcare package, they can be assisted to complete secondary school studies. Moreover, they are offered financial support and childcare services to pursue full-time education up to undergraduate level.

Fourth, research studies show that some respondents are disappointed with existing training arrangements. For example, respondents complained that the training provision offered by their PAs was 'too basic and of little value because it was mostly non-accredited' (Osgood et al, 2002). For some who wanted to upgrade their skills or train for an alternative career, however, the available training was 'adequate' (Osgood et al, 2002). Respondents of Perkins' study (2001) had mixed feelings about their skill levels after participating in the New Deal options. Some 'believed skill levels had been raised significantly, whilst others felt it was marginal or not at all' (Perkins, 2001, p 120).

As illustrated earlier, different groups of unemployed people have unequal access to education and training. Adult workers aged over 25 and older workers receive only limited support for full-time and higher education. They can engage only in two-week full-time courses (or the equivalent in part-time courses) because they are expected to take up jobs at any time regardless of their existing qualifications and personal expectations. Jobseekers have the opportunity of obtaining higher education only through their own savings and with the help of a Career Development Loan. On the other hand, unemployed young people aged 16–19 as well as lone parents have been provided with more financial and childcare support for pursuing full-time and higher-level qualifications. Thus, the existing measures limit the career development of adult and older workers, who only have limited opportunities to enhance their job-related skills. With the government's support, unemployed young workers have more opportunities to get higher qualifications and to take up technical or professional jobs.

Other weaknesses of existing labour training policies include short-term programmes and financial constraints. The most significant problem associated with intermediate labour market programmes is 'the lack of secure and regular funding. Administration of the paperwork associated with funding is the second main problem' (Marshall and Macfarlane, 2000). These two problems diverted operators from the programmes' primary objectives.

More importantly, PAs find it hard to deliver personalised services for their unemployed clients. Despite the NLG's emphasis on professional skills and personalised programmes for jobseekers, research studies, as illustrated earlier, have consistently brought to light mixed experiences among unemployed respondents. Some respondents were dissatisfied with the employment knowledge and counselling skills of their PAs. On the other hand, PAs admitted the inadequacy of the information about benefits and the difficulty of handling complicated problems. To help unemployed workers to overcome their problems, PAs need to be equipped with professional skills in order to provide effective assessments and interventions.

Self-determination

By restructuring the UK's welfare system, the NLG has stressed the welfare duties of citizens. The fulfilment of welfare duties justifies extending the state's power over recipients' daily activities as well as imposing sanctions on those failing to fulfil their responsibilities. The freedom of JSA claimants is restricted by the NLG's social security measures, which require all new claimants for JSA to attend Jobseeker's Interviews. In these interviews, PAs 'make sure you understand the rules for JSA' and 'discuss the kinds of work you are looking for and the best ways of finding a job' (Jobcentre Plus, 2004a). The work requirement of recipients has further been consolidated by a 'Jobseeker's Agreement', which details

- your availability for work
- the kind of work you are looking for

- what you will do to look for work and improve your chances of finding work
- how JCP aims to help you. (Jobcentre Plus, 2004a)

In short, recipients of JSA are required to be active jobseekers, making a commitment to ending their unemployed status. The use of the agreement formalises and legalises the work of PAs on the one hand, and provides a clear direction for recipients to follow on the other. The Jobseeker's Agreement is implemented through regular meetings between a jobseeker and his or her PA. As the government states, 'you must also come to regular, more detailed interviews to look at your situation' (Jobcentre Plus, 2004a). During the Gateway period, recipients have to meet their PAs at least every two weeks, while those who are pursuing one of the 'options' need to see their PAs every two months. Also, extra guidance can be provided for the unemployed who need more advice on choosing options. This can be done by staff of the sub-contracted adult guidance network, who are trained guidance advisers and make recommendations to the PAs. Unemployed persons in the Gateway may have to undertake a literacy and numeracy test and a 'Job Readiness Self-Assessment Test'. Results of the test are passed to PAs, who arrange the next steps to be taken.

Two groups of unemployed persons face tighter government control: young unemployed and long-term unemployed persons. According to the requirements of New Deal, unemployed youths aged 18–19 have to register with the Connexions Service before claiming JSA. If they fail to get a job in the first six months, they have to take action based on the options provided. As mentioned earlier, jobseekers aged over 25 need to participate in the Gateway for four months. If they are still unemployed, they have to attend 30 hours a week in arranged activities during a so-called Intensive Activity Period. Clearly, the autonomy of these two groups of claimants has been limited; their daily lives are being managed by the government, which aims to enhance their employment skills, making them more competitive in the labour market.

JSA recipients who fail to meet the government's work requirements are subject to sanction. For example, participants of NDYP and New Deal for 25 Plus who did not start the option or left without good cause are penalised. For the first failure, there is a two-week sanction. For a second failure, a three-week sanction is applied. For a third failure, recipients are sanctioned for 26 weeks (Saunders et al, 2001). When sanctioned, recipients receive a reduced amount of JSA under the 'hardship provision'. The above welfare requirements show that some degree of control has been placed on the behaviour of recipients, such as regular meetings with PAs and attending employment training.

Although the government also stresses the provision of tailor-made services for jobseekers, existing welfare practices are inconsistent with a personalised service. First, personal choice is to some extent illusory. Perkins' (2001, p 124) study found that JSA claimants were 'coerced into options not of their choosing' or there were 'few or no opportunities within their desired option'. Second, a claimant's personal difficulties in taking up employment are not considered as the main target of intervention, but are subordinate to the 'work first approach'. The government's 'top priority is rapid re-entry into employment for those who are unemployed or economically inactive' (Macleod, 2003, p 8). Accordingly, all unemployed persons are required to follow the same procedure, from 'Gateway' to 'Options' for NDYP or from 'Gateway' to 'Intensive Activity' for New Deal for 25 Plus. The idea of personalised services and individual plans advocated by the NLG is far from the reality. This type of arrangement may fail to address the needs of recipients with multiple problems. For example, Dean's (2003, p 452) respondents complained the JCs 'push a bit too much, 'cos they're always writing you letters saying have you found work yet and stuff like that'. Dean further found that some respondents resented the authority and would 'sign off (ie withdraw their claims to benefit) rather than go through the New Deal process' (Dean, 2003, p 451). Several negative feelings were expressed by Perkins' (2001, p 97) respondents, who felt 'looked down upon' by their workers, their independence being eroded, and being treated not as 'an individual but were part of a very impersonal system'. Two respondents expressed strong feelings about the signing process:

> ... you walk in, you wait for five or ten minutes or whatever in the queue and then it is just hand your form over and you go along, they ask you the same questions, you give the same answers, you give the same answers as the person before you and the person before that. They're bored out of their brains; you're bored out of yours. Both of you want to get out of there as fast as you can. They want to get everybody dealt with. (Perkins, 2001, p 97)

> They don't treat you as a person they treat you as cattle. It's like their job to prod you, so they prod you but they make it personal when you do it. It leaves you feeling of less

worth than you probably do already on the dole. (Perkins, 2001, p 98)

The loss of autonomy, the facing of interpersonal services and the encountering of stigmatised welfare arrangements may discourage unemployed workers from living on state benefits. This may partly explain why a large number of participants are 'missing', especially before entering the period of options. For example, 32% of claimants left NDYP for an 'unknown destination' (Table 6.7). The suppression of unemployed persons' freedom may lead to their giving up welfare rights in order to retain their sense of control over their lives.

Jobseekers also have limited participation in the policy-making process. They can only indirectly influence social security policies through their elected representatives in the House of Commons and their trade union representatives on government advisory committees. The UK is a parliamentary democracy in which the legislative process involves both the House of Lords (the upper house) and the House of Commons (the lower house). Elected members can express the concerns of jobseekers through the Work and Pensions Select Committee, which 'examines the expenditure, administration and policy of the Department for Work and Pensions and its associated public bodies' (UK Parliament, 2004). Pressure groups may be invited by relevant committees of the House of Commons to express their views. For example, in discussing the issue of child poverty, the Work and Pensions Select Committee invited various organisations to express their views, such as Save the Children, the End Child Poverty Campaign, Child Poverty Action Group, Citizen's Income Trust, Disability Alliance, and One Parent Families. One Parent Families submitted a report calling for an increase of £5 per child in the Child Tax Credit, and urging an improvement in welfare administration so that recipients could receive 'the right amount of tax credit at the right time' (House of Commons, 2004a). However, the influence of

Table 6.7: New Deal leavers with 'unknown destination', 1998–2003

	New Deal for Young People	%	New Deal 25 Plus	%
1998	19,540	25	2,460	18
1999	54,410	28	12,870	10
2000	54,080	27	12,110	9
2001	51,080	29	13,200	11
2002	53,120	32	19,270	18
2003	61,720	34	23,390	20

Source: House of Commons (2004b)

elected MPs on unemployment policies and benefits is subject to the willingness of key policy makers – the Cabinet, and especially the Prime Minister – to respond to the needs of unemployed persons.

Another form of participation is policy consultation initiated by the government. There is often consultation and discussion before bills are introduced to parliament (UK Parliament, 2004). Welfare groups can use the consultation process to air their concerns. Again, the government can still ignore any suggestions.

A further channel of influence is through trade union representatives on the Social Security Advisory Committee. The duties of the committee (SSAC, 2005) are:

1. to give advice on social security issues as it sees fit;
2. to consider and report on social security regulations referred to it;
3. to consider and advise on any matters referred to it by the Secretary of State for Work and Pensions or the Northern Ireland Department responsible for social security;
4. to scrutinise information produced by the Department for Work and Pensions.

It is said that the committee has frequent meetings with outside organisations, visits the department's local and national delivery sites and maintains a close interest in developments in the social welfare field. Apart from the chairman, the committee has 13 members. Under the Social Security Act 1980, one member should represent employers and one should represent employees. In addition, at least one member is expected to have experience of chronic illness or disability. It seems that the Social Security Advisory Committee has provided some degree of participation for welfare recipients. But it should be stressed that its influences on overall government policies is limited by its consultative nature and the concentration of political power in the Cabinet, especially in the hands of the Prime Minister.

As the above discussion reveals, living on JSA is associated with restrictions on JSA claimants' behaviour. Because of rigid and pre-scheduled welfare arrangements, from 'Gateway' to 'Options', recipients find it hard to formulate their personalised plans or tackle their personal barriers to employment. Recipients' self-determination, therefore, has been suppressed in a 'work-first' welfare system.

Equal value

As illustrated previously, claimants have different degrees of access to learning and training opportunities. Two issues might affect the nature of support for unemployed persons. The first is the desire to reduce the number of workless families. The second is the increasing number of people claiming IB. Against this background, special support has been provided for enhancing the employability of disabled persons, lone parents and older workers. Disabled persons who study higher education courses (for example, for qualifications such as BSc, BA, DipHE, HND, or HNC) are entitled to the Disabled Students' Allowance, which consists of three types of allowances:

- *Special Equipment Allowance:* a one-off payment for large items such as personal computers, cassette recorders, and so forth.
- *Non-Medical Helpers Allowance:* an annual allowance to cover the costs of practical help including signers, readers, note-takers, and personal assistants.
- *General Allowance:* an annual allowance for small items and consumables, which can also be used to supplement the other allowances.

As for lone parents, if they study full time they can obtain childcare grants or lone-parent's grants to cover the costs of childcare. Those who study up to A-level or equivalent can also obtain IS if they are not living with their parents and cannot get support from them. Young parents aged 16–19 studying at sixth form or college qualify for up to £5,000 for registered childcare. In addition, they can apply for 'learner support funds' to cope with expenses such as books, equipment, transport, and accommodation. Those aged over 18 with dependent children under 15 can apply for a Childcare Grant Package to pay for registered childcare, and a Parents Learning Allowance for books, travel, and equipment.

On the other hand, the focus of government policies towards adult and older workers is on 'work priority'. Although older workers are entitled to a Training Grant of up to £1,500 and extra financial aid for the first 26 weeks in work, they receive less support for studying full-time. Unemployed workers aged over 25 also face similar constraints on full-time education. On the other hand, young unemployed workers, as discussed earlier, can obtain career and psychological counselling and are also provided with financial support for full-time studies. Clearly, there is a 'learning gap' between young and adult or older workers. As a result, the former have more opportunities to pursue better-paid jobs, while the latter may have to settle for low-skilled work. After examining post-16 learning opportunities, the LSDA (2003, p 7) criticised government policies for being 'in favour of full-time education and training programmes for young people, up to the age of 22'. It further points out that 'The rules governing job-seeking benefits mean that individuals cannot enter into full-time or part-time programmes at will' (2003, p 8). Obviously, unequal learning opportunities exist between different age groups (young workers versus older workers) and between different family patterns (lone parents versus traditional families). The present welfare measures reinforce the low skills and low job status of adult and older workers, who are the most vulnerable workers in declining manufacturing industries. It is only through improved skills and systematic training that mature and older workers are able to change their career paths from low incomes to higher incomes, from temporary jobs to permanent jobs, from part-time jobs to full-time jobs, and finally from being welfare recipients to being taxpayers.

Conclusion

The NLG has restructured the UK's welfare system around work, and welfare-to-work has become the main strategy for tackling poverty and social exclusion. As illustrated in this chapter, compulsory measures such as 'Jobseekers' Interviews', the 'Jobseeker's Agreement', 'Gateway', 'employment or training options' and 'Intensive Activities' have been used to maintain work motivation and enhance the employability of unemployed persons. The New Deal has also been promoted as a personalised and effective programme to assist the career development of unemployed persons. However, the existing rigid welfare arrangements from 'Jobseekers' Interviews' to New Deal 'options' or 'Intensive Activities' are inconsistent with or may even pose a threat to a personalised service, which should focus on the uniqueness of individuals and their problems. As asked in Chapter One, how acceptable is a government's control over the activities of welfare recipients? The existing rigid welfare requirements fail to meet the special needs of claimants. With limited training and a heavy workload, PAs also fail to provide sufficient and appropriate support for jobseekers, especially those with complicated problems. For this reason, JSA recipients perceived the meetings with PAs to be 'perfunctory'; they felt 'processed' without being involved in the interview, and 'did not believe that sufficient information or advice was provided on the different options available to them' (Davies et al, 2004, p 9). As Worth (2003, p 618) points out, 'an employability-focused policy agenda, expressed through programmes like the New Deal, is unlikely to improve the long-term employability of participants when its focus is on job-readiness at the immediate point of labour market entry'. If welfare services are not based on a detailed assessment of a person's needs, the effectiveness of the New Deal in solving the personal barriers of unemployed workers is in question.

The second issue is the levels of JSA, which have been shaped by the NLG's views on labour market participation as the key to tackling poverty. Those who are unable to get sufficient income in the labour market are compensated through tax credits. However, those who are unable to find jobs have more limited incomes. As illustrated earlier, levels of JSA are still too low for recipients to participate as full citizens. As a nationwide study concludes, 'in 2002 there were still families that went without items and activities that many would regard as necessities' (NCSR and DWP, 2004, p 310). In short, the existing welfare measures provide little security for long-term unemployed persons; nor can they provide effective assistance for adult and older workers to improve their skills and career paths.

SEVEN

Sweden and human dignity

Sweden has always been regarded as 'the archetype of a universal model' (Palme, 2002) as well as 'the most expensive welfare state' (Rothstein, 1998, p 6). After comparing a wide range of welfare states, Doyal and Gough (1991, p 290) conclude that the Swedish welfare state 'emerges as the global leader, the country most closely approximating optimum need-satisfaction at the present time'. Sweden was also ranked second on the United Nations' Human Development Index (United Nations Development Programme, 2004). The Swedish government has consistently attributed this to class and gender equality and the dominant role of government in welfare provision. The Social Services Act clearly states that it is the responsibility of the Swedish government to 'promote people's financial and social security' (National Board of Health and Welfare, 2000). In pursuing this welfare goal, the Swedish government has provided comprehensive welfare services to meet the needs of different age groups at different stages of their lives.

To fulfil its welfare objectives, the Swedish government allocates substantial public resources to the social services; nearly one third of Sweden's GDP is devoted to welfare expenditure, and progressive taxation measures have been adopted. The social expenditure in Sweden is 32.3% of its GDP, in contrast to 26.8% in the UK and 20.1% in Spain in 2001 (Nordic Social-Statistical Committee, 2003). As a result of progressive taxation and cash transfers favouring deprived social groups, the gap between rich and poor in Sweden is smaller than that in other countries (Behrendt, 2002). As illustrated in the earlier part of this book, human dignity consists of more than economic well-being; it also includes human autonomy and development, and social relationships. This chapter attempts to examine the effectiveness of the Swedish model in enhancing the dignity of unemployed persons.

The Swedish government's policies on unemployment

Sweden is one of the most developed economies in the world. With a population of 8,878,000, Sweden's GDP per capita in 2003 was ranked 22 (US$25,400) (CIA World, 2003). Compared with other countries, Sweden 'stands out as a country that spends large resources on active market policy' (Holmlund, 2003, p 16). The Swedish labour movement has been guided primarily by the 'Rehn–Meidner model', characterised by 'an active labour market policy', 'a restrictive finance policy and a solidaristic wage policy' (Green–Pedersen and Linbom, 2002, p 16). The principle of the Swedish employment policy has been that 'everyone who wants to work and can work should be given this opportunity' (Forsberg et al, 2002, p 1). Accordingly, full employment is 'the top of the Government's agenda' because 'a well-functioning labour market and an efficient labour market policy are important prerequisites for both growth and welfare' (Government Offices of Sweden, 2004a).

Sweden, however, is 'a success story in the 1980s and a failure in the first half of the 1990s' (Green–Pedersen and Linbom, 2002, p 9). The Swedish government maintained a low unemployment rate of 2–3% throughout the 1980s. In the early 1990s, the unemployment rate rose to 8%, but improved in the late 1990s. From 1997 to 2000, the number of jobs rose by more than 200,000. As a result, the unemployment rate fell from 8% in 1997 to 4% in 2001 (Table 7.1). In April 2004, the unemployment rate was 4.9% (219,000 persons), and another 2.4% unemployed workers (103,000) participated in various types of labour market programmes (AMS, 2004).

By achieving the objective of full employment, the Swedish government aims to:

- channel work to the unemployed and labour to employers;
- take measures against shortage occupations and bottlenecks; and
- take initiatives to help those who have difficulty obtaining work. (Government Offices of Sweden, 2004a)

Table 7.1: Sweden's unemployment rate, 1990–2004

Year	Number of unemployed persons	% of workforce
1990	75,100	1.6
1995	344,100	7.9
1996	372,300	8.6
1997	299,200	7.1
1998	256,500	6.0
1999	244,400	5.7
2000	203,100	4.7
2001	175,200	4.0
2002	184,700	4.2
2003	244,000	5.5
2004	241,200	5.4

Sources: Nordic Social-Statistical Committee (2003); Statistics Sweden (2005)

In practice, Swedish labour market policies are guided by the 'work-first principle' and the 'work and skills principle' (Government Offices of Sweden, 2004a). Thus, the government emphasises career training in order to:

- enhance or renew the skills of workers through training or retraining so that they can meet the new demands from their jobs;
- provide on-the-job training for workers through wage subsidies so that employers are motivated to increase their labour force; and
- create employment opportunities for those who find it difficult to compete with others, especially during times of economic recession.

As for financial assistance for unemployed workers, Sweden has one of the 'most generous unemployment protection systems' (ILO, 2004). Unemployment insurance in Sweden is administered by 38 independent Unemployment Insurance Funds, which were previously regulated by the Insurance Division of the AMS. In 2002, the Riksday (parliament) legislated to set up an Unemployment Insurance Inspectorate to supervise unemployment insurance. Also, there are 418 Public Employment Service Offices (PESOs) nationally where career counsellors offer matching, training and activating services. In Sweden, more than 80% of workers (3.7 million) are protected by two types of unemployment insurance schemes: voluntary income-related insurance (VIRI) and basic insurance (BI).

Voluntary income-related insurance

To be eligible for VIRI, one has to meet the following conditions:

- *Membership condition.* Applicants must have been members of an unemployment fund for at least 12 consecutive months. To be a member, one must work four weeks and at least 17 hours a week in a five-week period. The average membership fee is SEK 100 (£7.36) (AEA, 2004).
- *Work condition.* During a period of 12 months, immediately prior to becoming unemployed, applicants must have been working for a minimum of six months. They must also have worked at least 70 hours a month. The alternative requirement is a total of 450 hours' work during six consecutive months, with at least 45 hours work a month.
- *Study condition.* Applicants must have completed at least a one-year full-time course in addition to the nine years of compulsory

schooling. Also, they must have registered with the Employment Service (ES) and/or worked for at least 90 days in the 10 months immediately after completing their study.

- *Employment registration.* Applicants must register with the PESO as a jobseeker.
- *Labour programme participation.* Applicants must accept any reasonable job offers or participate in a labour market programme.

There is a minimum and a maximum daily cash benefit for insured workers. The maximum benefit is SEK 730 (£55.01) for the first 100 days, followed by SEK 680 (£51.24) per day. The minimum benefit is SEK 320 (£24.11) per day. The benefit, however, is taxable and is counted as pensionable income.

Basic insurance

BI is a fixed daily allowance, which is paid to all workers or self-employed people who pay taxes and social insurance contributions but who are not members of insurance funds or fail to meet the membership requirements for at least 12 months. A recipient of BI can receive a maximum of SEK 320 (£24.11) a day. However, the recipient has to:

- actively seek work;
- be able to work for at least three hours a day and an average of 17 hours a week; and
- register with the local PESO and draw up an action plan within three months of unemployment.

Both VIRI and BI provide benefits for five days a week for 300 days.

The discussion earlier shows that both labour market programmes and financial assistance have been used to tackle the problem of unemployment. In some countries, labour market programmes are used to punish the poor, while the amount of financial support is too low to provide unemployed workers with a decent life. The following section discusses whether Swedish labour market policies meet the basic needs of the unemployed and help develop their potential.

The dignity of unemployed recipients

Based on the concept of human dignity proposed in this study, we need to evaluate a welfare system, in addition to the level of financial assistance, from social and psychological dimensions. This section aims at examining whether the Swedish welfare measures can safeguard the dignity of unemployed persons.

Meeting physical needs

The Swedish model provides generous benefits for unemployed workers. It is said that recipients of VIRI can receive as much as 80% of their previous salary. In fact, Swedish unemployment insurance mainly benefits lower income groups rather than higher income groups, since only lower income earners can receive as much as 80% of the replacement rate; most beneficiaries receive less (Figure 7.1). In addition, the upper limit of earnings-related benefits has not been raised for several years. As a consequence, only a small number of workers can receive up to 80% replacement rate (Ahlberg, 2003).

After examining social and material deprivation among young unemployed youths aged 18–24, Julkunen (2002) found that a significant proportion of Swedish respondents were unable to buy necessary clothes (33%) and participate in social activities such as 'Going to the movies' (35%), 'Visiting friends and relatives' (31%) and 'Going to a pub/restaurant' (30%) (Table 7.2). Compared with other well-developed welfare states such as Finland, Iceland, Norway, Demark, and Scotland, the living quality of unemployed Swedish young people

Figure 7.1: Disposable incomes of normal and insured childless couples, 2001

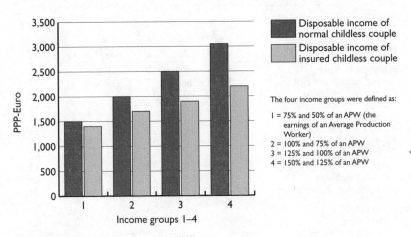

The four income groups were defined as:

1 = 75% and 50% of an APW (the earnings of an Average Production Worker)
2 = 100% and 75% of an APW
3 = 125% and 100% of an APW
4 = 150% and 125% of an APW

Source: Nordic Social-Statistical Committee (2003)

was in the middle. The evidence earlier shows that existing Swedish unemployment insurance mainly benefits the lower income groups rather than the higher ones. Unemployed young people also find it difficult to lead a normal social life.

In Sweden, those who fail to meet the criteria of unemployment insurance, such as new graduates, immigrants and workers with unstable employment history, can apply for Social Assistance (SA). In 2002 237,000 households with 434,000 individuals received this benefit. Among them, 3% were unemployed recipients or registered jobseekers (National Board of Health and Welfare, 2002). Accessing financial assistance is a right of Swedish citizens. As the Social Services Act clearly states:

> An individual who cannot themselves provide for their needs or can have them provided for through another way, has a right to support from the social welfare board (municipality) for their support and for their way of life in other respects according to the conditions set forth in the rest of Section 6. (quoted in Jewell, 2002, p 9)

The aim of the Swedish government is to provide everyone with 'the resources necessary to live in accordance with human dignity' (Ministry of Health and Social Affairs, 2003a, p 25). The Social Services Act of 1982 declares:

Table 7.2: Deprivation among young unemployed people: percentage frequently going without particular activities or items, by country

Items	Finland	Iceland	Norway	Sweden	Denmark	Scotland
Having a hot meal	6	8	12	6	2	6
Buying necessary clothes	32	24	30	33	11	27
Paying rent on time	15	20	16	7	4	18
Inviting friends home	5	7	9	11	3	15
Going to the movies	36	33	28	35	15	45
Visiting friends/relatives	24	18	27	31	14	34
Buying gifts	22	16	18	22	6	32
Travelling abroad	56	31	42	51	31	63
Subscribing to a newspaper	38	23	24	35	14	13
Pursuing hobbies	19	24	20	20	10	29
Going to a pub/restaurant	29	34	31	30	18	46
Mean total	26	22	23	26	10	30
Mean index	6.3	5.4	5.7	5.8	3.6	6.1

Source: Julkunen (2002)

Society's social services shall on the basis of democracy and solidarity promote people's economic and social security, equality in living conditions and active participation in social life. (quoted in Giertz, 2004, p 25)

Under these welfare principles, the poor are expected to enjoy 'a reasonable standard of living' (National Board of Health and Welfare, 2000). Swedish SA has two components. One consists of 'livelihood support' and 'other assistance', as set out by the central government. The other consists of 'assistance in another form' such as furniture, equipment, debt management and major dental care, which is determined by local authorities (Figure 7.2).

Comparative studies show that Swedish social security transfers play a key role in tackling poverty. Based on the household data of the Luxembourg Income Study, Behrendt (2000, p 33) found that the Swedish SA scheme had reduced poverty by 7% in 1992. In effect, the income of poor households had increased to 18% above the poverty line. Similar findings were reported by Riley (2003), who estimated

Figure 7.2: The content of Swedish Social Assistance (SA)

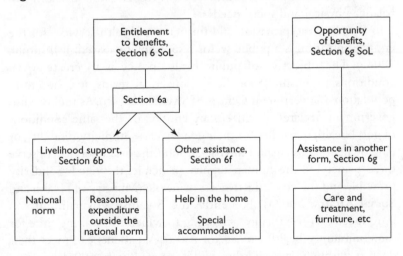

Source: National Board of Health and Welfare (2000)

that the Swedish poverty rate had been reduced by social security transfers from 28% to 9% in 1999. A further study reveals that the poorest 10% of households received 92% of their income from social security transfers, especially from SA, in contrast to the top 25% of households, who received only 5% from this source (Nardi, 2000). To meet rising living costs, the Swedish government regularly adjusts the level of SA in the light of price changes and National Consumer Agency calculations of the maintenance needs of different types of families. The adjustment, therefore, takes changing consumption patterns into account (Nordic Social-Statistical Committee, 2003).

As noted above, access to financial support is 'a basic right' of Swedish citizens. The concept of basic right is further linked to 'a reasonable and normal standard of living'. This shows that the Swedish government aims to provide the resources poor people need to lead a normal life. Although comparative studies show that poor Swedish people have a higher income after social security transfers, young unemployed persons still suffer from social deprivation. This suggests that present social security measures mainly benefit particular groups of people, especially lower-income households and families with children (see later). Single, able-bodied unemployed workers, however, are still struggling to balance physical and social needs.

In Sweden, 'the provision and financing of health services for the entire population is a public sector responsibility' (Swedish Institute, 2004a). The objective of public health policy is to create social conditions to 'ensure good health, on equal terms, for the entire population' (Government Offices of Sweden, 2004b). As the Swedish government declares, all citizens are entitled to 'the same conditions of good health' regardless of their gender, class, ethnicity, disability, or employment status. Against this background, the health services observe three principles: the human dignity principle, the needs/solidarity principle and the cost-effectiveness principle (Ministry of Health and Social Affairs, 2003a). Recently, the Swedish government has introduced a '0–7–90 rule', according to which the waiting time for the community health care sector is 0 days, patients can meet their doctors within 7 days, and they will be treated within 90 days.

Health services are provided by 20 county councils and one other local authority (Gotland). These are financed by local income tax and central government grants, with payments for certain services as well as fees from patients. The total cost of medical services in Sweden is about 8.5% of GNP. The charge for staying in hospital is SEK 80 (£6.03) per day, while for consulting a doctor it is from SEK 100 (£7.36) to SEK 150 (£11.30) due to variations between county councils. A high cost ceiling is set to limit the burden on patients. A patient who has paid a total of SEK 900 (£67.82) is entitled to free services for the rest of the 12-month period.

Based on existing health services, unemployed persons can receive relatively cheap and comprehensive treatment, with their medical costs limited to a certain level. Social Assistance recipients are exempt from charges such as dental treatment, medical treatment, spectacles, equipment for the home and removal expenses. Overall, Sweden has achieved very good health. The infant mortality in the first year of life was 3.4 deaths per 1,000 and the average life expectancy was 77.1 years for men and 81.9 years for women (National Board of Health and Welfare, 2003).

Meeting psychological needs

In many countries, the needs of the poor are mainly dealt with by finance and welfare administrators with little psychological knowledge and counselling skills. Research studies, however, consistently show that unemployed persons suffer psychological and behavioural problems such as low self-esteem, anxiety, depression, restlessness, excess weight, lack of appetite and an increasing use of alcohol, tobacco, narcotics and drugs. In Sweden, trained social workers are responsible for assessing the personal needs of SA recipients within a framework of vague and general programme regulations as well as working with them on an 'active plan'. With lower caseloads, social workers have more opportunities to deal with recipients' educational or rehabilitation goals (Jewell, 2002, p 20). After comparing welfare workers in the United States, Germany and Sweden, Jewell (2002, p 27) concludes:

> Sweden does seem to create a comparatively high level of individual programme orientation in a sort of *ad hoc* system of temporary social workers. Caseworkers have the skills and authority to approach people in a holistic fashion and, what's more, the relative simplicity of regulations and the limited obligations in meeting administrative requirements actually allows them to realize, at least partially, the potential for responsive encounters with their clients.

Also, qualified career counsellors in PESO have completed three years of university study; they work with recipients of unemployment insurance. The objectives of the Public Employment Service (PES) are 'uniformity, legal security and efficiency', and 'the day-to-day work of the Employment Service is to be characterised by job satisfaction and professionalism' (AMS, 2003, p 8). There are 6,500 placement officers, who are stationed at over 400 PESOs to help jobseekers obtain work. The placement officers are required to 'listen to jobseekers and help them to arrive at a clear appreciation of their situation and of what it will take for them to find work as quickly as possible' (AMS, 2003, p 38).

In addition, social workers from special sections of municipalities help young unemployed people to overcome employment barriers. Respondents of a study noticed that unemployed young people encountered low self-esteem and other problems such as alcohol and drug abuse. They also had poor educational qualifications and lacked work experience. Young single mothers had particular difficulty in caring for their children. In response to these difficulties, social workers, together with other relevant organisations, attempted to enhance the self-confidence of young people and developed special plans with them (Forsberg et al, 2002).

Integrated services are also provided for young people. Individual plans for unemployed young people can be developed by several services including (1) the social welfare agency, (2) the unemployment office, (3) the labour market institute, (4) a municipal project and (5) the social insurance office. A respondent working for the Swedish Association of Local Authorities in Varmland pointed out that the individual programme aims to meet the different educational needs of unemployed young people so that 'there is no set curriculum; rather an individual curriculum is drawn up for those that choose this programme' (Forsberg et al, 2002, p 13). Some can participate in the programme from one to four years until they are aged 20; some may be focused on academic studies. Students with special needs may study at an adult education centre for dyslexics.

Intensive services have been designed to help the long-term unemployed. Workers from government departments, trade unions and schools reported that key problems of the long-term young unemployed people included poor educational attainments, negative social attitudes, lack of structure in their daily lives, lack of contact with working life, a feeling of being outsiders and poor self-confidence (Forsberg et al, 2002). For the long-term unemployed, the key objectives of the activation measures are to improve 'the well-being and self-esteem of the individuals' (Kvist, 2001, p 5). The Labour Market Institute (LMI) provides guidance and career-oriented rehabilitation for jobseekers whose needs cannot be met by the unemployment office. There are 120 LMIs in Sweden, at least one in every county.

The LMI employs different experts such as social welfare consultants, psychologists, occupational therapists and physiotherapists, specialists in learning disabilities and visual impairments, and neuro-psychologists. Thus, the LMI can conduct extensive investigation, rehabilitation, and work preparation programmes. For some young people this can be 'a very long process before the goal of work or training is achieved' (Forsberg et al, 2002, p 17).

The impact of using counselling and employment professionals in providing services for unemployed persons is mixed. After reviewing research studies on employment programmes, Giertz (2004, p 29) concludes that 'The work was bureaucratic, decisions discretionary and recipients often experienced distress or shame'. On the other hand, some programme officers and welfare recipients gave positive feedback. According to a welfare administrator from Social Services in Karlstad, the ASPEN (an acronym [in Swedish] for work, studies, internship, experiences and usefulness) provides 'a daily structure and routine as well as a social context' (Forsberg et al, 2002, p 12). ASPEN is (Forsberg et al, 2002, p 33). For young people who find that services from ASPEN are insufficient to help them, Social Service workers contact the LMI, which will help the young people 'develop an individual plan of action'. As the respondent observed, with help from ASPEN programmes young people could 'overcome their passivity, seem happier and develop important social contacts' (Forsberg et al, 2002, p 12).

As illustrated earlier, trained social workers and career counsellors have been recruited in Sweden to tackle the employment barriers of unemployed workers. Accordingly, welfare practitioners have adopted a holistic approach to the needs of unemployed persons. However, professional workers have to perform both controlling and empowering functions. Difficulties in balancing these two roles may have a negative impact on the psychological well-being of recipients. Nevertheless, the use of professional workers and a variety of programmes show the Swedish government's intention to tackle the psychological and social factors that prevent a person from entering the labour market.

Fulfilling caring duties

In Sweden, the duty of caring for children is shared by both parents and the government. The objective of the Swedish government is to 'enable equal terms for all children when they are growing up' (Government Offices of Sweden, 2004c). The Social Services Act also states that it is the responsibility of municipalities to ensure children and young people grow up in good and safe conditions (National Board of Health and Welfare, 2000). The government's commitment to children's welfare directly enhances the caring capacities of parents.

As illustrated earlier, a 'reasonable living standard' is the objective of Swedish social assistance policy. The minimum income guarantee for those receiving SA can be as much as 60% of the national median income. Also, unemployment insurance mainly benefits lower-income groups. More importantly, Child Benefit in Sweden directly boosts the income level of families with children. The benefit is non-taxable and relatively generous. The allowance for the first child can be as high as 6% of the median disposable income. In 1982, the Swedish government even introduced increments for the third and subsequent children (Table 7.3).

Added to this, children in the later years of their secondary education can receive a monthly allowance of SEK 950 (£71.59) for nine months of the year. As the Swedish government put it, the ultimate goal of financial support for families is more than tackling poverty; it is 'reducing disparities in living conditions between households with children and those without' (Ministry of Health and Social Affairs, 2003b, p 1). As a result of government financial support (including Child Benefit, SA and unemployment insurance), poor parents' caring capacities have been enhanced although they live on public benefits.

International comparative figures further demonstrate that the levels of Swedish social assistance are higher than those of her European counterparts (Table 7.4).

As for physical health, children and young people aged under 20 are entitled to free medical and dental care. Regarding education, the Education Act of Sweden states that all children and young people aged 7–16 years must attend school. In addition to free tuition, local authorities provide school children with 'all the materials necessary for school work. Particular emphasis is put on textbooks, etc covering essential parts of a specific subject or a group of subjects' (Sweden Information Smorgasbord, 2004a). As well, local authorities are required by the Education Act to provide free upper secondary education for

Table 7.3: Child Benefit and supplements for large families

Monthly allowance per child	SEK 950 (£71.59)
Supplements for large families	
The third child	SEK 254 (£19.14)
The fourth child	SEK 760 (£57.27)
The fifth child and additional child	SEK 950 (£71.59)

Source: European Commission (2005)

Table 7.4: The impact of the transfer system on families with children

	All families with children	Two-parent families[a]	One-parent families[b]
Italy			
Pre-transfer poverty rate	10.1	8.4	22.3
Post-transfer poverty rate	10.7	9.8	16.9
Poverty reduction %	−6.0	−16.0	24.2
UK			
Pre-transfer poverty rate	26.9	16.8	79.3
Post-transfer poverty rate	20.3	14.3	57.2
Poverty reduction %	24.5	14.9	27.9
Sweden			
Pre-transfer poverty rate	17.3	11.9	36.7
Post-transfer poverty rate	2.8	2.3	4.3
Poverty reduction %	83.8	80.7	88.3

Notes: [a] Families where there are only two adults married or cohabiting, with one or more children under 18.

[b] Families where one adult cares for one or more minor children under 18, without other adults in the household (older children, parents, etc).

Source: Solear (1999)

all pupils completing compulsory schooling. As a result of these supportive education measures, most young people are enrolled in secondary schools. Of those who completed compulsory school in 2002, 97.8% continued studying at upper secondary school (National Agency for Education, 2003). Because of the Swedish government's commitment to children's welfare, parents have been given the required resources to meet the financial, medical and educational needs of their children.

Social integration

To some extent, the amount of resources shapes the interactions between unemployed people and their social networks. Unemployment may have only limited effects on the lives of unemployed workers who receive income-related insurance as high as 80% of their previous salaries. However, most unemployed persons may have to reduce their expenditure on social and cultural activities. Unemployed persons living on SA are provided with resources to maintain a certain degree of social activity and community life. Based on the concept of a 'reasonable standard of living' (National Board of Health and Welfare, 2002), SA in Sweden consists of two elements: 'livelihood support' and 'other assistance'. Livelihood support has six budget items, including food, clothing and footwear, play and leisure, disposable articles, health and hygiene, and a daily newspaper or a telephone or a television licence. Other items consist of housing, domestic electricity supply, journeys to and from work, household insurance, medical care, emergency dental care, spectacles, membership of a trade union and unemployment insurance contributions. By including the expenses of 'play and leisure' and by giving recipients the resources to pay for newspapers, TV licences and membership fees of trade unions, the Swedish welfare system has treated humans as social beings, recognising the importance to poor people of maintaining a normal social life to some degree. However, both young unemployed people (Julkunen, 2002) and long-term unemployed workers (Clasen et al, 1997) were reported to be unable to afford holidays, visits to restaurants and pubs, and trips to the cinema. Some even saved money by not visiting a dentist or a doctor. This reveals that the amount of assistance still constrains the extent to which recipients can participate fully in a normal social life.

Human learning and development

One of the key features of the Swedish welfare system is its emphasis on human learning, expressed in terms of active labour market policies. The Swedish government uses two main strategies to improve the labour market. The first is to create 'a better match between available labour and the existing demand for labour' through labour training; the second is to 'encourage demand for labour and generate employment' through subsidised jobs (Swedish Institute, 2004b). A wide range of labour programmes have been used to help unemployed workers return to the labour market. Over recent decades, 2–5% of the labour force participated in labour market programmes (Carling and Richardson, 2001). The details of active labour market policies are as follows (AMS, 2003):

Guidance and job-matching

The basic services provided by the public employment offices include standard job information, matching of vacancies to applicants, search skill-enhancing activities, and motivation-raising activities. The PES tries to achieve 'efficient matching' by providing job vacancies for jobseekers so that the labour market can run smoothly. The expansion of self-service tools on the Internet is one of these programmes.

Hiring support

This targets the long-term unemployed and occupationally handicapped persons by providing a wage subsidy of about 50% of wage costs for a worker for six months. This measure aims to increase the number of transitions from subsidised to unsubsidised employment. The employees receive wages at the usual level from their employers during the employment period.

Vocational rehabilitation

This offers individualised vocational rehabilitation for persons with occupational disabilities or in need of in-depth guidance.

Employment training

This targets unemployed workers aged 20 or more. Training can take the form of necessary general education or preparation for career-oriented training. In addition, jobseekers are offered training in occupations in which there is a labour shortage. Participants can receive a grant which is equivalent to the unemployment insurance benefits. In 2002, 61% of unemployed persons obtained jobs within 90 days of completing their training (AMS, 2002).

Work experience

Unemployed workers can participate in workplace training for up to six months. They are paid at a rate similar to that of unemployment insurance benefits or SA.

Computer/Activity Centres

Computer training programmes are provided for unemployed persons, and are combined with jobseeker and guidance activities.

Municipal programmes for young people aged under 20

Young people are regarded as a priority group so that training and jobs are offered to those who are out of work for more than 100 days. Municipalities are required to provide unemployed young people aged 18–20 with some form of programme. They also decide the level of compensation for the participants.

Projects with a labour market policy focus

PESOs design special projects, in association with other labour market agencies, to strengthen individual persons' prospects of obtaining and keeping a job.

Business start-up grants

These grants pay the living costs of unemployed people who attempt to start their own businesses. Those entitled to receive income-related unemployment benefits can obtain 'activity support' at an equivalent amount. The grant is particularly beneficial to 'occupationally handicapped persons' and those over 55 years old (AMS, 2003).

The Youth Guarantee (YG)

The YG is a range of programmes for unemployed persons between the ages of 20 and 24.

The YG has several advantages. It offers young people employment practice through internships. Also, it provides participants with a chance to earn employment references. Other benefits include improvements to the self-esteem and social skills of the unemployed persons, in particular a chance to take control of their own life situations (Forsberg et al, 2002, p 10).

Activity Guarantee/Activation Guarantee (AG)

The AG is for long-term unemployed workers registered with the ES. Its objective is to get them back to work through full-time, structured activities. The AG has the following features (AMS, 2000):

- services are provided by qualified counsellors based on individual plans, called 'jobseeker plans';
- there are group programmes with 10–15 persons;
- participants can receive an activity allowance or training allowance; and
- compensation is provided for partners (voluntary organisations or private companies).

Wage-subsidised employment

The government provides grants for employers hiring persons with occupational disabilities.

Public sheltered employment

These programmes are mainly for the 'occupationally handicapped'. In 2002 a monthly average of 60,800 were employed by means of wage subsidies or OSA (public sheltered employment) (AMS, 2003, p 42).

The labour measures cited earlier have successfully helped unemployed people to obtain jobs in the open labour market. It was reported that 70% of people obtained work within six months of completing job training; and 86% claimed they had found jobs that were related to their vocational training (AMS, 2002).

Apart from this, the Swedish government promotes adult education by offering basic, upper secondary and supplementary education for those over 20 years old. It is a right of residents of municipalities to receive basic adult education (National Agency for Education, 2003, p 82). The objective of basic education is to 'give adults the knowledge and skills they require to take part in social and working life' and also to provide 'a foundation for further studies'. Further, the Swedish government implemented the 'Adult Education Initiative' by giving extra subsidies for municipalities to provide upper secondary and supplementary education for unemployed persons. To support their studies, participants can obtain grants that are similar to unemployment benefits. In the 2001/02 school year, 287,584 students attended courses organised by municipalities and county councils, and 94.2% of them attended day-time courses. The median age of students was 32 (National Agency for Education, 2003).

As shown earlier, the Swedish government has used a wide range of measures to develop the potential of the unemployed. Several features can be identified in these labour programmes. First, an 'individualised job plan' is a key approach to the needs of an unemployed person. Disadvantaged groups such as long-term unemployed workers, school leavers, disabled persons, older workers and immigrants find it difficult to enter the labour market (AMS, 2003, p 18). This means that special programmes should be provided for them to overcome employment barriers. They have been helped by their mentors, who work out an 'individual plan' with them. In this way, each unemployed person is considered unique and as having particular needs. Second, the programmes aim to improve both unemployed people's occupational skills and their self-confidence. This recognises the impact of psychological well-being on a person's employment prospects. Third, intensive programmes involving various types of professionals and organisations have been developed for helping unemployed persons with special difficulties. Fourth, a group work approach has been used to enrich unemployed participants' learning experiences, encouraging them to support each other. For example, a 20-week 'good leader training' course has been offered to unemployed young people, with 15–20 persons on each course. The training teaches young people to independently lead a project and conduct market research. Fifth, the Swedish government also emphasises the provision of basic education for those lacking basic academic qualifications. The government understands that the education system is 'essential to enable people to acquire the knowledge they need for active citizenship' (Ministry of Health and Social Affairs, 2003a, p 26). Also, it was reported that one third of participants of the AG lacked 'compulsory school or high school leaving certificates'. Basic skills were offered to these participants. Of 2,045 participants, 80% were aged between 30 and 60, and 7% over 61 (AMS, 2003, p 18). The National Labour Market Board (AMS) (2002b) also reported that 10% of the YG participants come back to the PESO with a higher academic degree. Thus, the provision of basic education provides a foundation for unemployed people to develop training and career opportunities.

Self-determination

The evidence cited earlier shows that unemployed persons in Sweden have received relatively generous financial support under the existing welfare arrangements. This subsection examines whether the Swedish welfare system can enhance the self-determination of unemployed recipients. Sweden is a 'parliamentary democratic monarchy' and 'All public power in Sweden comes from the people' (Sweden Information Smorgasbord, 2004b). General elections in Sweden are held every four years and citizens can choose their representatives to sit in three decision-making bodies: the national parliament, the local county council, and the municipality. The Swedish parliament (Riksdagen) is the highest decision-making body, with 349 members. However, 'Sweden has a long tradition of local self-government' (Swedish Association of Local Authorities and Federation of Swedish County Councils, 2003, p 1) and 'decentralisation' is one of the key features of its public administration. This means that 'both responsibility for services and decision-making should be placed as close as possible to the people affected by decisions' (Ministry of Finance, 2005, p 11). There are 290 municipal authorities and 20 county councils in Sweden. Gotland is a special case because it has no county councils; instead, county council responsibilities are exercised by the Gotland municipality. Those responsibilities include the provision of health care and the development of public transport at the regional level. Both municipalities and county councils have their own parliaments and governments, which are elected at the general election. Based on the concept of local self-government, local authorities are 'independent bodies, free to make their own decisions within certain limits' (Ministry of Finance, 2005, p 6). They have the power to levy taxes to finance the services they provide. The average tax rate was 20.80% for municipalities and 10.71% for county councils. This means that the total average local tax was 31.51% in 2004.

'Democracy in the Swedish sense fully expects citizen participation' (Gay, 2003). The Swedish government understands the limitations of direct elections and encourages the participation of civil organisations. As the government points out, 'There is a clear connection between social and political equality', and disadvantaged groups tend to be 'marginalised in political terms and to feel powerless' (Ministry of Health and Social Affairs, 2003a, p 44). Therefore, the Swedish government adopted the 'Democracy in the New Century' measure in 2002, which aims at providing more channels for citizens to voice their concerns, allowing different levels of organisations and different arenas to make political decisions (Ministry of Justice, 2002). For example, fathers' rights organisations were invited to review and comment on proposed legislation before it was submitted to the parliament.

Labour policy-making in Sweden also exhibits principles of 'decentralisation' and 'participation'. The board of directors of the AMS and the County Labour Council (LAN) 'decide major questions' (Forsberg et al, 2002, p 4), even though the Labour Market Administration (AMV) at the central level is mainly responsible for overall labour policy. The AMV includes the AMS and County Labour Board in each of 21 counties (Figure 7.3). The AMS, which reports to the Ministry of Industry, Employment and Communication, works on behalf of the government to make decisions on all labour training and employment issues.

At the local level, the County Labour Boards (CLBs) are responsible for labour affairs in each county. In 1999 local Employment Services Committees (ESCs), cooperative bodies, were established at the local

Figure 7.3: The Swedish National Labour Market Administration

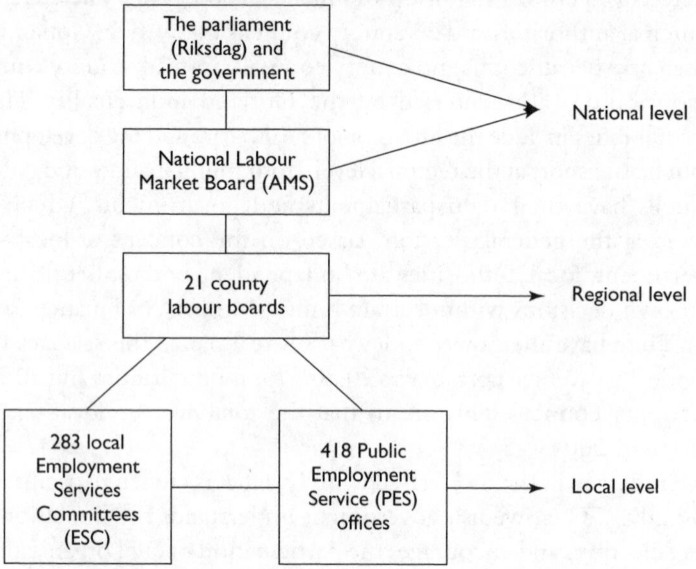

```
        ┌─────────────────┐
        │  The parliament  │
        │  (Riksdag) and   │
        │ the government   │
        └────────┬────────┘
                 │                    ──────► National level
        ┌────────┴────────┐
        │ National Labour │
        │ Market Board (AMS)│
        └────────┬────────┘
                 │
        ┌────────┴────────┐
        │   21 county      │
        │  labour boards   │          ──────► Regional level
        └───┬─────────┬───┘
            │         │
  ┌─────────┴──┐   ┌──┴──────────┐
  │  283 local │   │ 418 Public  │
  │ Employment │   │ Employment  │
  │  Services  │───│ Service (PES)│ ──────► Local level
  │ Committees │   │   offices   │
  │   (ESC)    │   │             │
  └────────────┘   └─────────────┘
```

Source: Lundin and Skedinger (2000)

level, one in almost every municipality. Each ESC has between 8 and 16 members who are representatives from the PES, the CLB, trade unions and the business community.

The main duties of ESCs are to:

> Initiate different projects, suggest changes in labour market policies when necessary and co-ordinate the activities of various actors (for example, the municipalities and the PESOs) that are carrying out and financing labour market projects.... The task of drawing up budgets and working plans is however the responsibility of the PESOs. Through this process the ESCs lay down the broad outlines for the work at the local level. (Lundin and Skedinger, 2000, p 9)

As the above administrative structure reveals, there is a close link between central government and local authorities as well as between county councils and local business and labour organisations. Such a decision-making process provides opportunities for participation by local politicians, trade unions and business organisations.

In Sweden, labour can influence employment policies through formal and informal mechanisms. Swedish workers have strong and well-

Table 7.5: Rate (percentage) of unionisation of Swedish workers, 1980–2002

	1980	1990	2002
Blue-collar workers	80	84	85
White-collar workers	84	84	83
All employees	82	84	84

Source: Swedish Trade Union Confederation (2003)

organised labour organisations. Over 80% of both white-collar and blue-collar workers are members of trade unions (Table 7.5). The most influential trade union in Sweden is theSwedish Trade Union Confederation (LO), which represents a total of 2.2 million individuals and has 21 regional trade union ombudsmen and offices. Its membership includes over 80% of Swedish workers.

The LO has a close relationship with the Social Democratic Party (SDP). The president of the LO is traditionally a member of the Executive Committee of the SDP. The personal connections between trade unionists and the SDP are strong at 'all levels of society' (LO, 2003, p 13). Through such relationships, trade unionists have 'important roles, centrally, regionally, and locally, as representatives in consultative committees of various authorities' (LO, 2003, p 13). As a result of the close relationship between LO and the SPD, labour unions in Sweden participate more strongly in economic policy making (including fiscal policy, monetary policy, investment, overall industrial planning, trade policy, job creation and training, and employment law) than their European counterparts (Table 7.6). Labour unions' mean participation score was 9.2 in contrast to 3.8 in the UK. In practice, the SDP takes account of the attitudes of trade unions towards labour policies. For example, because of the opposition of the LO, the SDP scrapped the time limit on unemployment insurance benefits (Anderson, 2002).

Because of the government's promotion of public participation, representatives of trade unions can directly influence labour policies

Table 7.6: Mean union participation index scores in selected European countries, 1970–92

Country	Mean score	Country	Mean score
Austria	9.7	Ireland	6.1
Sweden	9.2	Netherlands	5.9
Switzerland	8.0	Belgium	5.3
Finland	7.1	Germany	4.4
Norway	6.9	Britain	3.8
Denmark	6.9	France	3.0
Italy	6.6		

Source: Comston (1996)

through their involvement in ESCs. Moreover, trade unions can shape central government's labour welfare measures through their informal but close relationship with SDP politicians. The views of unemployed workers can largely be expressed through their representatives on both local and central decision-making bodies.

Human dignity is related to the degree of participation and freedom that a recipient enjoys in claiming and receiving benefits as well as in politics. The Social Services Act of 1997 subjects SA recipients to the following conditions in order to participate in an 'activation programme' organised by municipalities (Giertz, 2004; Minas, 2005). They must be:

- under 25 years old;
- 25 or more years old and needing to improve their competency; or
- students receiving study allowances but without having a job during a study break.

Local government has developed three models of activation programme. The first is the 'Hallstahammar model', a combination of work, social training, studies and other useful activities. The second is the 'Uppsala model' which requires that recipients seek jobs intensively. The third is the 'temporary municipal job' model, whereby recipients are treated as employees with a wage accepted by unions. After completing their spells of employment, recipients can leave SA and are qualified for unemployment insurance. Clearly, SA recipients have limited choice but to receive training and subsidised employment once they are living on benefits. There are two issues regarding this arrangement. First, there is no reciprocal obligation between the government and recipients. As Giertz (2004, p 36) points out, 'the municipality can demand participation while the individual has no right to require participation in a training programme'. Second, this directly threatens the objective of the 'individualised plan' because social workers have little choice but to ask recipients from different backgrounds to participate in 'activation programmes'. In short, recipients who do not get a job or attend education 'can routinely be diagnosed as in need of competence increasing measures' (Giertz, 2004, p 36). In practice, the implementation of this policy depends on the municipality. For example, social workers in Malmö have accepted or terminated counselling for people lacking motivation or abusing alcohol or drugs (Giertz, 2004, p 36).

Recipients of unemployment insurance, for their part, have to fulfil several requirements mentioned earlier in this chapter. These include registration at the PESO and drawing up a 'job search contract' and an 'action plan' which identifies suitable types of jobs by skill level and geographical location. Unemployed persons work with staff of PESO to develop a plan which 'should be individualized for the particular jobseeker' (FUIF, 2002, p 5). The Unemployment Insurance Act in 2000 introduced some restrictions on unemployed recipients. The government abolished the use of 'active labour market programmes' as a condition for re-qualifying for benefits. Instead, the period of protection has been limited to 300 days, after which only one renewal is allowed. Then recipients have to participate in the AG in order to continue receiving unemployment benefits. Under this new arrangement, unemployed workers can be asked to take up a proper job or participate in training activities for up to 40 hours a week. In addition, the range of occupations and localities within which work is sought has to become broader after each 100-day period. If an unemployed recipient refuses 'a suitable job' or programme, his or her daily benefit is reduced by 25% for 40 days for the first refusal, and by 50% for a further 40 days for the second. If he or she turns down a job for the third time, the benefit is stopped. Several criteria determine whether a job is 'suitable':

- Previous occupational experience might affect one's ability to cope with the job.
- The place of work should satisfy the requirements of the work environment legislation with regard to the prevention of ill health and accidents.
- The salary offered should not be substantially (more than 10%) lower than the daily cash benefit that a person receives from the unemployment insurance fund.

As illustrated earlier, a wide range of programmes have been offered to young unemployed persons. Unemployed young people under 20 who do not attend high school or training programmes have to join a youth programme, which takes the form of education, internship, or a mixture of the two. The internship can also be pursued outside Sweden. A respondent of a research study felt that the programme 'constitutes an offer, which is not coercive in any way' (Forsberg et al, 2002, p 8).

The above job requirements show that a certain degree of control has been exerted over the behaviour of unemployed recipients, who are required to draw up an action plan and accept jobs offered if they fail to get one in the open market. The features that mitigate these control measures in the Swedish welfare system are the relatively generous benefits and the use of professional social workers and career counsellors.

Equal value

Unemployed persons are economically weak citizens whose experiences reveal whether the economically weak also become socially and politically weak. The discussion of equal value concerns whether the unemployed receive the same respect as employed citizens and whether unemployed people of different genders, ages and races have similar employment opportunities. Equality is a key objective of the Swedish government, and has been expressed through different dimensions. The first is the 'national norm of living standard' for recipients of SA. Unemployed persons receiving SA are expected to continue to participate in certain types of customary activities such as reading a newspaper, using a telephone, watching television and joining trade unions. In other words, unemployed citizens are treated as social beings and are provided with resources to maintain a certain degree of community life. Such an approach to welfare is different from the three other societies discussed in this book, which mainly provide basic subsistence for the poor. However, about one third of unemployed young people, as illustrated earlier in this chapter, were unable to participate in some customary social activities, and the present level of financial support seems not to meet the Swedish government's objective of providing a national norm of living for claimants of SA.

The second dimension is equality between families with or without children as well as between working and unemployed families. Unemployment insurance recipients with lower income and more children can get a higher replacement rate, more assistance from Child Benefit and supplements for large families. As illustrated in Table 7.4, by means of cash transfers the Swedish government has reduced the poverty rate of families with children from 17.7% to just 2.8%. As a result, the gap between unemployed families with children and working families has been minimised.

The third dimension is employment equality for different age groups. The Swedish government's principle is: 'everyone who wants to work and can work should be given this opportunity' (Forsberg et al, 2002, p 1). Also, developing employability is a priority theme of the 'equality initiative' in Sweden (Ministry of Health and Social Affairs, 2003a, p 19). The government has 'a commitment to ensuring that everyone can participate in society and to preventing social exclusion' (Ministry of Health and Social Affairs, 2003a, p 25). Those who are facing employment barriers, such as older people, young people, disabled persons and women, have been provided with extra assistance. Since more than four out of every five children aged 3–6 years in Sweden can receive day care services, Swedish women are able to 'choose to enter the labour market if they can find a job' (Kvist, 2000, p 11). This is evident from the female economic participation rate, which is 83.8% of the male rate for people aged 15 and above (United Nations Development Programme, 2004). Young people can receive 12 months' full-time training and education under programmes such as the YG.

Decentralised decision-making involves local authorities in designing application procedures and determining some items of assistance. This policy 'opens the door to arbitrariness' and creates regional variations (Minas, 2005, p 20). As illustrated earlier, central government sets levels only of 'livelihood support' and 'other assistance', while the municipality 'has the opportunity, but is not obliged, to provide assistance in another form'. In short, municipalities can determine 'how their work is carried out' and 'the payment of assistance on the basis of varying local conditions and needs'. As a consequence, research studies show that 'there are substantial variations across municipalities' (Arslanogullari, 2000, p 6). Other studies further illustrate that SA is 'discretionary on at least three levels, the municipal political board, the local office and the individual social worker' (Giertz, 2004, p 27). In addition, municipalities have different approaches to activation programmes. Their interests are related to taxation and unemployment figures in their areas. Very often, they use 'low-level programmes rather than passivity' (Giertz, 2004, p 31). Such differences in the rate of assistance and in welfare-to-work programmes jeopardise the national objective of equality and also adversely affect the dignity of unemployed recipients.

In recent years, academics have argued that the Swedish welfare system creates institutional inequalities. There is an obvious inequality between unemployed claimants of SA and recipients of unemployment insurance. As Giertz (2004) observes, the former are required to participate in activation programmes organised by municipalities which limit choice, in contrast to the variety of programmes managed by PES. They also receive lower benefits than unemployment insurance recipients. On the other hand, recipients of unemployment insurance can participate in an AG to continue receiving compensation from unemployment insurance. As a result of these measures, 'the unemployed on social assistance are still in a second tier compared to the unemployed with insurance' (Giertz, 2004, p 210). New immigrants seem to be the most vulnerable group in Swedish society, and need more employment support. However, their status as SA recipients restricts their training opportunities, and they suffer financial disadvantages. This is the fundamental structural problem created by the Swedish welfare system.

Conclusion

This chapter has attempted to examine whether the Swedish welfare state can safeguard the dignity of unemployed workers. The discussion earlier shows that the dignity of unemployed persons has been shaped by three fundamental objectives of the Swedish government: full employment, active workforce, and equality. By pursuing equality, the government attempts to provide 'a normal standard of living' for recipients of SA. Poor unemployed persons and their family members can expect that their physical, medical, educational and to some extent their social needs will be met. Based on the goal of full employment and an active labour strategy, unemployed persons in Sweden have been provided with a wide range of opportunities to improve skills and educational qualifications. As the AMS (2000) stresses, 'Through intensive measures such as competence development and training, the Activity Guarantee will improve these people's [those with difficulties in getting jobs] chances of landing the new jobs that are going'. Also, professional workers and career counsellors provide intensive services for the most disadvantaged groups. It should be stressed that Sweden's labour policy has moved in the direction of 'differentiation, individualization and the shift in responsibility to the municipalities' (Forsberg et al, 2002, p 33). As one respondent of a study pointed out, 'Certain young people require directed resources or resources devoted over a longer period of time before results are achieved' (Forsberg et al, 2002, p 8). The Swedish experience clearly shows that active labour market policies can 'affect the structural level of unemployment and help the labour force to adapt to changing economic circumstances' (Green-Pedersen and Linbom, 2002, p 21). Thus, it can be said that to a great extent, the dignity of unemployed persons in terms of meeting basic needs, fulfilling caring duties, developing potential, and self-determination has been safeguarded by the Swedish welfare system.

The most controversial issues, however, are the exercise of autonomy and the disadvantaged position of unemployed persons receiving SA. Unemployed SA recipients who have limited opportunities to participate in the labour market, such as new immigrants and young people, receive lower benefits and more limited training programmes than their counterparts receiving unemployment benefits. The problem is fundamentally linked to a better-rewarded unemployment insurance scheme that excludes ineligible unemployed workers. A second issue concerns the legitimacy of state control over the behaviour of welfare recipients. Like the governments of other welfare states discussed in this book, the Swedish government exercises strict control over unemployed citizens. As illustrated earlier, present insurance policies require unemployed workers to register at PES offices and to participate in employment programmes. It should be stressed that this kind of control is mitigated by the better unemployment benefits received by insured workers and the still reasonable living standard enjoyed by recipients of SA. As Kvist (2000, p 18) notices,

> Relatively generous benefits in the Scandinavian model for low-income groups are thus circumscribed by tough work conditions in order to combat unemployment traps and benefit dependency. In this way 'activation' stimulates the unemployed to seek and get work ... 'Activation' also aims to endow participants with more qualifications ... the conditioning of benefits on 'activation' aims to secure people against marginalisation, against entrapment on benefits or in precarious jobs.

An informant who is responsible for labour market policy pointed out that the lack of education has been regarded as the main barrier to young people seeking to enter the labour market. Many of them have poor academic results in basic subjects such as Swedish, English and mathematics (Forsberg et al, 2002). Also, according to an expert on employment, one of the values of activity is to ensure that a young person 'develops structured daily routines and does not turn night into day' (Forsberg et al, 2002, p 7). For those who have difficulties in entering the labour market, the Nordic countries still provide 'some sort of daily activities' (Kvist, 2001, p 5). Thus, the positive aspects of subsidised employment and labour training have been used to justify generous Swedish benefits. However, as Giertz (2004, p 179) argues, 'A more systematic structuring of interventions of different types and intensities could be more beneficial for the development of knowledge about interventions that work'. This implies that a state needs to improve its quality of intervention. In short, the Swedish system of control has two distinguishing features. The first is the use of professional social workers and career counsellors to generate 'personalised plans' in various programmes. The second is wider participation in labour market policies through decentralisation and consultations at various levels. The

Swedish experience shows that control should be based on a person's unique needs, and implemented by relevant professionals in the context of broad-based citizen participation.

Part Three:
Comparisons

EIGHT

Comparing human dignity in four welfare systems

By using different perspectives for evaluating a welfare system, we can reach different conclusions. The selection of an assessment tool is very important because its results might shape the public's attitudes towards the living quality of the poor and also affect a government's policies on the levels of welfare benefits. Thus, welfare evaluation can be a verdict on the fate of poor people, suppressing or pursuing equality and social justice in a society. In Chapters four to seven, human dignity has been used to assess the treatment of unemployed persons in four welfare systems. This chapter compares the welfare measures of the four systems and their impact on the dignity of unemployed persons. Also, welfare measures that enhance or suppress the dignity of welfare recipients are identified and discussed. As the unemployed are economically and very often politically weak, the treatment of unemployed persons tells us a lot about the nature of a welfare state, its distribution of political power and the social and economic positions of poor citizens.

Meeting physical needs

A person's physical and psychological well-being is fundamental to his or her survival and daily functioning. Three of the four selected countries use national insurance schemes to provide unemployed workers with income protection. Only Hong Kong does not have a state-managed unemployment insurance scheme, which reflects strong opposition from the business community since the 1960s. The Hong Kong government also uses the principle of the free market to justify its minimal labour welfare. For example, by rejecting seven labour ordinances granting more power to workers over collective bargaining, the former Chief Secretary of the Administration explained that these ordinances would adversely affect 'harmonious labour relations' and 'Hong Kong's economic competitiveness and attractiveness to overseas investments' (Chan, 1997). Hong Kong has been institutionalised as a free economy with an undemocratic polity. Politically, Article 16 of the Basic Law in Hong Kong's constitution states, 'The Hong Kong

Special Administrative Region shall be vested with executive power' (*The Basic Law of the Hong Kong SAR of the People's Republic of China*, 1990, p 10). Economically, Article 108 of the Basic Law requires the HKSAR to continue the 'low tax policy previously pursued in Hong Kong' (Basic Law, 1990, p 39). Thus, Hong Kong's lack of a national insurance scheme is fundamentally related to its polity, which provides limited political participation for the working class (see Chapter Four for details).

As for the levels of unemployment benefits, there are variations between China, the UK and Sweden. An unemployment insurance scheme was established in China in 1999 following the publication of the Unemployment Insurance Ordinance. The level of unemployment benefit is not based on any scientific studies but set in relation to other types of benefits. It is expected to be higher than the MLA but lower than the minimum wage. Thus, the state unemployment insurance scheme is designed to maintain work incentives and to reflect workers' previous insurance contributions. In the UK, the government has never adopted any scientifically validated benefit scales. Various studies have reported that unemployed families are unable to maintain a balanced diet and have difficulties in paying bills when subsisting on unemployment benefits (Table 8.1). In contrast, the unemployment insurance in Sweden gives more protection for unemployed workers, who can receive as much as 80% of previous salaries. However, unemployed young people were found to be unable to participate in a customary social life such as 'buying necessary clothes', 'going to a pub or restaurant' and 'buying gifts' (Julkunen, 2002, pp 242-3). Long-term unemployed persons also encountered similar problems (Clasen et al, 1997).

The three welfare systems also differ in the maximum period of entitlement to unemployment benefits. Unemployed Swedish workers can receive up to 300 days of benefits with a possibility of renewal for an additional 300 days. After that, unemployed workers can participate in the AG to continue receiving the same amount of benefits. This means that the Swedish unemployment scheme provides unlimited benefits for recipients, although unemployed workers can be required to do subsidised jobs or attend career training for up to 40 hours a week. Actually, during high unemployment in the 1990s, the Swedish government reduced the replacement rate of unemployment insurance benefits and also considered limiting the duration of entitlement. Faced with strong opposition from trade unions, the government finally adopted a more acceptable approach by slightly changing the re-qualifying conditions. This incident clearly reveals the impact of Swedish labour unions on welfare measures.

In the UK, the time limit for receiving the contribution-based JSA is 26 weeks. Unemployed workers are then transferred to the means-tested income-based JSA. The period of receipt of unemployment insurance benefits in China, however, varies according to a worker's contribution records. The maximum period is 24 months for those working for more than 10 years.

To summarise, the unemployment insurance schemes of the three countries display the following features:

- The Swedish scheme can compensate to a great extent for the income of unemployed workers, especially those previously on low incomes. In this way, unemployed workers are able to continue to enjoy a reasonable standard of living.
- The British scheme has provided a basic income and a limited period of protection for unemployed workers.
- Both the Swedish and the British governments use active labour programmes as a means to enhance skills and tackle welfare dependency. The Swedish system provides more options, supported by professional careers counsellors.
- The Chinese scheme links unemployment protection to unemployed workers' previous financial contributions so that their benefit period is associated with the number of years they have contributed. Also, unemployed workers' eligibility for benefits is associated with their behaviour. They cannot receive medical benefits if their health problems are caused by illegal actions. Therefore, an insurance-based unemployment system has been linked with the Chinese government's desire to exercise control over its citizens. In short, being a good worker and a good citizen are the criteria for receiving unemployment benefits.

As for medical care, state-managed health schemes in the UK, Sweden, and Hong Kong play a dominant role in providing medical services for the general public (Table 8.1). Under collective medical services, poor unemployed families in these three countries receive free treatment. However, the sources of their funding vary, which affects the quality of the services. Hong Kong's medical care is mainly financed by general taxation. Facing increasing medical costs as a result of the ageing population, expensive drugs and equipment, and a deterioration of public revenues due to economic recession, the Hong Kong government in recent years has required patients to contribute more to the cost of health services by charging fees. As pointed out by the CE of the Hong Kong Hospital Authority, William Ho (2002):

> The government has the ultimate responsibility for people's health, but to achieve that, it cannot do it alone. We must leverage the strengths of both the public and private sectors, and let consumers understand that they, too, must make a contribution to make the system work.

Given more itemised charging measures, low-income households and unemployed families who are not living on public benefits have to pay more for their treatment.

In the UK, the NHS is largely financed out of general taxation, with some revenue from National Insurance contributions. Together these account for about 90% of its income. As revealed in the Hospital Plan in 2000, the NLG's objective is to increase health expenditure in order to match European average spending on health care by 2008. Accordingly, health expenditure in the UK will increase from 6.7% of GDP when the NLG came to power to 9.4% by 2007–08 (Brown, 2002). However, the NHS is still largely free to all patients at the point of receipt, even though the financial pressures have been tremendous in recent years. As the NLG declares, 'We believe that any system for delivering health care must uphold the founding principle of the NHS – that it is free at the point of use based on need, not ability to pay' (DH, 2002). Unemployed persons claiming income-based JSA or Income Support are exempt from the following expenses (DH, 2005):

- NHS prescriptions
- NHS dental treatment
- NHS wigs and fabric supports
- sight tests, glasses and contact lenses
- travel for NHS treatment under the care of a consultant.

Like the Hong Kong government, the NLG also has to face the issue of financing the expansion of the NHS because it has promised the voters not to increase the standard and top income tax rates. However, it increased National Insurance contributions from employers, employees and the self-employed by one percentage point on all earnings above £4,615 (Brown, 2002).

In Sweden, the 'fundamental principle is that the provision and financing of health services rests primarily with the county councils' (National Board of Health and Welfare, 2003, p 5). In this way, the quality of medical care is mainly shaped by local politicians in 21 geographical areas. Over 80% of health expenditure is financed by local taxation; patients have to pay only a small amount towards their treatment. Also, the policy of placing a ceiling on charges implies that the government takes the ultimate responsibility for the health treatment of patients regardless of the nature of the illness. This is an important protection for low-income unemployed families who are not living on public benefits.

China, by contrast, has fundamentally changed its health care system from a collective free service to a marketised one, especially through employment insurance-based protection. Under decentralisation, health care has become 'a local matter, dictated by the ability to pay' (Liu et al, 1998, p 120). As Médecins Sans Frontières (2004) observes,

> The commercialization of the health system means that many people, and especially the poorest, are left without basic medical care. Because their income often comes directly from the services they provide, health workers in China increasingly prescribe drugs and treatments that are inappropriate or expensive in order to boost their income. As a result, because preventive medicine is not very lucrative, it is often neglected. The expanding economy, combined with this laissez-faire style of health care, has had an enormous impact on the care being provided throughout the country.

Due to the privatisation of health services, access to health care now depends on one's wealth and entitlement to work-related benefits as well as the health policies of local authorities. Unemployment insurance contributors can claim back only 70% of medical costs, and the government provides free or subsidised treatment only for patients with special diseases such as AIDS. As a consequence, a large number of urban poor people and of the rural population are being excluded from health treatment (Table 8.1). An official study conducted by the Ministry of Health showed that 36% of patients in cities and 39% in rural areas did not consult doctors because of financial difficulties (*Ming Pao*, 2004g). Therefore, health inequality and the affordability of medical treatment have become the biggest problems in China that adversely affect the dignity of a large number of Chinese people in a mixed economy.

The above discussion shows that poor unemployed persons can get access to health care in collective health care systems in the UK, Sweden and Hong Kong. However, the quality of health care and its perceived of financial burden are also affected by a government's commitment to health equality and the extent of its financial constraints. Following a low taxation policy, the Hong Kong government finds it difficult to continue financing health services from general revenues. As a result, fees have been introduced to increase patients' financial contributions towards their treatment. Facing the same problem in financing health services, the UK government, however, has increased its revenues partly through higher National Insurance contributions. The experiences of Hong Kong and the UK illustrate how ideology and politics shape a government's fiscal strategies. The Chief Executive of Hong Kong is elected by an economic and social elite and pro-China organisations. As a result, he mainly pursues the objectives of the business community and the Chinese government in order to preserve Hong Kong as a free enterprise zone with a simple and low taxation policy. By maintaining a low tax system, the HKSAR has little choice but to increase patients' contributions to their health care.

In contrast, the Swedish government makes good health and equal access to health care as national objectives under the leadership of the Social Democratic Party. Apart from a democratic system at the central level, the Swedish government also promotes active citizen participation through decentralisation of power and the consultation of various labour and business organisations. For example, representatives of employers and employees can voice their concerns about labour market policies through the nationwide Local Employment Services Committees.

China, by contrast, is a one-party state where all power lies in the hands of the Chinese Communist Party. In practice, the Standing Committee of the Political Bureau (SCPB) makes all major decisions, although a limited degree of consultation has been initiated by local authorities. For example, the Shanghai municipal government seeks advice from experts on major welfare policies, especially academics from higher education institutions. The final decisions, however, rest with senior government officials. Under the existing decision-making process, the needs of unemployed persons may not have been effectively addressed. It seems that recent welfare interventions of the Chinese government are mainly motivated by the need to maintain social stability and to create favourable conditions for economic development rather than any well-planned and long-term benefits to the general public. According to a senior official of the Shanghai Municipal Civil Affairs Bureau, 'As the unemployment rate is closely connected with social stability, we are obliged to help more people shake off poverty' (*China Daily*, 2005). This might partly explain why the three major social security systems (the basic living guarantee for laid-off workers, the unemployment insurance system and the minimum living standard guarantee) were formally established only in the late 1990s, about 20 years after the open-door policy began. In short, the experiences of the four welfare systems and their strategies towards health care policy illustrate how the physical health of unemployed persons has been shaped by the politics and economics of a society.

All four welfare systems have social assistance schemes providing financial support for poor unemployed persons. Their rules of entitlement and levels of assistance, however, vary. Based on the free market economy, Hong Kong's CSSA mainly provides minimal and temporary assistance for poor people. To prevent welfare dependency and control expenditure on social security, the Hong Kong government shifted its social assistance criteria from 'basic needs' to 'below market wages'. Accordingly, the rate of the CSSA scheme has been set no higher than that of the poorest 25% by expenditure. This change reveals that the Hong Kong government is little concerned by the adequacy of benefits for meeting survival needs, but stresses the importance of labour market incentives to the spirit of capitalism.

In China, the MLSG seems to be a coping strategy of the CCP in response to the contracting welfare capacity of state enterprises and increasing pressures on unemployment. It also amounts to compensation for former state workers as well as residual financial assistance for helping poor unemployed workers in a mixed economy. For the Chinese government, the purpose of MLSG is to promote China's capitalism and maintain social stability. Against this background, MLSG is mainly financed by local authorities and at a level lower than the minimum wage. Research studies found that recipients were unable to buy adequate food or pay for their children's education (Tables 8.1 and 8.3). As a remedial welfare strategy, the MLSG is also administered by existing political networks such as street committees (SCs) and resident associations (RAs). The MLSG is therefore shaped by local effort and supported by non-professionals with limited human resources. Like the unemployment insurance scheme, the CCP's control over its citizens has been strengthened through the release of recipients' names and the requirement that recipients follow national family planning policies and uphold law and order.

Like the Hong Kong government, the UK government is unwilling to establish scientifically validated benefit levels. Instead, it uses 'household income below 60% of median income' as a poverty threshold, though this has not influenced the determination of benefit scales. Against this benchmark, social security benefits have not provided unemployed families with an income sufficient to protect them from poverty. Research findings cited in Chapter Six show that unemployed households faced a 75% risk of poverty, many poor people could not afford good-quality food and more than one in ten families was unable to buy new clothes. It is only by having a paid job that their living standard can be improved.

The Social Services Act in Sweden clearly proclaims the right of each citizen to receive financial support from the state (see Chapter Seven). The concept of citizenship is mixed with the national objective of equality. Comparative studies commonly point out that social security transfers in Sweden have dramatically reduced poverty by as much as 19% (Riley, 2003), and the poorest 10% of households even receive over 90% of their income from state benefits (Nardi, 2000). As these figures suggest, poverty arising from unemployment in Sweden has been very largely tackled. However, as reported by Julkunen (2002), a significant number of unemployed young persons suffer from material and social deprivation. This implies that the existing social security benefits target the needs of families with children but are inadequate for meeting the needs of unemployed youth.

The discussion earlier clearly shows that low levels of social assistance for unemployed persons have been adopted in three of the four welfare systems – China, Hong Kong and the UK. Although the benefit rates in Sweden have taken recipients' social needs into account, the social activities in which recipients can afford to engage are limited. Benefit levels are still a long way from providing recipients with the lifestyle that is customary in the society in which they live. Both the Chinese government and the Hong Kong government clearly state that the income of people living on public benefits should be lower than the minimum wage (in China) or should not be higher than the income of the poorest 25% by expenditure (in Hong Kong). In fact, a similar approach to public assistance was adopted in Britain under the Poor Law Amendment Act of 1834. According to that Act, the condition of the pauper in the workhouse should be 'in no case as eligible as the condition of persons of the lowest class subsisting on the fruits of their own industry' (quoted in Jones, 1994, p 13). Under active labour market policies or workfare measures, poor unemployed persons in China, Hong Kong and the UK are expected to evade poverty or lead a decent life through labour participation. Based on the concept of human dignity, a reasonable standard of physical health should be provided for all unemployed persons so that they can develop educationally and maintain some degree of social participation.

Table 8.1: Meeting the physical needs of unemployed persons in four welfare systems

Area	China	Hong Kong	UK	Sweden
Unemployment insurance	Unemployment Insurance Ordinance in 1999.	The Hong Kong government persistently refuses to set up any unemployment scheme that limits the operation of the free market economy.	Contribution-based JSA and income-based JSA.	Voluntary Income-related Insurance and Basic Insurance.
Eligibility for unemployment insurance	Involuntary unemployment. Workers with urban residency. Having made contributions for at least 12 months.	No unemployment insurance scheme.	Pay National Insurance contributions for the contribution-based JSA. Income-based JSA is a means-tested benefit	Recipients of Voluntary Income-related Insurance have to fulfil membership and work conditions. Recipients of Basic Insurance should have paid taxes and social insurance contributions.
Level of unemployment insurance benefit	Higher than the MLA but lower than the minimum wage.	No unemployment insurance scheme.	Benefits up-rated annually in line with the Retail Price Index.	The upper limit of earnings-related benefits has not been raised for several years. Therefore only a small number of workers receiving Voluntary Income-related Insurance can receive up to 80% replacement rate (Ahlberg, 2003).
Public assistance objective	MLSG established in 1999 by providing 'a basic subsistence assistance for poor people' (Information Office of the State Council, 2004).	CSSA was set up in 1996 (previously known as Public Assistance). CSSA provides financial support to 'bring the income of needy individuals and families up to a prescribed level to meet their basic needs' (Social Welfare Department, 2004a, p 2).	Provide financial help for those whose income is below the means-tested benefit (Income Support) scales.	A person 'is entitled to assistance from the social welfare committee towards his livelihood (livelihood support) and for his living in general (general assistance)' (1998 Social Services Act, quoted in National Board of Health and Welfare, 2000) The government's objective is to provide everyone with 'the resources necessary to live in accordance with human dignity' (Ministry of Health and Social Affairs, 2003a, p 25).

(continued)

Table 8.1: Continued

Area	China	Hong Kong	UK	Sweden
Public assistance objective (continued)				A national benefit standard was introduced in 1998, which includes items in a household budget drawn up by the National Board for Consumer Policy. But, items such as housing and travelling costs and childcare expenses are left to be decided by local authorities (Minas, 2005).
Level of public assistance benefits	The lowest level of assistance among the three protection systems (unemployment insurance, minimum wage, and MLSG): 'Should meet the needs of their basic daily necessities such as food, clothing, and housing. Expenses such as water, gas, electricity, and education for children should also be considered' (State Council, 1999). The national average of MLSG was reportedly 29% of the average income of urban residents (Shang and Wu, 2004).	'The levels of benefit should be kept down so that they are more in line with market wages for low-end jobs' (Social Welfare Department, 1998, p 23). The level of assistance should not be higher than the income of the poorest 25% of households.	The UK government persistently rejects any calls for scientific determination of benefit levels. It is believed the benefit levels have been justified and held 'below the level of low wage rates' (Veit-Wilson, 1999, p 101). Unemployment benefit in the UK was about 23% of workers' previous income (Clasen et al, 1997).	The poor are expected to live on 'a reasonable standard of living' (National Board of Health and Welfare, 2000). Social assistance includes two parts. Part I consists of 'livelihood support and other assistance' set out by the central government. Part II is 'assistance in another form', which is decided by local authorities.
Recipients' living conditions	'Difficulty getting food and clothes. No money to pay heating, rent. Cramped living space' (Cook and Jolly, 2000, pp 18–19).	A recipient claimed, 'it is not enough, not even for food' (*Far Eastern Economic Review*, 1995). Benefit levels are too low to provide a decent living (Wong and Chua, 1998).	Recipients could not avoid real hardship. Long-term unemployed persons were reported being unable to afford basic necessities. They generally run into debt (Clasen et al, 1997).	The rate of poverty was reduced from 28% to 9% after social security transfers (Riley, 2003). The lowest 10% of households received 92% of their income from social security transfers (Nardi et al, 2000).

(continued)

Table 8.1: Continued

Area	China	Hong Kong	UK	Sweden
Recipients' living conditions (continued)	Most recipients could only buy the cheapest food regardless of its nutritional value (Tang, 2003)	A respondent said 'I eat two meals a day' and 'seldom cook rice because you need other dishes to go with it' (Catholic.org.hk, 2004).	Benefits were inadequate to pay for household bills (Kempson, 1996). Deprivation exists in a significant number of households, especially lone parents: 10% could not afford 'meat/fish every other day'; 12% could not buy 'new clothes when needed' (NCSR and DWP, 2004).	Long-term unemployed persons could not afford holidays, visits to restaurants, pubs and cinemas. Some saved money by not going to see the dentist or the doctor (Clasen et al, 1997).
The extent of health protection	Unemployed persons can claim only up to 75% of medical costs. Medical assistance for those with chronic illnesses. Occasional and temporary medical assistance provided by local authorities and charitable organisations. Limited medical assistance for the poor: The Shanghai Municipal Government issues the 'health help cards' for poor chronically ill patients. The Ministry of Health reported 36% of patients in cities and 39% in rural areas did not go to see doctors because of financial difficulties (BBC News, 2004).	CSSA recipients are exempt from paying for medical treatment at public clinics and hospitals. Expenses for spectacles were scrapped in the 1998 social security review. It becomes a 'discretionary item' following public pressure. CSSA recipients cannot claim for some special dental treatments.	NHS provides free medical services for poor citizens.	'The provision and financing of health services for the entire population is a public sector responsibility' (Swedish Institute, 2003). The objective of public health is to create social conditions to 'ensure good health, on equal terms, for the entire population' (Government Offices of Sweden, 2004b). Poor citizens are exempt from paying for medical costs. A high-cost ceiling is set for limiting patients' burden.

Meeting psychological needs

One of the biggest problems with social security in many countries is that the social and psychological needs of human beings have not been adequately addressed in the process of benefit applications and of calculating benefit entitlement. An unemployed worker and his family need more than money and a job. Some unemployed workers associate unemployment with a number of underlying problems such as lack of self-confidence, low qualifications, inadequate social skills, and even mental health problems. Also, unemployment might threaten the normal functioning of a family and cause tensions among family members. Therefore, the problems of unemployed persons and their families are a big challenge to social security staff.

In Hong Kong, welfare staff who deal with CSSA applications are required only to have completed secondary school education and to attend a four-day induction programme and a ten-day basic course (Hong Kong Government, 1996). However, their duties include interviews, home visits, and providing employment guidance for participants of the Support for Self-reliance Scheme (SFS). The negative feedback from CSSA recipients suggests that the existing service quality and training of staff of the Social Welfare Department is far from adequate (Table 8.2 and Chapter Four).

In China, street committees and resident associations, the traditional neighbourhood organisations, have been used to provide the MLA. Because of the traditionally political nature of these organisations and the low education levels of their staff, the administration of the MLSG scheme has become an uneasy mixture of welfare and political control. The central government's request for the release of the names of applicants is not only an invasion of personal privacy but also an extension of the authoritarian style of the official organisations into the administration of social assistance.

In the UK, Personal Advisers (PAs) are key to the provision of financial assistance and employment guidance for jobseekers. Although the Customer's Charter of Jobcentre Plus (2004b) aims to achieve a high quality of service based on personalised plans, the training of PAs cannot match their duties. Newly recruited PAs can receive about 73 days training, but existing PAs have attended only eight (House of Commons, 2002a). Research found that PAs felt their knowledge and skills were insufficient for their work. Unemployed persons also expressed mixed feelings about the service quality of PAs (see Chapter Six). Some considered PAs polite and supportive, while others felt that they failed to provide detailed benefit information or accurately

Table 8.2: Meeting the psychological needs of unemployed persons in four welfare systems

Area	China	Hong Kong	UK	Sweden
Application procedure for public assistance	SC and RA workers check applicants' information from various sources. 'Applicant's name, age, number of family members, address and the amount of support will be made public in the neighbourhood, and comments from residents in the neighbourhood will be invited as part of the process of means testing' (Shang and Wu, 2004, p 267).	Applicants have to provide detailed evidence about financial conditions. Home visits are arranged.	Sign 'Jobseeker's Agreement', attend 'Jobseeker Interviews'.	Apply at Social Welfare Office, processed by trained social workers.
Training of staff	Most staff of SC and RA who are dealing with public assistance applications have low education qualifications. They attend only short-term training in public administration. A few social workers may also deal with financial assistance. Shanghai is the first province to recognise the social work profession. However, 'Social workers currently are qualified after training for three to six months' and experts 'worry that the training is inadequate' (*Shanghai Star*, 2005). Unemployment services are provided by ESVs. Most of them are former SOE workers who were retrained after being made redundant.	Welfare staff do not have any professional qualifications. They have completed secondary school and attend a four-day induction programme and a ten-day basic course provided by the Social Welfare Department (Hong Kong Government, 1996).	JSA is administrated by staff of JC/JCP. Short-term on-the-job training. Newly recruited PAs receive 73 days' training; existing PAs get an average of eight days' training (House of Commons, 2002a). Staff of Connexions Services are trained PAs.	*Social Assistance:* Trained social workers are responsible for social assistance cases. 'Caseworkers have the skills and authority to approach people in a holistic fashion' (Jewell, 2002, p 27). *Unemployment Insurance:* 'The day-to-day work of the Employment Service is to be characterised by job satisfaction and professionalism' (AMS, 2003, p 8). Career counsellors who have completed three years' university study are responsible for providing job information and training for the unemployed. Various professionals provide assessments and intensive services for long-term unemployed workers or people with special needs.

(continued)

Table 8.2: Continued

Area	China	Hong Kong	UK	Sweden
Recipients' experience when receiving benefit	Government publishes the names of recipients in the form of public notice. Some felt loss of face, isolation and felt they had no-one to talk to (Cook and Jolly, 2000). Recipient felt ashamed to apply for educational assistance.	'Worker was unwilling to help me. It was like begging' (Hong Kong Polytechnic University, 1995, p 39). Staff from Social Welfare Department and Labour Department are 'unable to provide total care to jobseekers, especially on psychological needs' (Hong Kong Council of Social Service, 2001b).	Mixed feelings among respondents. Some form good relationship with PAs (Lakey et al, 2001). Some felt they were being treated with a lack of respect and did not have the right sort of information (Millar, 2000).	Mixed impact reported by researchers. According to the long-term unemployed respondents, active labour market programmes provided 'valuable, enjoyable and character forming experiences' (Clasen et al, 1997, p 4). One welfare administrator claimed young people could 'overcome their passivity, seem happier and develop important social contacts' (Forsberg et al, 2002, p 12). 'The work was bureaucratic, decisions discretionary and recipients often experienced distress and shame' (Giertz, 2004, p 29).

assess recipients' readiness for work. Thus, the training of PAs seems to be unable to prepare them for their role in providing personalised services, which is one of the key arguments justifying recipients' regular meetings with welfare staff.

Swedish employment and social assistance emphasises the use of professional workers. The career counsellors of the Public Employment Service (PES) are expected to complete three years of relevant training. The municipalities also use social workers to deal with social assistance applications. In addition, the Labour Market Institute (LMI) uses various experts such as psychologists, physical therapists, labour therapists, and specialists in intellectual and visual handicap to meet the needs of unemployed workers whose problems cannot be handled by the staff of PES (see Chapter Seven). But it should be stressed that social workers who are unable to balance their social control and welfare functions will make the system bureaucratic and recipients feel shame and stress (Giertz, 2004). Nevertheless, Sweden is the only one of the four welfare systems that provides various types of individualised and group training for unemployed persons conducted by trained professionals.

To summarise, an official picture has been presented of a well-organised, client-centred and professionalised employment service, which promises personalised plans and tailor-made training programmes for unemployed workers, particularly in the UK and Hong Kong. However, research studies consistently show that welfare recipients experience mixed feelings about the service quality of PAs. Some PAs even admitted their inadequacy and incompetence in their work. Instead of comprehensive assessments to explore a recipient's individual needs, the 'work-first' approach and 'work-focused interview' are widely practised in Hong Kong and the UK. Therefore, the personal needs of unemployed workers have been suppressed in the receipt of state benefits because 'work' dominates the relationship between unemployed workers and their advisers. In short, the work-focused approach already narrows the scope of assessment and the time and types of interventions that a personal adviser can offer to clients. By making work the top (and maybe the only) priority for unemployed persons, existing workfare policy may assume that everyone can work and should work immediately. Under this welfare approach, unemployed persons' underlying barriers to work might be wrongly interpreted by poorly trained PAs as a 'motivation problem' or even a moral problem of laziness.

Fulfilling caring duties

In this section, a person's caring duties mainly concern parents' ability to meet their children's health, education and social needs. By comparing parents' caring capacities in the four societies, it becomes apparent that collective welfare provisions can better meet the needs of poor children (Table 8.3). As discussed in Chapter Five, China has experienced rapid welfare changes over the past two decades. Since the introduction of the market economy and the contraction of state-owned enterprises (SOEs), poor families can no longer rely on state welfare but have to depend on their earnings in the labour market. Family members of laid-off workers receive limited welfare protection, especially after leaving re-employment service centres (RSCs) and formally ending their employment relationships with state enterprises. Despite being in charge of the most prosperous province in China, the Shanghai municipal government provides only temporary and limited medical assistance for poor families. With low levels of both unemployment insurance benefits and the minimum living standard guarantee (MLSG), poor parents struggle to finance children's social and leisure activities. More seriously, research studies commonly point out that many families cannot access medical treatment due to financial difficulties. For example, a recent study with 1,876 respondents from cities and another 2,102 from rural areas reported that 70% of respondents did not have any medical insurance and 25.1% of respondents claimed that they and their family members, for financial reasons, could not visit doctors (*Ming Pao*, 2005). Poor parents also cannot finance their children's studies. This is revealed from a low enrolment rate for higher schools (42.8%) in China, whose people put much emphasis on educational achievement (Ministry of Education, 2004). In short, the Chinese government has re-established a new welfare relationship between the state and the family. Parents in a mixed economy can no longer rely on collective welfare. Instead, the duty to care for children has now been transferred from the state back to the family. As a result, poor unemployed parents can get only limited financial assistance from the MLSG, which hardly meets their children's educational and social needs (see Chapter Five for details).

By contrast, poor children in the other three welfare regimes can access better education and health services because of collective provision. As a result, poor parents are exempt from paying for education and medical costs. Also, the social assistance schemes of these three countries provide extra support for families with children. Parents can apply for help in meeting children's education-related expenses such

Table 8.3: Unemployed parents' caring capacity in four welfare systems

Area	China	Hong Kong	UK	Sweden
Health	Temporary and irregular medical assistance for families receiving MLA. Parents without savings are forced to 'delay obtaining treatment for their sick children' (*Shanghai Star*, 2004).	Government provides free medical care for CSSA families. Children cannot get financial support for some types of dental treatment and need to undergo a complicated process to get assistance on spectacles (see Chan, 1998, on service quality of welfare staff).	NHS gives free prescription to children.	Free medical and dental care for people under 20.
Education	Complicated application procedures cannot effectively pay for the tuition fees of poor children. Although the government provides nine years' free education, poor parents find it difficult to pay for children's education-related expenses. 77% of respondents could not pay for school expenses; 7% would stop children attending schools (Tang, 2003).	Hong Kong provides nine years' free education for all residents. Children from CSSA families can get financial support for tuition fees and relevant education expenses of primary and secondary school education.	The UK government provides free primary and secondary education for children and young people. Free school meals and other local authority education welfare services cover some education expenses for low income families on a means-tested basis. 'Failed to enable low-income families to meet the extra, unavoidable costs associated with education' (*Guardian*, 2004b).	Free education is provided in Sweden from nine years' compulsory education to university. Local authorities also provide school children with 'all the materials necessary for school work, particular emphasis is put on textbooks, etc. covering essential parts of a specific subject or a group of subjects' (Sweden Information Smorgasbord, 2004a).
Social life	Basic assistance cannot meet basic and other daily necessities. Poor children are unable to get resources to lead a normal social and school life.	Failed to provide extra resources to participate in social activities (MacPherson, 1994). It was reported 64% of CSSA families could not afford extra-curricular activities (*Ming Pao*, 2004a).	Out-of-work benefits are too low to provide social activities for children, but little is yet known about the impact of new tax credits on low-paid families. However, a range of new initiatives outside the tax benefit system, such as Sure Start and the Children's Fund, have given children from low-income families access to recreational opportunities.	Social activities are elements of social assistance. 'Play and leisure' are included in the 'livelihood support'. Opportunities for social and cultural activities of children are enhanced by generous child allowances. The amount of allowance for the first child is as high as 6% of the median disposable income. Supplements were also introduced for the third and subsequent children.

as books, stationery and travel. In the UK and Sweden, parents' capacity to finance children's social activities has been enhanced by the provision of child benefits. In particular, Sweden provides supplements for large families to reduce their burden of care. Clearly, these two governments are playing a greater role in helping parents to fulfil their caring duties. Hong Kong, however, has no child benefit schemes. The levels of Comprehensive Social Security Assistance (CSSA) Scheme, as shown in Chapter Four, are inadequate to provide recipients with a healthy diet, not to mention extra resources to pay for children's social activities. More importantly, poor parents have to squeeze CSSA benefits to pay for children's spectacles and some dental treatment, which were not included as basic needs in the 1998 social security evaluation (Social Welfare Department, 1998). It was only after strong pressure from members of the Legislative Council and welfare organisations that the Hong Kong government made spectacles a discretionary item for the CSSA in 2005. Thus, children of unemployed parents in Hong Kong can access education and health services, but have difficulties in participating in after-school activities and leading a life that is customary in Hong Kong society.

Comparing parents' caring duties of the four welfare systems clearly reveals that state provisions in key welfare areas such as health and education directly contribute to the well-being of children. This is because collective provision creates a more equal basis for children from various income groups to develop their potential and secure better health. In contrast, with limited state provision or with very low levels of social assistance, poor parents find it hard to fulfil their caring duties. As a consequence, children will be excluded from basic education, health care and a normal social and school life.

Social integration

The four welfare systems vary widely in their impact on the social integration of welfare recipients. Chinese policy is ambivalent on this issue (Table 8.4). It requires local authorities to release the names of MLSG recipients on the one hand, while asking local government officials to take action to meet the needs of the poor on the other. For example, following the instructions of the central government, the Shanghai municipal government mobilised senior officials and social organisations to visit unemployed families, giving them financial and material assistance. However, it put the names of MLSG recipients on the public notice board, asking for comments. Recipients of MLSG are also excluded by limited resources from a normal social life. As illustrated earlier, the MLA has been deliberately made the most meagre of China's three income-protection systems. The MLSG includes only basic items for meeting survival needs and disregards recipients' social needs, which explains why 39% of respondents in a study did not visit friends or relatives even during the Chinese New Year, the most important annual festival (J. Tang, 2003). This implies that poor people in China are being progressively isolated from their social networks, friends and relatives.

The Hong Kong government's policy on public assistance is close to the ideology of the free market. The government expresses overt suspicion towards CSSA recipients even though only 57 fraud cases were reported in the CSSA review (Social Welfare Department, 1999). The Hong Kong government has adopted several measures to tackle welfare abuse such as increasing home visits of CSSA applicants, setting up a hotline for the public to report cases of suspected fraud, and recruiting more staff to investigate fraud. The Hong Kong Social Welfare Department has occasionally publicised unusual fraud cases in the mass media. In addition, the levels of CSSA have been cut to the income level of the bottom population quartile by expenditure. Because of the low benefit rate, poor unemployed persons have been excluded from a normal social and cultural life. Because of the negative images associated with CSSA recipients, unemployed persons are detached from their social networks. The stigmatisation of CSSA recipients has reached such a degree that some unemployed persons choose to commit suicide rather than live on public benefits (see Chapter Four for details). The Hong Kong government's measures have created two distinct lifestyles for CSSA recipients and labour market participants. As a CSSA respondent put it, 'This is not my world; it is the world of those who have money' (Catholic.org.hk, 2004). In short, CSSA recipients are not expected to have a normal social life, a privilege reserved for income earners.

With low levels of JSA, unemployed recipients in the UK also experience exclusion from customary social and cultural activities. Like their counterparts in Hong Kong, they have fewer contacts with friends and relatives. It was reported that 9% of poor respondents could not afford to have a meal with friends and relatives, and 6% were unable to buy presents on special occasions (NCSR and DWP, 2004). Clearly, the low level of benefits is a great barrier to recipients' social integration. Also, the attachment of negative images to the unemployed further pushes them out of normal social circles.

The evidence earlier shows that social assistance benefits in China, Hong Kong and the UK have been set at a level that is too low to take the social needs of recipients into account. As a result, recipients of the

Table 8.4: Unemployed persons' social integration in four welfare systems

Area	China	Hong Kong	UK	Sweden
Participation in social and cultural life	The rate of MLSG is at subsistence level without taking recipients' social needs into account. 39% of respondents did not visit friends and relatives even in the Chinese New Year (Tang, 2003). Sometimes, local government officials mobilise community resources and organise a 'warmth for the poor programme'.	Changed from 'basic needs approach' to 'comparison to the lowest 25% expenditure groups'. No consideration for social and cultural life. 'In order to pay for food, households cut back on clothing, transport, household goods and social activity of all kinds' (MacPherson, 1994, p 3. 70% of CSSA respondents said they did not have a 'reunion meal' celebrating Chinese New year (Ming Pao, 2003e).	Benefit levels are too low to provide recipients with opportunities to participate in social and cultural activities. 20% of lone parents could not afford to invite 'friends/relatives for a meal once a month'. 14% of lone parents were unable to have 'celebrations with presents at special occasions' (NCSR and DWP, 2004).	Aims at providing a reasonable standard of living for benefit recipients. The level of assistance includes play and leisure, a daily newspaper/ telephone/TV licence and membership of a labour union. However, Julkunen (2002, pp 242-3) found that a third of young unemployed respondents could not participate in a customary social activity, such as 'going to the movies', visiting friends/relatives, and 'going to restaurants'. Long-term unemployed workers also reported being excluded from a normal social life (Clasen et al, 1997).
Public image of unemployed benefit recipients	Information about MLSG applicants is published on public notice boards, including their names, age, family members, addresses and the amount of support.	Government occasionally releases details of some exceptional benefit fraud cases. Set up hotline reporting suspected cases of welfare fraud. Set up a special team to investigate suspected CSSA cases. These measures 'portrayed CSSA recipients to be lazy, creating social division' (Ming Pao, 2003b).	Set up hotline for members of the public to report suspected cases of benefit fraud.	Recipients of social assistance are 'portrayed as cheaters and persons lacking the will to be self-supporting' (Arsianogullari, 2000, p 1).
Recipients' social experience	'Families refused to apply for MLSG for fear of their children suffering discrimination' (People's Daily, 2002b). They seldom visit their friends and relatives even for important Chinese festivals.	Respondents felt shame and seldom visited friends and relatives because of being unable to buy gifts. 'I do not have money so I do not visit anymore' (Catholic.org.hk, 2004). 'I fear they will look down on me and think I am after their money' (Catholic.org.hk 2004).	Recipients felt shame living on state benefits. Only after having a job do welfare recipients feel they are 'fitting in more with peers and losing the stigma of claiming benefits' (Farrell and O'Connor, 2004, p 6). One respondent from Perkins' (2001, p 90) study said: 'If you say you want to go to the pub you can't buy a round. You just feel cheap and you just don't want to go with them.'	Some respondents were reported feeling lonely, isolated and stigmatised, and lost self-respect (Clasen et al, 1997).

MLSG in China, CSSA in Hong Kong, and JSA in the UK have difficulties in buying gifts, have fewer social contacts, and feel isolated from the rest of society. The exclusion of recipients from social activities and cultural life makes public assistance socially undesirable, which is likely to have deterred a large number of needy people from seeking public assistance.

In contrast, the Swedish government expects social assistance claimants to enjoy 'a reasonable standard of living' (National Board of Health and Welfare, 2000) and social services should promote 'active participation in social life' (Social Security Act as quoted by Giertz, 2004, p 25). In practice, a reasonable standard of living means 'play and leisure', a daily newspaper, a telephone, a television licence, and being a member of a trade union. However, a research study found that a significant number of unemployed young people were unable to participate in customary social activities such as going to a restaurant or buying gifts (see Chapter Seven). This suggests that the range of social activities that are open to people on social assistance benefits is limited even in Sweden, an exemplar of collective welfare provision. Nevertheless, the recognition of the right of unemployed persons to a normal living standard, and of welfare recipients as social beings, sets the Swedish welfare state apart in its commitment to principles of human dignity.

Human learning and development

Helping displaced workers to upgrade their skills, especially those who suffer from various disadvantages in the labour market, is the main concern of many welfare states. As illustrated in Chapters Four to Seven, all four welfare systems are playing an active role in providing a wide range of training courses and support services for unemployed workers. Their strategies, however, have some differences (Table 8.5).

Basic and further education

In Hong Kong and China, free vocational training courses have been offered to unemployed workers. Middle-aged and older unemployed workers in Hong Kong mainly attend short-term training courses lasting from two weeks to three months. In effect, unemployed persons can learn only some basic computing skills, job-search skills, or skills for low-paid jobs (such as training as a local domestic helper). In Shanghai, unemployed workers can attend training courses put on by the public sector or use government financial support for attending their preferred courses. After completing career training, they are expected to seek unskilled and semi-skilled jobs in, for instance, Chinese or Western catering and gardening. However, no training courses in advanced skills or general education such as primary and secondary schooling are offered to unemployed workers. Thus, adult and middle-aged unemployed workers cannot obtain financial assistance for improving their basic education. They are expected to continue taking up low-skilled jobs. Inadequate educational qualifications make it hard for them to change their career path and social class.

In contrast, several schemes have been provided for the UK's unemployed workers to improve their general education. They can even study at higher education institutions. The Adult Learning Grants provide financial support for adult learners aged under 30 to study up to higher education Level 3. Those who are receiving JSA can study part-time for undergraduate courses offered by the Open University. Lone parents can also get financial and childcare support for studying full-time undergraduate courses. In Sweden, the Adult Education Initiative provides opportunities to unemployed persons to complete secondary and supplementary education. Participants of the scheme can receive financial assistance that is equal to unemployment benefits (see Chapter Seven). Under the Youth Guarantee, young unemployed persons can choose full-time education. Clearly, young and adult unemployed workers in the UK and Sweden have more opportunities than their counterparts in Hong Kong and China to improve their general academic knowledge, study for higher qualifications or attend highly skilled technical training. In this way, unemployed workers can be equipped with the required qualifications and skills to change their career path and secure professional jobs with better salaries.

Job placement and subsidised jobs

The four welfare systems have launched job-placement initiatives for unemployed workers. In China, the Shanghai government provides 6–12 month placements for participants to work in companies or industries that are expected to have good prospects. Such a policy helps train workers to meet the future needs of a developing industrial and commercial sector. Similarly, the Hong Kong government offers training opportunities for university graduates to work in big companies. CSSA recipients are also offered job placements in voluntary organisations or private companies to learn job-related skills. In the UK, subsidised jobs are one of the options under the New Deal that are offered to those who are unable to get jobs in the open market. In

Sweden, unemployed workers can participate in workplace training for six months. Thus, subsidised jobs and work placements have become an important employment strategy, especially for young people, for obtaining work experiences and learning new skills.

It should be stressed that job placements in China and Hong Kong are temporary measures, which aim to tackle the serious unemployment problems of some sections of the population. For example, university graduate placement schemes in both Hong Kong and China are a response to the increasing difficulties this group of people face in getting jobs in the open market. In Hong Kong, the temporary nature of employment measures allows the government to stop them once the economy recovers. On the other hand, job placements in the UK and Sweden are an integral part of their welfare programmes. This means that both governments may consider unemployment as unavoidable in a free market economy. As a result, job placements have become a long-term strategy to enhance the skills of labour.

Support for self-employment

With the expansion of the free market economy, the Chinese government has provided training courses and various incentives such as tax and fee exemptions to encourage laid-off workers to start businesses. In Hong Kong, the government has launched a so-called Youth Self-employment Support Scheme, which provides training and mentoring to assist unemployed people to run their own businesses. However, no financial support has been given. In the UK, self-employment is one option of the New Deal for Young People. The UK government provides personal advisers and financial support for younger and older unemployed workers to start their businesses. In Sweden, business start-up grants have been used to pay for the livelihood of unemployed people who plan to set themselves up in business.

The discussion earlier shows that middle-aged unemployed workers in China and Hong Kong are mainly expected to seek low-skilled jobs because they can attend only short-term training courses. Also, temporary jobs have been offered to them in the form of specific projects (in China) or special duties for government departments (in Hong Kong). With limited training opportunities, middle-aged workers with low qualifications are vulnerable to economic change. They are marginalised workers in a highly skilled and knowledge-based economy. On the other hand, unemployed young people and university graduates have been offered full-time training (such as YPTP and YWETS in Hong Kong) and job placements (such as the Youth

Placement Scheme in Shanghai) ranging from 6 to 12 months. In Hong Kong, the amount of financial support for young people (HK$2,000, £136.89) is even better than that for middle-aged unemployed workers (HK$1,805, £123.55). Clearly, the Hong Kong government has different expectations of these two groups of unemployed people. The young people are encouraged to upgrade their knowledge in order to take up skilled jobs in a knowledge-based economy, while middle-aged unemployed workers are expected to learn some basic skills and quickly leave the welfare system. As a result, middle-aged unemployed persons have been poorly equipped to work in a changing economic environment. Nor have they the required skills to work at technical jobs. In short, limited career development opportunities have been offered to middle-aged and older workers. Even some highly motivated low-skilled workers have to struggle to pay the tuition fees of evening secondary school classes due to the Hong Kong government's withdrawal of subsidies for adult evening education. Clearly, with little support from the Hong Kong government, it is hard for adult unemployed workers to improve their general academic qualifications.

By contrast, unemployed workers in the UK and Sweden have been financially supported to study from basic and general education up to university-level courses. (In the UK, lone parents receiving Income Support can study full-time undergraduate courses, while recipients of JSA can study part-time courses with the Open University). In this way, they have more opportunities to change their career paths and to work in more stable and well-paid jobs. Different training policies have different impacts on the developmental needs of unemployed persons. Older unemployed workers in China and Hong Kong leave the CSSA by taking up low-skilled and low-paid jobs, while their counterparts in the UK and Sweden may leave benefits by finding stable and technical jobs. Chinese people stress education, considering it as a means to improve life quality. With little educational support, hundreds of thousands of adult and middle-aged workers in China and Hong Kong do not enjoy the educational opportunities that are available to their counterparts in Sweden and the UK.

Self-determination and participation

The welfare-to-work approach has shaped the degree of autonomy of unemployed persons in all four societies. The four welfare systems have different policies on community work (Table 8.6). In Hong Kong, unemployed workers are required to do the maximum of 30 hours

Table 8.5: Unemployed persons' learning and development opportunities in four welfare systems

Area	China	Hong Kong	UK	Sweden
Support for studying at primary and secondary education level	Without any support.	Without any support.	Financial support for NDYP (18–24) and lone parents to pursue full-time courses, including GCSE, 'A' level and NVQs at Levels 2 and 3.	The YG can help young people back to full-time education. 'Adult Education Initiative' which gives subsidies to municipalities for providing upper secondary and supplementary education. 'Individualisation and flexibility in the education system will make it possible for people to study at various levels and in various subject areas in parallel' (Ministry of Health and Social Affairs, 2003a, p 27).
Support for studying higher education	Without any support.	Without any support.	Financial and childcare assistance for lone parents to study up to undergraduate level. JSA recipients can study part-time courses offered by the Open University.	Employment training can be in the form of higher education.
Support for short-term (less than six months) training course/ job placement	Shanghai Government pays for all or a half of the training fees for those attending designated vocational training courses. Those obtaining a Certificate of Training Subsidy can choose any training programmes.	Various types of short-term courses have been offered to unemployed people. Special Job Attachment Programme for CSSA recipients and non-CSSA unemployed persons. Youth Pre-employment Training Programme for young people aged 15–19.	Participants of NDYP can choose a subsidised job with training.	Participants of 'Work Experience' training can attend training courses for up to six months.
Support for long-term (more than six months) training course/ job placement	Youth Placement Scheme for university graduates aged 16–30. The training period lasts 3–12 months.	Youth Work Experience and Training Scheme for young people aged 15–24. Graduate Employment Training Scheme for university graduates.	Participants of NDYP 18–24 can study for a recognised qualification for 12 months. Participants of New Deal for 25 Plus who have been unemployed for two years can study a full-time employment-related course for up to one year.	The YG provides unemployed young people with 12 months' full-time training and education.

(continued)

Table 8.5: Continued

Area	China	Hong Kong	UK	Sweden
Special assistance for special groups	Community Beneficial Jobs for those with special difficulties in obtaining jobs. '40–50 Project' helping unemployed women aged over 40 and men aged over 50 to get employment in 'jobs beneficial to the community' such as cleaning, planting, public security and the maintenance of public facilities. Special assistance for unemployed aged 40–50. Special training programmes for unemployed young people, especially for secondary school leavers and fresh university graduates. Occasionally, the Shanghai Municipal Government creates short-term jobs for the unemployed.	Ending Exclusion Project for single parents. Re-employment training programme for the middle-aged. Special Incentive Allowance Scheme for Local Domestic Helpers.	Disabled people get Disabled Students' Allowance. Lone parents with childcare problems can apply for Childcare Grant Package or Parents Learning Allowance. New Deal for 50 Plus gives a Training Grant of up to £1,500 and extra financial support for the first 52 weeks in employment.	Municipal programmes for young people under 20. Grants for employers to hire people with occupational disabilities. Public sheltered employment for occupationally disadvantaged people.
Incentives for self-employment	Various measures to help those setting up businesses such as training programmes, exemption from paying tax, commercial administrative fees and assistance on loans.	YSSS provides training courses, guidance, and facilities for young people.	Participants of NDYP can set up business for six months. New Deal for Self-employment provides guidance and living allowance as well as a top-up grant.	Business start-up grants for those running businesses.

community work with no extra financial assistance. As pointed out by the Hong Kong government, community work can sustain recipients' work habits, develop their social skills and make contributions to society (Social Welfare Department, 1999). Added to this, unemployed recipients have to actively search for jobs and meet their personal advisers every fortnight. In China, although the central government mentions a community work requirement in its guidelines, it has put in place no clear policies. Thus, its implementation mainly depends on local authorities. In Shanghai, those who have 'special employment difficulties' can obtain employment assistance services (Shanghai Employment and Social Security Bureau, 2000). They have to sign a 'mutual employment agreement' under which they are guaranteed a job offer in three months in a community organisation or a public enterprise. The work is related to hygiene, gardening, security and maintenance, and the salaries are 50% of the minimum wage. Unemployed workers can also receive a subsidy to help pay social insurance contributions. This initiative seems to combine subsidised jobs and community service. In the UK, the New Deal for Young People offers the two options of work experience in the non-profit sector and in the environmental task force. Also, it is only after the Gateway period that those who fail to find a job have to choose an option. In principle, recipients are given some degree of choice and community work is just one option. However, Perkins (2001) reported that some respondents of his study had been coerced into one particular option, or not all options were available in their region. This means that choice is limited in practice. In Sweden, unemployed workers are required to 'contribute to the preparation of an individual action plan together with the Public Employment Service' as a condition of receiving unemployment insurance benefit (Ahlberg, 2003, p 8). The Individual Action Plan sets out measures that can help an unemployed worker to get a job. Community work is not a compulsory requirement, but can be part of the Individual Action Plan or a programme activity of the YG.

Clearly, community work has different functions in the four societies. In Hong Kong, community work is a duty of CSSA recipients. In China, community work is a job with extra financial support. In the UK, community work has been considered as a training opportunity for unemployed young people. Similarly, the Swedish welfare regime treats community work as an option for developing employment-related skills. Thus, even if we treat community work as a means of exerting social control over unemployed workers, the extent of autonomy given and its impact on unemployed persons' career skills differ according to its purpose and organisation. The experience of the UK shows that nearly a third of participants in the environmental task force option were subject to welfare sanctions, compared with fewer than 10% of 'full-time education and training' participants. This implies that there could be resentment towards what might be perceived as 'involuntary community work'.

Another issue is the government's control over recipients' job-search activities and daily lives. In Hong Kong, welfare recipients are required to apply for at least two jobs per fortnight, and to report job-search progress regularly to their welfare advisers. Furthermore, they need to attend job interviews or employment training arranged by the Social Welfare Department (see Chapter Four). If recipients fail to comply with community-work and job-search requirements, their benefits can be terminated. In Shanghai, unemployment benefit recipients are required to report their job-search efforts and to attend job interviews and vocational training courses recommended by social security service centres. Those who fail to fulfil the requirements of job search and community work risk losing their benefits (Shanghai Municipal Government, 2004g; Shanghai Ministry of Civil Affairs et al, 2003; State Council, 1999). It should be stressed that the welfare administrators of Shanghai, unlike Hong Kong's welfare administrators who systematically monitor the implementation of active labour market policies, might not systematically and consistently carry out the requirements of welfare regulations. In the UK, participants of the New Deal for Young People have to discuss regularly their job seeking experiences with PAs. Those who are unable to get jobs in the open market need to choose one of the four options. Participants of New Deal for 25 Plus, for their part, have to undertake 30 hours per week of programmes in the Intensive Activity Period. In Sweden, recipients of unemployment benefits have to attend job interviews and training programmes. If they refuse jobs or training programmes, their benefits can be reduced by 25% for the first offence and 50% for the second.

A key issue regarding a government's control over unemployed workers' autonomy is the causes and impact of control. A good cause may justify government restrictions on welfare recipients' behaviour; while the positive and long-term well-being of recipients may secure public support for the government's welfare-to-work policy. However, it is difficult to defend the tight control over recipients' daily lives in the four welfare systems in our study. The Hong Kong government argues that community work helps to enhance recipients' social skills and maintain good working habits. However, no comprehensive assessment has been conducted to provide sufficient evidence to show that unemployed workers benefit from community work and need regular meetings. Similarly, the UK requires jobseekers to attend Gateway and intensive training after six months' unemployment for young people and one and a half years for those aged over 25, without any detailed assessments of the individual needs of unemployed persons. These requirements have been automatically imposed on welfare recipients regardless of their training background and experiences. PAs in Hong Kong and the UK, as well as welfare workers on street committees and resident associations in China, lack the professional skills and time (as is evident from a wide range of studies from Chapter Four to Chapter Six; see also Table 8.6) to formulate individualised plans and implement personalised services. As a result, welfare workers' interventions are unable to help recipients overcome their social and psychological problems, nor give them the qualifications and skills to enter the labour market (to a great extent in Hong Kong and to some extent in the UK). Thus, the three welfare systems fail to fulfil their promise to provide 'individualised plans' to overcome personal employment barriers, a key argument justifying their control over the unemployed. The Swedish welfare system has a better arrangement in which professional career counsellors and social workers provide various types of active market programmes for the unemployed. To some extent, this arrangement gives people 'self-determination in realising their own capacities' (Kvist, 2001, p 5).

With regard to participation in policy making, Hong Kong and (especially) China provide no direct opportunities for unemployed benefit recipients to express their concerns. The political elite of the CCP mainly dominates the decision making of the central government. Although the Shanghai government consults relevant experts, especially academics, on some policies, the final decisions rest in the hands of senior officials of both local and central governments. Hong Kong is a bureaucratic–capitalist regime; its welfare polices are mainly decided by the Chief Executive and senior government officials with the support of representatives of the business community and pro-China organisations in both Legislative and Executive Councils (Chan, 2005). The general public elects only half of the members of the Legislative Council; the rest are representatives of industrial and commercial associations as well as professional bodies. As a result, the influence of the poor on government welfare policies is constrained by a powerful administration and a weak and divided Legislative Council.

In the UK, the Labour Party has a poor relationship with the trade union movement, its traditional power base. Leaders of trade unions believe that NLG policies such as privatisation and contracting out of public services, especially in the NHS through the implementation of foundation hospitals and the private finance initiative, threaten the wages and conditions of workers. In response to the perceived hostility of the NLG towards the welfare of members, some trade unions have reduced financial contributions to the Labour Party. As a result, the trade union contribution to Labour Party funds has fallen from 90% of total contributions in the late 1980s to only one third (*Socialism Today*, 2002). Some leaders have even discussed the establishment of an alternative party which 'can genuinely represent the interests of the majority of Britain's disenfranchised population' (*Socialism Today*, 2002). Against this background, the influence of trade unions on British welfare policies seems to have been weakened. Although the UK's unemployment benefit recipients can indirectly influence government policies through their MPs in parliament, their impact will be limited by the 'neo-liberal' attitudes of Prime Minister Tony Blair. He showed people that 'he would never be influenced by the Left and that he was the Party' (Moss, 2001). Thus, the participation of unemployed persons in unemployment policy is very limited because of the concentration of power mainly in the hands of the Prime Minister and the Chancellor of the Exchequer. As former Prime Minister John Major (25 February 2005) observes:

> New Labour's style of governing has emasculated decision-making by Cabinet and cabinet committees; they still exist, of course, but only to take minor decisions and rubber-stamp important ones. Mr Blair and Mr Brown decide policy outside a collective decision-making process.

Thus, it is mainly the ideologies of Tony Blair and Gordon Brown that shape the UK's policies on the unemployed.

As illustrated in Chapter Seven, decentralisation is a key feature of the Swedish polity, under which municipalities have been granted power to decide issues affecting the well-being of local people. Also, trade and labour organisations have been formally co-opted into the local Employment Service Committees to voice their views. Moreover, the Swedish Social Democratic Party has close links with the Swedish Trade Union Confederation, which effectively blocked government proposals to reduce both benefit levels and the duration of entitlement. To some extent, unemployed persons can shape the Swedish government's welfare measures through the formal and informal relationship between labour unions and government officials at both central and local levels.

Table 8.6: Unemployed persons' degree of self-determination in four welfare systems

Area	China	Hong Kong	UK	Sweden
Direct participation – The unemployed directly participate in the decision-making process.	No.	No.	No.	No.
Indirect participation – Representatives of the unemployed participate in decision making or consultative bodies.	Representatives of the NPC are elected by various social and economic organisations. The actual political power, however, rests in the SCPB dominated by senior members of the CCP.	Representatives of labour unions have been co-opted to the Employee Retraining Board. Representatives of some voluntary organisations have been appointed as members of the Anti-Poverty Committee. The above committees are mainly consultative in nature and representatives represent different interest groups. Despite these constraints, unemployed workers' interests may be indirectly voiced by particular individuals but cannot be effectively safeguarded. Half of the LC members are directly elected by the public. The rest are representatives of business and professional organisations. It is difficult to pass welfare reform motions because the Basic Law requires that any laws should be passed by these two groups of members.	Members of both central and local government are directly elected by the public. Members of the House of Commons who sit on the Work and Pensions Select Committee might express views on unemployment and welfare issues. Sometimes, the Committee invites relevant academics and voluntary organisations to give evidence on welfare issues. This is also an indirect means of participation.	Members of both central and local government are directly elected by the public. Representatives of trade unions are involved in Local Employment Services Committees to give their views on labour training. The Swedish Government regularly consults with social partners, especially its close relationship with the Swedish trade unions.

(continued)

Table 8.6: Continued

Area	China	Hong Kong	UK	Sweden
Mechanism for dealing with unemployed persons' appeals	Claimants can make appeals in the form of administrative review, which is administrated by civil servants.	Members of the Social Security Appeal Board are appointed by the government.	Recipients can appeal to the Appeals Service, which operates a tribunal, a non-departmental public body. All members of the tribunal are appointed by the Lord Chancellor.	Recipients can appeal the decisions of municipalities at the County Administrative Court.
Compulsory meeting with welfare staff	Do not have systematic requirements on regular meetings, only irregular meetings.	Unemployed CSSA recipients have to participate in SFS, sign a Jobseeker's Undertaking, and meet their welfare workers at the social security field unit every fortnight.	All new JSA applicants have to attend a Jobseeker Interview. Participants of NDYP have to meet their PAs every fortnight. Participants of New Deal for 25 Plus also have to meet their PAs regularly.	The Social Services Act of 1997 requires recipients of social assistance to participate in an 'activation programme'. Unemployment insurance benefit recipients are required to register at an office of the Public Employment Service, draw up a job research contract and an action plan.
Compulsory community work	Has this requirement but can be an strictly and regularly implemented.	Community work up to a maximum of three days or 24 hours a week (Social Welfare Department, 2004a).	After the Gateway, NDYP participants can choose to work with an environmental taskforce or in the non-profit sector.	Not compulsory but can be an element of an individual plan.
Compulsory job training/ placement	Welfare staff can ask unemployed recipients to receive vocational training. This policy, however, is not strictly implemented.	CSSA unemployed recipients are asked by their PAs to attend training courses.	One of the options for NDYP. Participants of New Deal for 25 Plus have to attend an Intensive Activity Period for a minimum of 13 weeks to a maximum of 26 weeks.	Recipients can participate in a wide range of employment programmes, which 'should be individualised for the particular jobseeker' (FUIF, 2002, p 5). However, the Social Service Act of 1997 increased the power of local authorities by asking unemployed youths aged under 25 to participate in labour market programmes (Giertz, 2004; Minas, 2005).

(continued)

Table 8.6: Continued

Area	China	Hong Kong	UK	Sweden
Degree of freedom on job search and employment acceptance	Has to sign an 'acceptance of employment services contract'. Benefits terminated if recipients reject job offered or other employment services twice.	Have to accept jobs offered regardless of salaries and working patterns. 'Any job is better than no job'; 'Low pay is better than no pay' (Social Welfare Department, 1998, p 15).	Young people under 25 are allowed six months for jobs search before entering the Gateway Period. Those who are not actively seeking jobs or do not have Jobseeker's Agreement or do not take part in a New Deal Option are subjected to sanctions. Basic benefit will be deducted by 40% for single persons. Families with seriously ill or pregnant members suffer a 20% deduction. Unemployed persons over 25 have to join the Gateway only after being unemployed for one-and-a-half years.	For the first 100 days, jobseekers are free to choose the nature of jobs and have a right to refuse jobs that are not relevant to their training and are outside their workplace locality. After the first 100 days, jobseekers have to seek employment outside their localities and accept any 'suitable work'.
Special restrictions	Recipients cannot get medical benefits if their injuries are caused by violation of public order.			

To summarise, as stated at the beginning of this book, workfare supporters have to address a question: 'What justifies a state's control over the behaviour of unemployed persons?' The welfare measures of the four societies show that a 'work-first' approach is being adopted to enhance the employability of unemployed persons. However, no systematic assessment has been undertaken on the beneficiaries of workfare requirements, and the types of programme that can overcome employment barriers. As a result, access to services has been determined by the duration of unemployment and the age of unemployed workers, rather than by a detailed assessment of personal needs. Also, the welfare staff in China, Hong Kong and the UK lack the skills to assess needs and to plan effective interventions. As a result, regular meetings become just a check on recipients' work motivations. Without sufficient reasons for controlling the behaviour of the unemployed, and without well-planned programmes for upgrading their skills, 'workfare' has become purely a government tool for deterring welfare applications and pushing unemployed claimants back to the labour market with little protection. This is especially true in Hong Kong.

Equal value

Unemployed persons are financially weak and this readily translates into political weakness. The social status and opportunities of unemployed people in different circumstances reveal how far a welfare system pursues the principle of equal value. The Hong Kong government, as illustrated in Chapter Four, is suspicious towards the behaviour of able-bodied CSSA recipients. Negative characterisations of unemployed people are found in the government's policy papers, expressed in its deliberate release of the details of unexceptional fraud cases to the mass media. Unemployed workers in Hong Kong have been construed as 'dependent, irresponsible, lacking motivation, and abusive'. The implementation of harsh welfare measures in terms of compulsory community work and regular meetings with welfare staff further degrades welfare recipients almost to the status of offenders. Thus, unemployed persons in Hong Kong have been presented as inferior citizens enjoying little social respect. New unemployed immigrants suffer further discrimination in Hong Kong by the extension of the residency requirement for CSSA entitlement from one year to seven. This means that poor unemployed immigrants are excluded from public assistance. As for age discrimination, middle-aged unemployed persons, most of whom have to bear a heavy caring burden, suffer disadvantage in terms of training time and allowances compared with the young unemployed. As revealed in Chapter Four, most training courses offered to middle-aged people are mainly short term and do not aim at equipping them with technical skills to improve their career path.

In the UK, middle-aged and older unemployed workers, unlike their young and lone-parent counterparts, get less financial support for full-time and higher education. As shown in Chapter Six, they can study only part-time courses before losing their entitlement to benefits. From the limited full-time training opportunities and little financial support for middle-aged and older unemployed workers, it is clear that welfare-to-work policies in some societies are age-biased. Governments emphasise improving educational qualifications for young people rather than for middle-aged people who missed out on education in the past. Because of age discrimination, people of different ages access different training opportunities that directly shape their work opportunities and salaries.

The welfare of unemployed workers in China varies by region and type of locality (Table 8.7). Rural unemployed people are not entitled to the MLSG, which provides minimal income protection only for poor city residents. The amount of MLSG also varies from city to city, since it is shaped by the financial circumstances of a provincial government as well as its officials' attitudes towards public assistance. Social welfare based on permanent urban residency puts migrant workers in cities in a disadvantaged position. They can obtain only a little compensation for being unemployed and may even be totally excluded from unemployment insurance protection. On the other hand, the central government gives extra support for middle-aged workers (women aged over 40 and men aged over 50) and those who have been classified as having 'special employment difficulties'. Local authorities such as the Shanghai municipal government offer subsidised jobs for these two groups of unemployed workers in public enterprises and community organisations. In addition, they can get government subsidies for paying social insurance premiums. Thus, extra support has been provided for the most disadvantaged groups in pursuit of equal opportunities in employment.

In Sweden, a wide range of active labour market programmes have been provided for unemployed workers. Since full employment is the objective of the Swedish government, all unemployed persons are offered training courses or work placements. In particular, adult unemployed workers can access full-time education that is not only beneficial to their personal development but also increases their career options in the long run. However, as mentioned in Chapter Seven,

Table 8.7: The equal value of unemployed persons in four welfare systems

Area	China	Hong Kong	UK	Sweden
Equal social respect	Government always emphasises the potential of unemployed persons. Personal information of recipients is made public. One of the policy directions in Shanghai is to put social pressures on those with working ability but judged to be lazy.	Government shows little trust of unemployed recipients. Hotline set up for reporting cases of welfare fraud. Welfare staff asked to make home visits to prevent welfare fraud. Government occasionally releases details of extraordinary fraud cases to the mass media.	Based on 'welfare around work', the UK Government promotes employment rather than living on public benefits as the normal life for all citizens. The government targets specific groups such as young unemployed persons and those unemployed for 18 months.	Equality is the key objective of the Swedish government. The Swedish government has 'a commitment to ensuring that everyone can participate in society and to preventing social exclusion' (Ministry of Health and Social Affairs, 2003a, p 25).
Equal development opportunities	Special programmes for secondary school leavers and university graduates. '40-50 Project' provides employment assistance for middle-age unemployed workers.	Although young people and middle-aged unemployed workers can obtain training and job placements, the latter get shorter periods of training (a maximum of six months with limited places) and receive less financial support than the former.	Adult unemployed workers aged over 25 receive less support for studying full-time in general education or higher education. Disabled persons and lone parents can receive financial, equipment and childcare assistance for pursing vocational training and further education.	Good childcare policies so that women are able to 'choose to enter the labour market if they can find a job' (Kvist, 2000, p 11). Recipients of social assistance obtain lower benefits and participate in activation programmes organised by municipalities with limited choice compared with those who are receiving unemployment insurance benefits. Thus, 'the unemployed on social assistance are still in a second tier compared to the unemployed with insurance' (Giertz, 2004, p 210). Extra support has been provided for young people (the YG) and disabled persons (wage-subsidised employment and public sheltered employment).
Equal access to public assistance	The MLSG provides financial assistance only for poor people who are permanent urban residents. Rural unemployed persons and unemployed migrant workers in cities are unable to get government financial assistance. The amount of MLSG is determined by the financial circumstances of local authorities and the welfare attitudes of senior officials.	New immigrants with financial difficulties are excluded from pubic assistance. The minimum residency requirement is seven years. Able-bodied unemployed recipients cannot receive special grants for long-term supplements (eg removal expenses, furniture and clothes) and spectacles.	The amount of assistance is designed by the central government. All recipients receive the same amount of assistance without regional variations.	Levels of financial assistance are decided by each municipality. 'There are substantial variations among municipalities' (Arslanogullari, 2000, p 6). Social assistance was 'discretionary on at least three levels, the municipal political board, the local office and the individual social worker' (Giertz, 2004, p 27).

unemployed workers living on social assistance and those receiving unemployment insurance benefits receive different amounts of benefits and have different training opportunities. The former receive lower benefits and have more limited training options than the latter. This type of inequality is the consequence of the Swedish welfare system's exclusion of those who fail to meet the contribution conditions of unemployment insurance.

The discussion earlier shows that the status of unemployed workers has been shaped by political factors and social attitudes. As a traditional follower of the free market economy, Hong Kong's control over the behaviour of the unemployed is based on the concept of welfare rights and duties as well as the maintenance of self-reliance. Without a political system which is accountable and responsive to public demands, the Chinese government is too slow to tackle the division of welfare between unemployed workers in rural areas and those in cities, as well as the wide regional variations in social security provision. Driven by market efficiency and quick returns, both the Hong Kong and UK governments provide more support for the training of young people than older workers. In contrast, following its traditional emphasis on equality, the Swedish government provides equal education opportunities for both young and old. Thus, the political system and welfare ideologies shape the status and experiences of unemployed workers in a particular society.

Conclusion

The study of welfare practices in China, Hong Kong, the UK and Sweden suggests that several factors are positively associated with the dignity of unemployed workers. First, collective welfare can provide basic health protection for unemployed persons and also support parents in meeting their caring duties towards children's medical treatment and education. The governments of Sweden, the UK and Hong Kong play a key role in health services and education. Poor families in these countries can access medical treatment and basic education even when the main earners of their households are out of jobs. Their common objective is that nobody will be denied medical care as a result of poverty. Health care is a right of all citizens and its provision is accepted as a fundamental duty by the three governments. As health services in these three societies are financed from general revenues, some degree of wealth redistribution has been achieved. On the other hand, over 40% of respondents in a national survey in China have been excluded from medical treatment and many children (migrant workers' children in particular) cannot access education following the implementation of work-oriented financial benefits and medical insurance. At present, poor unemployed people can receive only a low rate of financial assistance in the form of the MLSG and only temporary (or even no) health care treatment. Only collective welfare provision can fundamentally relieve the financial pressures of unemployed workers so that their financial, medical and educational needs can be met and their caring duties fulfilled.

Second, unemployed persons' autonomy and self-determination is related to the degree of political participation in a welfare system. China is a one-party state; all political power is in the hands of the elite of the Chinese Communist Party. Hong Kong is a semi-democratic state, dominated by senior government officials and the business community. In China, recipients of the MLSG are required to have their names publicised. In Hong Kong, unemployed workers are required to participate in voluntary work without any options. It is obvious that government officials in China and Hong Kong have much power over unemployed workers' daily lives and family circumstances. In contrast, unemployed workers in both Sweden and the UK have been granted some degree of self-determination. Swedish unemployed workers can choose community work based on personal plans, while the UK's unemployed workers have a six-month gap (one and a half years for those aged over 25) before joining the Gateway and Intensive Activity Period. Participants of the New Deal for Young People can also choose from several options following the Gateway period. Differences in polity shape the power of the four governments. In Sweden and the UK, unemployment measures need to go through processes of formal and informal consultation as well as parliamentary debates. In this way, labour representatives and welfare activists can mobilise their members to put pressure on the two governments, especially in Sweden where the Swedish Trade Union Confederation and the Social Democratic Party have formal and informal communications over welfare issues. In this way, unemployment policies can be subject to radical changes or amendments. Against this background, unemployed workers and their representatives in the two democratic systems have more opportunities to influence government policies and, to some extent, determine their lives.

Third, the dignity of unemployed workers depends on national objectives and well-planned intervention. As an upholder of the free market, the Hong Kong government says little about the ultimate goals of social development such as tackling poverty. The Hong Kong government is not interested in establishing any poverty lines, nor does it have any long-term plans to tackle poverty and inequality. As a consequence, unemployed families lack sufficient resources to maintain physical health or to participate in normal social and school life. Hundreds of thousands of poor people are living in appalling housing conditions. As the Hong Kong government believes, the improvement of the economy directly benefits all social groups, and the provision of educational opportunities helps poor families to increase their income and quality of life. Such market-oriented social objectives have been promoted by both the British colonial administration before 1997 and the HKSAR following its reunion with China after 1997. Unfortunately, over the past three decades economic freedom has created extraordinary wealth for business communities and provided high salaries for civil servants and professionals, but it has failed to bring prosperity to poor families. The experience of Hong Kong's unemployed workers under the replacement of social planning by the free play of market forces shows that they are not valued equally with their better-off fellow citizens, they have limited self-determination, they do not participate in social activities, they cannot provide their children with a normal school life, they have insufficient resources for buying healthy food, and they receive little psychological support from welfare workers.

In contrast, both the Swedish government and the UK's NLG have clear visions of the type of society they want to achieve. The Swedish government clearly aims at achieving 'equality of health care', 'reducing the gap between families with and without children', 'full employment', 'political participation in civil society' and 'gender equality'. Its welfare policies are the expression of these objectives. According to the Social Services Act, local authorities have 'a responsibility to promote people's financial and social security' (National Board of Health and Welfare, 2004). In 2002, the Swedish government adopted a bill, 'Democracy in the New Century', which aims to 'safeguard representative democracy' and 'stimulate citizen participation in governance' (Ministry of Justice, 2002). Also, the objective of public health is to create social conditions that 'ensure good health, on equal terms, for the entire population' (Government Offices of Sweden, 2004b). As a result, unemployed persons in Sweden receive higher unemployment benefits than their European counterparts, have more opportunities in adult education and enjoy good-quality health care. In the UK, the NLG's objectives are to halve child poverty by 2010 and eradicate it by 2020. As for health care, it upholds the principle of an NHS that is 'free at the point of use based on need, not ability to pay' (DH, 2002). Also, it attempts to improve the quality of health care in the UK by raising the expenditure of health services above the European average by 2007. As a result, poor unemployed families can receive more financial support through the Child Tax Credit. In addition, unemployed persons still do not need to worry about health treatment, and receive health care of an improving quality. However, as mentioned previously, the Hong Kong government has attempted to raise health revenues through charging itemised fees. In China, a large number of Chinese people lack proper health care due to financial constraints. For achieving human dignity, the experiences of Sweden and the UK show that well-planned intervention is superior to reliance on market forces, as in Hong Kong, and on fragmented welfare measures such as those adopted in China.

Fourth, individualised services and professional skills are essential to unemployed persons' psychological well-being, self-determination and the development of human potential. All four welfare systems promise personalised services but in practice only the Swedish welfare system recruits professional social workers and career counsellors to provide psychological counselling and career guidance for unemployed workers. Swedish social workers were reported as having 'the skills and authority to approach people in a holistic fashion' and to promote clients' educational and rehabilitation aspirations (Jewell, 2002, p 27). Special plans have been developed by social workers and other organisations to enhance the self-confidence of young people with poor qualifications (Forsberg et al, 2002, p 12). Similarly, the key objectives of the activation measures for long-term unemployed workers are to improve 'the well-being and self-esteem of the individuals' (Kvist, 2001, p 5). For those who have complicated problems, a wide range of experts from the Labour Market Institute conduct extensive assessments. For some people, it is 'a very long process before the goal of work or training is achieved' (Forsberg et al, 2002, p 19). However, the Hong Kong and UK governments have adopted the 'work-first approach' based on 'work-focused interviews', implemented by PAs who have completed only short training courses. As shown previously, PAs admitted their incompetence in fulfilling their duties. As a result, regular interviews become only a routine check on the work motivation of the unemployed. Even so, only 25% of unemployed respondents in one study were receiving help from their PAs to tackle their problems (Britton, 2001). The 'work-first' approach also fails to address the underlying barriers faced by unemployed workers who need intensive services. The experience of Sweden shows how effective labour market measures need more investment in welfare staff to undertake need assessments and develop individualised plans. It is only by these means that effective support for unemployed persons can overcome barriers in the job market.

To conclude, unemployed persons in China, Hong Kong, the UK and Sweden experience different levels of human dignity that reflect variations in welfare ideology, in the structure of welfare services, in patterns of political organisation and ultimately in the objectives for the whole society. By comparing the seven dimensions of human dignity of the four welfare systems, it is revealed that traditional collective welfare with the social democratic objectives of equity and equality are positively related to the dignity of unemployed workers. This means that human society needs to tackle social problems with policies based on active participation in civil society and well-planned intervention. The belief that the free operation of market forces can improve human society is a dream that Hong Kong has being chasing for more than 150 years since the advent of British colonial rule. It is fast becoming a belief shared by the Chinese government. The cases of Sweden and (to a certain extent) the UK show that human dignity rests in a political system that allows active participation in civil society and in the objectives of political leaders who have a determination to eradicate human poverty and enhance human potential in well-organised and committed ways.

NINE

Human dignity and the classification of welfare states

Two issues have emerged from studying the dignity of the unemployed in China, Hong Kong, the UK and Sweden. The first is the application of human dignity to the classification of welfare systems. The second is the impact of welfare-to-work strategies on human dignity. This first issue addresses the debate about classification models and the importance of using human dignity to assess the achievements of a welfare state. The second examines whether welfare-to-work policies enhance the dignity of unemployed persons, as governments claim they do.

Welfare regimes and human dignity

It is argued in Chapters Two and Three that rationality and sociability are intrinsic human capacities and that human beings strive for mutuality and autonomy. Under this approach, welfare policies are evaluated not for their market efficiency and economic achievement, but for their potential to create the conditions for realising the seven elements of human dignity identified in Chapter Three that enable people to live with autonomy and in harmony with one another. In other words, welfare systems will be evaluated for their achievements in promoting both material and non-material aspects of human dignity.

Both Richard Titmuss (1974) and Gosta Esping-Andersen (1990) have made important contributions to the comparative study of welfare states. Titmuss's thesis focused on the welfare relationships between the individual, the family, the market, and the state. Accordingly, he identified three models of social welfare: Residual Welfare, Industrial Achievement-Performance and Institutional Redistributive. In a Residual Welfare State, social welfare is expected to be provided by the family and the market. It is only the failure of these two institutions that justifies state involvement in welfare provision. In a welfare state which stresses Industrial Achievement-Performance, 'social needs should be met on the basis of merit, work performance and productivity' (Titmuss, 1974, p 31). On the other hand, a country which follows the Institutional Redistributive Model considers social welfare to be 'a major integrated institution in society, providing universalist services outside the market on the principle of need' (Titmuss, 1974, p 31). Titmuss's classification guides us in our investigation of the welfare role of social, economic and political institutions in different societies.

The most influential classification of welfare states was proposed by Esping-Andersen in 1990. He observed that there were three types of welfare regime based on their decommodification of welfare and its stratification along social class lines. Decommodification measures the degree to which a person can live independently of the market as a result of welfare provision. Stratification measures the impact of welfare provision on the differentiation of social classes. Under Esping-Andersen's methodology, Hong Kong and the UK can be classified as Liberal Welfare Regimes. In contrast, Sweden is classified as a Social Democratic Welfare Regime. China, however, is a difficult case. In the past, we would have classified it as a Social Democratic Welfare Regime because of its emphasis on equality, wealth redistribution and collective welfare provision. However, it has experienced rapid social and economic changes over the past two decades; it is now no longer a planned economy but a mixed one, with regard to a rapidly expanding private sector and contracting public welfare. Now, China has some elements of a Social Democratic Regime (because of the state's major role in education, transport, water and electricity supply and its emphasis on gender equality), a Conservative Regime (because of better benefits for civil servants and the location of political power in the hands of the CCP, whose members have special social and political status), and a Liberal Welfare Regime (because of means-testing of MLSG and health and housing provision depending on the market).

Like China, Hong Kong is a mixed case. It should be a Liberal Welfare Regime in view of the low levels of benefits and complicated application procedures. On the other hand, it looks more like a Social Democratic Welfare Regime given the extent of government provision in education, health care and housing. The classification of the UK's welfare system has similar problems. The UK is 'a good example of a system that fits uneasily into any of the three regime types' (Cochrane et al, 2001, p 12). The UK reflects features of a Social Democratic Welfare Regime in its National Health Service and education system. However, it looks like a Liberal Welfare Regime from the low levels of Income Support and its welfare-to-work measures that deter welfare applications and strengthen market values. Thus, the UK reflects 'an odd mixture of the "socialist" and "liberal" types' (Ginsburg, 1992, p 23).

More importantly, there are big differences among countries with the same type of welfare regime. For example, Hong Kong and the UK can be broadly classified as Liberal Welfare Regimes. However, Hong Kong's welfare benefits are far lower than those of the UK. Also, Hong Kong, unlike the UK, does not have labour market and income maintenance programmes such as a national minimum wage, unemployment insurance, child benefit, and the old-age pension scheme. The discussion earlier shows that the use of regime type as a tool for classifying welfare states seems unable to reveal either the true nature of a welfare system or the impact of its welfare services on the social and psychological well-being of welfare recipients.

As illustrated in Chapter One, Esping-Andersen's classification has been challenged by the experiences of women and ethnic minorities, whose disadvantages have not been adequately addressed. After comparing the role of women in different welfare regimes, Sainsbury (1999) found that there are big variations in childcare among countries of the Conservative Regime type. The regime types even broke down when women's earnings were taken into consideration. She concludes:

> Regimes are ideal types – a conceptualisation that assumes the co-occurrence of all its defining properties. In the real world this co-occurrence hardly ever exists; politics and political imagination combine these attributes in a variety of ways. (Sainsbury, 1999, p 260)

Similar problems are encountered with Titmuss's model. This is because China, Hong Kong and the UK have welfare programmes that can be classified as either residual or collective services. For example, Hong Kong has a comprehensive health service for all citizens financed by general revenue. But it also has a social security system that emphasises mutual help among family members, with complicated application procedures and very low levels of assistance.

The limitations of the existing classifications may reflect their roots in traditional Marxist and socialist critiques of capitalism, so that economic conditions and class position are the focus of concern. The assumption is that economic well-being automatically leads to psychological well-being, social harmony, autonomy and ultimately the emancipation of human beings. However, as discussed in Chapter One, people have needs beyond economic ones, which include social and psychological needs, especially the pursuit of self-actualisation. A welfare classification needs to take account of these aspects of human welfare and reflect how well different welfare arrangements serve the

Table 9.1: The dignity of unemployed persons in four welfare systems

Welfare system	The condition of human dignity						
	Physical well-being	Psychological well-being	Fulfilling care duties	Social integration	Learning and development	Self-determination	Equal value
China	X	X	X	X	✓	X	X
	The benefit levels of MLSG are not enough to meet physical needs. Only temporary and limited assistance with medical costs.	Names of MLSG recipients are released to the public. Non-professional workers of SCs and RAs handle MLSG applications.	Unemployed parents do not have adequate resources to provide children's education, medical care, and social activities.	Benefits are too low to enable recipients to take part in social activities. Recipients are unable to celebrate important festivals.	Provides training courses and job placements for unemployed workers. Special assistance to women over 40 and men over 50. Job offered to those with special difficulties in seeking open employment.	All decisions are made by both central and provincial government with little participation by unemployed workers. Recipients may be required to do community work based on the practices of provincial government.	Only unemployed workers with city residency are entitled to the MLSG and unemployment insurance scheme. Migrant workers and rural workers with rural residency are excluded. Benefit levels affected by economic development as well as welfare attitudes of provincial government.
Hong Kong O	O	X	O	X	✓	X	X
	Provides free medical care services for unemployed people living on CSSA. The rate of CSSA is lower than the Basic Needs Approach and is too low for recipients to buy nutritional food.	Complicated application procedures. Welfare workers receive only short-term training courses with few professional skills.	Free medical care. Poor unemployed families can obtain financial assistance for studying at secondary school. The rate of CSSA is too low to enable children to play a full part in normal social and school activities.	The levels of CSSA are too low to enable recipients to take part in social activities. Negative image of CSSA recipients portrayed by the Hong Kong government.	A wide range of training courses and job placements for different age groups of unemployed workers.	Semi-democratic government dominated by senior government officials, professional and business bodies. Recipients are forced to meet PAs regularly and do 'voluntary' work without any options. In practice, no individualised plans offered, recipients have to follow the instructions of welfare staff.	Unlike young unemployed people, middle-aged workers get less on job placements and receive little support for improving basic education. Hong Kong government is suspicious of unemployed workers' work motivation and readily suspects welfare fraud.

(continued)

Notes: X = criterion not satisfied; O = criterion partly satisfied; ✓ = criterion largely satisfied.

Table 9.1: Continued

Welfare system	The condition of human dignity						
	Physical well-being	Psychological well-being	Fulfilling care duties	Social integration	Learning and development	Self-determination	Equal value
UK	O	O	✓	X	✓	O	O
	Benefit levels just meet survival needs. The NHS provides free medical care for poor unemployed people.	Non-professional workers at JCP provide work-focused interview and New Deal programmes. Professional workers in Connexion Services provide career guidance and psychological support for young people. Mixed feelings among recipients on services of the JCP.	Unemployed parents' caring duties are supported by free medical treatment from the NHS. Benefit levels are too low to meet children's social needs. When in work, parents' economic power is increased by Child Benefits and Child Tax Credit.	Benefits are too low to enable unemployed workers to participate in social activities.	Provides training courses and job placements for unemployed persons.	Parliamentary democracy with some degree of MP influence on unemployment policies. No direct participation for benefit recipients. Options offered to the participants of NDYP. Voluntary participation for some recipients (lone parents, disabled persons and unemployed workers aged over 50) on New Deal programmes.	Disabled people and lone parents are financially supported to study at higher education institutions. Limited support for unemployed people over 25 in full-time training and higher education.
Sweden	✓	✓	✓	O	✓	O	O
	Provides an acceptable standard of living for recipients of SA. Generous unemployment benefits for those who have lost their jobs. Free medical care for poor unemployed people.	Professional social workers and career counsellors provide psychological support and career guidance for unemployed persons. Various kinds of experts from the Labour Market Institute provide in-depth assessment for those with special employment needs.	Provides free medical treatment and free education for children. The economic power of unemployed families with children is increased by generous Child Allowances.	In practice, the normal standard of living provides access to only a limited degree of social activities for recipients.	Provides a wide range of training courses and job placements. Unemployed adults can access full-time education to improve their qualifications.	Open and democratic polity with a high degree of trade union participation in both central and local decision-making bodies. The Government encourages civil participation, especially at local level. However, no direct participation for unemployed recipients.	Variations between local authorities in benefit levels and active labour programmes for recipients of social assistance. A benefit and training gap between recipients of social assistance and unemployment benefits. Full-time adult education opportunities for middle-aged unemployed workers.

Notes: X = criterion not satisfied; O = criterion partly satisfied; ✓ = criterion largely satisfied.

social and psychological well-being of humans. In this way, we can assess the impact of a government's welfare strategy on human dignity. An alternative approach to the analysis of the performance of different welfare systems lies in appraising their impact on the dignity of welfare recipients. After examining the conditions of human dignity among unemployed workers in the four societies (Table 9.1), we have identified five new types of welfare system: the Dignity Suppressive State, the Human Instrumental State, the Social-deficit State, the Autonomy-limited State and the Dignity Enhancement State.

The Dignity Suppressive State

The Dignity Suppressive State achieves little, or even fails completely, in terms of meeting the seven conditions that directly contribute to human dignity. Unemployed persons are not treated as equal to citizens who are not living on public benefits. In receiving government assistance, they are portrayed as having poor characters and as lazy and prone to abuse public benefits. They have little opportunity to participate in the welfare decision-making process. Social welfare in this model is not considered to be a right of the poor but a gratuity from the state. The amount of social welfare provided is at the discretion of the rulers or dominant groups. Welfare administrators also have a lot of power in deciding the level of benefits and absolute power in setting the behavioural conditions that unemployed workers must meet, such as regular interviews, home visits, community work and other types of welfare duties.

Unemployed persons' lack of equal status and their limited autonomy in a Dignity Suppressive State is the result of the concentration of political power in the hands of a small number of people or social groups. Given that welfare policies have been framed with little public consultation or participation, the needs of the poor are ignored. As a result, only a minimal amount of social welfare has been provided for the public. Unemployed persons living in this system have inadequate resources to develop their sociability and rationality.

Because state support is minimal, temporary and stigmatising, people have to rely on selling their labour in the market and on the informal welfare networks of family members, friends, and charitable organisations to meet basic needs.

The Human Instrumental State

The Human Instrumental State mainly concerns the economic role of human beings and the economic functions of social services. In this type of welfare system, unemployed workers receive little social respect but are mostly portrayed as welfare dependants. Furthermore, they are subject to stigmatising means-tested benefits and to control over their behaviour. In addition, responsibility for handling welfare applications lies with non-professional welfare staff, who are mainly concerned with securing the employment of unemployed persons, taking little account of their personal and social problems. With restricted opportunities for political participation, the unemployed and their representatives have little power over welfare policies, which are mainly determined by government bureaucrats or dominant social and economic groups.

Human beings, to a great extent, are treated as a 'tool' for economic and political purposes. Economically, citizens are manipulated to increase the productivity of industrial and commercial sectors and to promote economic growth. Politically, the state provides special benefits and welfare services for particular social classes or small social groups in order to enlist their support. For achieving economic objectives, the economic function of welfare is stressed so that more resources are invested in education, career guidance, job training and placements for unemployed persons. For achieving political objectives, welfare benefits are provided for key social groups who help consolidate the political legitimacy and administrative operation of the state. Sometimes, social services are a response to urgent issues or particular social groups that threaten social stability.

Under this type of welfare system, the market is believed to be an effective mechanism for meeting needs, and public welfare mainly concerns the provision of sufficient conditions for maintaining the physical survival of labour and for reproducing the next generation for the economy. In short, the state stresses the economic role of welfare rather than its role in human development and social integration. Accordingly, financial support for unemployed workers is too low to provide them with social and cultural opportunities. As a result of minimal financial assistance, unemployed families have to obtain extra support from informal welfare sources, such as relatives, friends and voluntary organisations.

It seems that China and Hong Kong are examples of the Human Instrumental State. Both provide limited support for meeting recipients' social and cultural needs. The MLSG in China, for example, as a 'low level security tool for low income urbanites', is designed only to help people meet the basic needs for food and clothes. Health care, housing and education are 'all out of its reach' (*China Daily*, 2004a). On the other hand, both societies invest more in education and training. The former Chief Executive of Hong Kong, Tung Chee Hwa (2005, p 15) asserts that 'through education and training, we seek to provide individuals with the opportunity to give full play to their potential, enhance themselves and free themselves from poverty'. Also, since adopting the open-door policy, China's welfare development has been slow, and its social services have been fragmented and mainly initiated by local authorities. Such welfare patterns are related to the CCP's fear of social unrest. As Rocca (2003) notes:

> the invention is not a turn in the government strategy but the result of decisions taken by local authorities in order to control this new population.... They are not technocratic or rational policies applied by a bureaucratic apparatus but a series of policies adopted 'on the spot', as an emergency procedure faced with unintended phenomena and emergency. As a consequence, these policies are wavering and confused.

Both the Chinese and Hong Kong governments also provide limited opportunities for recipients to participate in the decision-making process. In short, the key feature of the Human Instrumental State is a strong government that emphasises human economic functions and provides limited welfare for maintaining the physical survival of recipients.

The Social-deficit State

In the Social-deficit State, unemployed persons are allowed some degree of participation in the process of welfare policy making and a certain degree of autonomy as welfare consumers. Moreover, programmes are offered to unemployed persons who face special employment barriers, such as lone parents and disabled or older workers. The autonomy of unemployed recipients and the special programmes for some unemployed persons may be related to the political impact of politicians and pressure groups in a more open polity. Such pressures also make a ruling party more accountable and responsive to public demands for the provision of a reasonable quality of social services such as public assistance, health care, education and housing.

However, the market is regarded as an effective system for meeting needs, so that work incentives need to be maintained in the process of welfare delivery. In light of this consideration, unemployment benefit and public assistance are not intended to meet recipients' social and cultural needs. Also, non-professional or semi-professional workers are used to handle unemployment applications. Thus, the psychological needs of the unemployed are not adequately addressed, nor can their sociability be developed. This type of welfare system stresses investment in human capital so that more resources are devoted to active labour market policy such as training courses, job replacements and careers guidance in order to enhance the employability of unemployed workers.

The UK welfare system has many of the features of the Social-deficit State. As illustrated in Chapter eight and Table 9.1, the NLG has improved the NHS and is tackling child poverty. On the other hand, it provides low levels of financial assistance for poor unemployed workers, who find it hard to meet their social and psychological needs. It is only through working in the market that they are able to obtain more resources to lead a decent life.

The Autonomy-limited State

In the Autonomy-limited State, unemployed citizens can access various types of welfare services such as healthcare, education, job training, and counselling. Moreover, they can participate in some kinds of social and cultural activities. All these services are provided either directly by the public sector or by highly subsidised voluntary and private sectors. However, political power in this welfare system is mainly in the hands of a small number of social, political or religious elite who are playing a dominant role in shaping social policies. The political and welfare roles of social organisations and the family are encouraged by the state; while their social control and caring functions have been assisted by the government's financial and ideological support. Unemployed recipients, however, are not given sufficient channels for expressing their views. Their political activities are regulated by the State's legislation or even suppressed by political power in order to maintain social stability. In short, an elite-dominated welfare system, strong informal caring practices, and limited political participation of welfare recipients are main features of the Autonomy-limited State. In other words, welfare recipients' social and physical needs are satisfied at the expense of their autonomous capacity.

The Dignity Enhancement State

Unemployed persons in the Dignity Enhancement State can secure the opportunities and resources for meeting the seven conditions of human dignity. They are allowed to exercise some degree of self-determination in the process of receiving benefits. The political structure of this type of welfare state is relatively open so that representatives of unemployed workers can participate in consultative and decision-making bodies to express the needs of the unemployed.

The Dignity Enhancement State gives priority to social justice and equality rather than the wealth accumulation of particular social groups. Accordingly, the state plays an active role in providing services such as health, education, and child welfare. Also, generous levels of financial assistance are provided for the unemployed not only in tackling poverty but also in reducing the wealth gap between the rich and the poor. In this way, unemployed citizens are expected to enjoy a normal standard of living. As well, professional workers are employed to provide individualised services that tackle the underlying causes of recipients' unemployment. In short, opportunities and resources have been provided for all citizens to develop their mutuality and autonomy.

Table 9.1 shows that the Swedish welfare system can be very largely classified as a Dignity Enhancement State (though more work is needed to promote some conditions of human dignity). This is because unemployed persons in the Swedish system are treated holistically. Physically, they get adequate resources to buy food and receive free medical care when needed. Psychologically, they are assisted by professional social workers and career counsellors in meeting financial needs and tackling personal problems and employment issues. Furthermore, unemployed persons with special problems are assisted by various experts through the services of the Labour Market Institute. Socially, recipients of social assistance are given extra resources to participate in certain types of social activities. Developmentally, unemployed people are provided with a wide range of training and educational opportunities to enhance their skills and improve their general academic qualifications. Trade unions are also given opportunities to express their members' concerns. The Swedish model has provided more resources and opportunities to enhance human autonomy and mutuality than the other three welfare systems.

As discussed in Chapter eight, several factors are positively related to human dignity: collective welfare provision of key services, social and political participation of citizens, a national commitment to pursue common well-being, and individualised and professional services. These features are about human needs and how social and political structures should be organised to meet them effectively. The Swedish welfare system has provided us with some directions on how collective efforts should be used to pursue common well-being rather than the benefits of some particular groups or social classes. This is because all citizens, regardless of their income, social status, ethnicity and gender, should be entitled to the resources and opportunities to strive for mutuality and autonomy.

Human dignity and workfare

Since the early 1990s, 'workfare' has become a new and dominant approach to social security policy, especially in developed economies. Many welfare states impose new demands on welfare recipients such as regular meetings with welfare staff, compulsory community work, training, and job placements. If recipients fail to fulfil these requirements, their benefits are reduced or even terminated. A central issue in this development is how much power a government should be given over welfare recipients and whether workfare can promote the dignity of recipients, as advocated by pro-workfare governments. The present study argues that autonomy and mutuality are two dimensions of human dignity through which human well-being can be achieved. As illustrated in this book, human dignity has been suppressed in workfare strategies by subordinating autonomous capacity to welfare bureaucrats, especially in the case of Hong Kong. In the implementation of workfare measures, the fundamental issues that need to be addressed are the objectives and outcomes of state control. If the control is mainly for the benefit of recipients and is based on personalised and well-planned intervention, it may help tackle a person's difficulties in overcoming the social and psychological barriers that prevent engagement in a positive social and economic life. In this way, control becomes a means to empower unemployed people, working for their long-term interests. Under a truly personalised plan formulated by the active and equal involvement of both unemployed people and their professionally trained advisers, the government's control can be justified and unemployed workers' barriers to work overcome. However, if the control is mainly for maintaining work incentives, based on some negative views about welfare recipients, and if its implementation is based on a pre-scheduled timetable and structured programmes for all recipients without assessing their personal needs (as in compulsory 'voluntary' work in Hong Kong, or the New Deal options in the UK), such control seems to be an expression of a traditional suspicion and even hostility towards claimants. It completely neglects the actual social and psychological barriers faced by unemployed persons. It does not have an effective means to help recipients to cope with their problems. 'Personalised plan' and 'personal adviser' are terms which are being used to mask workfare's suppression of people's autonomy and its damage to their self-image and social relationships.

The suppression of human dignity by current workfare practices will eventually cause the social and psychological disintegration of a welfare recipient. At the personal level, controlling people without providing them with long-term development will degrade them to the status of non-human beings without thinking capacity. At a societal level, the creation of abusive images of welfare recipients and the adoption of compulsory community work have stigmatised welfare claimants and criminalised their behaviour. This will widen the social and psychological gaps between welfare recipients and non-recipients. As a consequence, recipients lose control over their public image, and face barriers in establishing positive social relationships with others. This leads to suspicion, isolation, and the social exclusion of recipients from their social networks (Chapters Four to Six).

Positive social images together with personalised interventions should be the basis of effective workfare measures. This is because the first can promote social acceptance and support, while the second can maximise a recipient's choice and participation. Thus, workfare should be a type of client-centred intervention as well as a human investment, based on the concepts of state responsibility and human development. Unfortunately, present workfare practices in many countries (like China, Hong Kong and the UK) mainly aim to reduce the number of unemployed recipients and the level of public welfare expenditure. Welfare recipients seem to be treated as welfare stooges with little concern for their actual employability and social and psychological well-being. Workfare thus becomes a new form of social control based on the imposition of welfare duties. Any welfare measures that suppress human autonomy and threaten mutuality will force the needy out of the official welfare system with little protection. The present workfare strategies that simply stress the personal responsibilities of claimants are, in effect, an expression of the state's irresponsibility in failing to provide sufficient resources and well-designed training programmes for the poor. As Peck and Theodore (2000, p 130) notice, welfare-to-work has to use compulsion 'to enforce participation in sub-standard programmes, which have to rely on a "compulsion push" from welfare, rather than a "quality pull" from the programme itself, to achieve transitions'. Concerning compulsory jobs offered to unemployed persons, Deacon (1997, p 39) argues that 'A long-standing criticism of job creation schemes in general is that they do not offer proper training. This means that the jobs which are created are often "dead end" jobs, after which participants return to unemployment.'Therefore, effective programmes based on the workfare approach are not cheap but require more financial investment and well-trained professionals for conducting in-depth assessment and formulating personalised plans. As pointed out by Loumidis et al (2001, p 148) following a national study of the New Deal for Disabled People Personal Adviser Service: 'It will be important to find ways of supporting those clients who require more intensive help over long periods in order to make even gradual steps towards work.' In short, workfare can be an acceptable and effective welfare approach only if personal needs have been seriously taken into account, supported by individualised plans. In this way, a poor unemployed person can be provided with the resources and opportunities necessary to tackle one's employment barriers, and ultimately develop one's mutuality and autonomy.

References

Abacci Atlas (2004) 'Hong Kong's economy', (www.abacci.com/atlas/economy3.asp?countryID=218).

Adelman, L., Middleton, S. and Ashworth, K. (2003) *Britain's poorest children: Severe and persistent poverty and social exclusion*, London/Loughborough: Save the Children/CRSP.

AEA (Unemployment Fund for Graduates in Sweden) (2005) 'The unemployment insurance', Stockholm: AEA (www.aea.se/the_unemployment_insurance_.aspx).

Ahlberg, K. (2003) *Social protection for the unemployed: Sweden*, National Report to the XVII World Congress of Labour Law and Social Security, Montevideo, Uruguay, 3–5 September.

Alcock, P. (2001) 'The comparative context', in P. Alcock and G. Craig (eds) *International social policy*, Basingstoke: Palgrave, pp 1–25.

Allen County (2004) Workfare programme, Wayne Township Trustee Office, Indiana (www.waynetownship.org).

AMS (National Labour Market Board) (2002) 'Activity Guarantee for LTE: 45 communities poised for pilot projects', Press Release, Stockholm: AMS (www.ams.se/RDFS.asp?L=30234).

AMS (2003) *Annual report 2002*, Stockholm: AMS.

AMS (2004) 'The labour market situation in April 2004: increased labour market measures keep open unemployment under control', 23 June, Stockholm: AMS (www.ams.se).

Anderson, K. (2002) 'Welfare state adjustment in Sweden and the Netherlands', Paper prepared for the Biennial Conference of Europeanists, Chicago, 14–16 March.

Argyle, M. (1991) *Cooperation: The basis of sociability*, London: Routledge.

Arslanogullari, S. (2000) *Social assistance in Sweden*, Uppsala: Department of Economics, Uppsala University.

Bambra, C. (2004) 'The worlds of welfare: illusory and gender blind?', *Social Policy & Society*, vol 3, no 3, pp 201-11.

BBC News (2002) 'Church leaders enter Cuba row', 17 January (http://news.bbc.co.uk/1/hi/uk_politics/1766368.stm).

BBC News (2004) 'China's ailing health care', 7 December (http://news.bbc.co.uk/1/hi/world/asia-pacific/4062523.stm).

Beauvoir, M. (2003) 'The concept of human dignity', New York, NY: Max-G Beuvoir (www.vodou.org/human.htm).

Behrendt, C. (2000) 'Do means-tested benefits alleviate poverty? Evidence on Germany, Sweden and the United Kingdom from the Luxembourg Income Study', *Journal of European Social Policy*, vol 10, no 1, pp 21–41.

Behrendt, C. (2002) *At the margins of the welfare state: Social assistance and the alleviation of poverty in Germany, Sweden and the United Kingdom*, Aldershot: Ashgate.

Behrendt, C. (2004) 'The situation of families in Sweden in the 1990s', European Observatory on the Social Situation, Demography and Family (http://europa.eu.int/comm/employment_social/eoss/downloads/gm_01_sweden_bernhardt_en.pdf).

Boone, J., Fredriksson, P., Holmlund, B. and Ours, J. (2001) *Optimal unemployment insurance with monitoring and sanctions*, Tilburg: Department of Economics and Centre for Economic Research, Tilburg University.

Boulton, W. (1997) 'Hong Kong–South China electronics industry', in M. Kelly and W. Boulton (eds) *Electronics manufacturing in the Pacific Rim*, Baltimore: World Technology Evaluation Centre, Loyola College, Maryland (www.wtec.org/loyola/em/toc.htm).

Bowlby, J. (1953) *Child care and the growth of love*, London: Penguin Books.

Bowlby, J. (1969) *Attachment and loss. Vol. 1: Attachment*, New York, NY: Basic Books.

Britton, L. (2001) *Evaluating New Deal 25+*, Working Brief, May, London: Centre for Economic and Social Inclusion (www.cesi.org.uk/site/aboutus.asp).

Brown, G. (2002) 'The chancellor's Budget speech: part 1', *Guardian*, 17 April (www.guardian.co.uk/budget2002/story/0,11219,685920,00.html).

Brown, G. (2004) 'Gordon Brown's speech at the Labour Conference in Brighton', 27 September. (http://politics.guardian.co.uk/labour2004/story/0,14991,1313855,00.html).

Calmfors, L., Forslund, A. and Hemstrom, M. (2001) 'Does active labour market policy work? Lessons from the Swedish experience', *Swedish Economic Policy Review*, vol 85, pp 61–124.

Carling, K. and Richardson K. (2001) *The relative efficiency of labour market programmes: Swedish experience from the 1990s*, Stockholm: Office of Labour Market Policy Evaluation.

Carpenter, J. and Sbaraini, S. (1997) *Choice, information and dignity*, Bristol: The Policy Press, Joseph Rowntree Foundation and *Community Care*.

Catholic.org.hk (2004) 'Cuts in CSSA payments to the elderly are sufficiently well adjusted to hide suffering from public view', Diocese Centre, Hong Kong (http://sundayex.catholic.org.hk/hk).

Census and Statistics Department (2003) *Hong Kong annual digest of statistics*, Hong Kong: Census and Statistics Department.

Census and Statistics Department (2004a) *Key economic and social indicators,* Hong Kong: Census and Statistics Department (www.info.gov.hk/hkecon/kesi/index.htm).

Census and Statistics Department (2004b) *Unemployment and underemployment statistics for April–June 2004*, Hong Kong: Census and Statistics Department (www.info.gov.hk/censtatd).

Census and Statistics Department (2005) 'Unemployment by sex and age', Hong Kong: Census and Statistics Department (www.info.gov.hk/censtatd/eng/hkstat/fas/labour/ghs/unemp_by_s.a.html).

Central Television International (2004) 'Workers from non-public enterprises will be protected by health insurance', (www.83666.gov.cn/dtzz/zxdt/t20040223_2206.htm).

Chan, C.K. (1996) 'Colonial rule, Chinese welfare ideologies, and the reproduction of social policy: the case of Hong Kong', PhD thesis, Sheffield: Department of Sociological Studies, Sheffield University.

Chan, C.K. (1998) 'Welfare policies and the construction of welfare relations in a residual welfare state – the case of Hong Kong', *Social Policy and Administration*, vol 32, no 3, pp 278–91.

Chan, C.K. (2003) 'Protecting the ageing poor or strengthening the market economy – the case of the Hong Kong Mandatory Provident Fund', *International Journal of Social Welfare*, vol 12, no 2, pp 123–31.

Chan, C.K. (2004) 'Placing dignity at the center of welfare policy', *International Social Work*, vol 47, no 4, pp 227–39.

Chan, C.K. (2005) 'Manging welfare in post-colonial Hong Kong', in A. Walker and C.K. Wong (eds) *East Asian welfare regimes in transition: From Confucianism to globalisation*, Bristol: The Policy Press, pp 95-116.

Chan, F.O.S (1997) Speech by the Chief Secretary for Administration in moving the second reading of the Legislative Provisions (suspension of operation) Bill 1997 at the Provisional Legislative Council, 9 July. (www.info.gov.hk/isd/speech/1997bill.htm).

Chan, J. (2003a) 'Social discontent escalates in China', World Socialist Web Site, 12 February (www.wsws.org/articles/2003/feb2003/chin-f12.shtml).

Chan, J. (2003b) 'Chinese capitalism: industrial powerhouse or sweatshop of the world?', World Socialist Web Site, 31 January (www.wsws.org/articles/2003/jan2003/chin-j31.shtml).

Chan, J. (2003c) 'Political crackdown in China as leadership prepares mass privatization', World Socialist Web Site, 26 November (www.wsws.org/articles/2003/nov2003/chin-n26.shtml).

Chan, J. (2004) 'Chinese regime amends constitution to protect private ownership', World Socialist Web Site, 2 April (www.wsws.org/articles/testdir/apr2004/npc-a02.shtml).

China Daily (2003) 'City poor to receive cash boost', 28 July (www.chinadaily.com.cn/chinagate/doc/2003-07/28/content_252195.htm).

China Daily (2004a) 'China faces shortage of psychologists', 7 September (www2.chinadaily.com.cn/english/doc/2004-09/07/content_372385.htm).

China Daily (2004b) 'Guangdong province plans farmer welfare system', 28 September (www.china.org.cn/english/null/108289.htm).

China Daily (2004c) 'Employment challenge for Shanghai', 21 October (http://service.china.org.cn/english/Life/109942.htm).

China Daily (2004d), 'New proposal to help migrant kids into school', 8 November (http://service.china.org.cn/english/2004/Nov/111494.htm).

China Daily (2004e) 'Aiming to improve social security net', 28 April (http://service.china.org.cn/english/china/94278.htm).

China Daily (2004f) 'China's employment situations and policies', 25 June (http://english.people.com.cn/200404/26/eng20040426-141553.shtm).

China Daily (2005) 'Shanghai does its bit to bail more out of poverty', 4 February (www.chinadaily.com.cn/chinagate/doc/2005-02/04/content_415071.htm).

China Internet Information Center (2002a) 'Labor and social security profile', 12 November (http://service.china.org.cn/english/2002/Nov./48592.htm).

China Internet Information Center (2002b) 'Shanghai Municipal Government takes lead in poverty aid' (http://service.china.org.cn/english/government/25693.htm).

China Internet Information Center (2004) 'Education hard for migrant workers' children', 3 November (www.china.org.cn/english/null/111064.htm).

China Labour and Protection Post (2004) 'Putting social security system to the constitution, workers are better', 16 March (www.83666.gov.cn/dtzz.zxdt/t20040316_2358.htm).

Chow, W.S. (1982) *Poverty in an affluent city: A report of a survey on low income families in Hong Kong*, Hong Kong: Department of Social Work, Chinese University of Hong Kong.

Chung, K. (2004) *Confucianism*, thespiritualsanctuary.org (http://thespiritualsanctuary.org/Confucianism/Confucianism.html).

CIA World Factbook (2003) Sweden Photius Coutsoukis, (www.photius.com/rankings/gdp_per_capita_2003_0.html).

Clasen, J., Gould, A. and Vincent, J. (1997) *Long-term unemployment and the threat of social exclusion: A cross-national analysis of the position of long-term unemployed people in Germany, Sweden and Britain*, Bristol/York: The Policy Press, Joseph Rowntree Foundation (www.jrf.org.uk/knowledge/findings/socialpolicy/sp127.asp).

Cochrane, A., Clarke, J. and Gewirtz, S. (eds) (2001) *Comparing welfare states*, London: Sage in association with the Open University.

Compston, H. (1996) 'Trade unions, policy-making and unemployment: a comparative study of 13 west European democracies', Political Studies Association annual conference, 9–12 April, University of Glasgow.

Conachy, J. (2001) 'Chinese think-tank warns of growing unrest over social inequality', 15 June, World Socialist Web Site (www.wsws.org/articles/2001/jun2001/chin-j15.shtml).

Cook, S. and Jolly, S. (2000) *Unemployment, poverty and gender in urban China: Perceptions and experiences of laid off workers in three Chinese cities*, Brighton: Institute of Development Studies, University of Sussex.

Costello, M., Davies, V., Johnson, C., Sirett, L. and Taylor, J. (2002) *Qualitative research with clients: Longer term experiences of a work-focused service*, London: DWP.

Davies, V., Hartfree, Y., Kellard, K. and Taylor, J. (2004) *Delivering the Jobcentre Plus vision*, London: DWP.

Deacon, A. (1997) 'Welfare to work options and issues', in M. May, E. Brunsdon and G. Craig (eds) *Social Policy Review 9*, London: Social Policy Association, pp 34–49.

Dean, H. (2003) 'Re-conceptualising welfare-to-work for people with multiple problems and needs', *Journal of Social Policy*, vol 32, no 3, pp 441–59.

Deng, X. (1984) 'Building a socialism with a specifically Chinese character', Excerpt from a talk with the Japanese delegation to the second session of the Council of Sino-Japanese Non-Government Persons, 30 June, China Internet Information Centre (www.china.org.cn/english/features/dengxiaoping/103371.htm).

Deng, X. (1991) 'Remarks made during an inspection tour of Shanghai – addressed to leading cadres of Shanghai', 28 January–18 February China Internet Information Centre (www.china.org.cn/english/features/dengxiaoping/103332.htm).

Department of Employment (1988) *Employment for the 1990s*, London: HMSO.

DH (Department of Health) (1999) *Reducing health inequalities: An action report*, London: DH.

DH (2002) 'Delivering the NHS Plan: next steps on investment, next steps on reform', (www.dh.gov.uk/PublicationsAndStatistics/Publications PublicationsPolicyAndGuidance/PublicationsPAmpGBrowsableDocument/fs en?CONTENT_ID=4097252&MULTIPAGE_ID=4911797&chk=8/VTR1).

DH (2005) 'Basics about help with NHS charges' (www.dh.gov.uk/PolicyAndGuidance/MedicinesPharmacyAnd Industry/ Prescriptions/NHSCosts/NHSCostsArticle/fs/en?CONTENT_ID=4049391&chk=qoqspx).

Dignity USA (2003) 'What is dignity?', (www.dignityusa.org/whatis.html).

Direct.gov.uk (2005) 'Tax Credits' (www.direct.gov.uk/Topics/Money/TaxCredits/TaxCreditsArticle/fs/en?CONTENT_ID=4015478&chk=ZfM9c9).

Dominelli, L. (1991) *Women across continents: Feminist comparative social policy*, New York, NY: Simon & Schuster.

Douji, C. et al (2004) *Urban poverty and minimum living security: Main report of China urban anti-poverty forum*, Beijing: MCA.

Downie, R. and Telfer, E. (1969) *Respect for persons,* London: George Allen and Unwin Ltd.

Doyal, N. and Gough, I. (1991) *A theory of human need*, Basingstoke: Macmillan.

DSS (Department of Social Security) (1998) *A new contract for welfare: Principles into practice*, Cm 4101, London: DSS/The Stationery Office.

DTI (Department of Trade and Industry) (2004) 'The national minimum wage' (www.dti.gov.uk/er/nmw/index.htm).

DWP (Department for Work and Pensions) (2003) *Opportunity for All, fifth annual report 2003*, London: The Stationery Office.

Economic Analysis Division of the Financial Services and the Treasury Bureau (2004) *Labour*, Financial Services and the Treasury Bureau of the HKSAR (www.info.gov.hk/hkecon).

Economic and Employment Council (2004) *First meeting of the Economic and Employment Council, EEC paper 2/04,* Commerce, Industry and Technology Bureau of the HKSAR (www.gov.hk/fso/eec/eng/pdf/EEC-P%204-04.pdf).

Economist (2004) 'Behind the mask', 18 March (www.economist.com/displaystory.cfm?story_id=2495113).

Education and Manpower Bureau (2004) 'Employee Retraining Board', Education and Manpower Bureau of the HKSAR (www.emb.gov.hk/index.aspx?langno=1&nodeid=675).

Esping-Andersen, G. (1990) *The three worlds of welfare capitalism*, Oxford: Polity Press and Blackwell.

European Commission (2005) 'Sweden: family benefits' (http://europa.edu.int/comm/employment_social/missoc2001/sv_part9_en.htm).

Evening News Post (2004) 'Reemployment scheme: Touching Net – developing business in internet can get training subsidy', 20 April. (www.83666.gov.cn/dtxx/zxdt/t20040420_2722.htm).

Far Eastern Economic Review (1995) 'State expectations: poor want a helping hand, not an invisible one', 7 November.

Farrell, C. and O'Connor, W. (2004) *Low-income families and household spending*, London: DWP.

Farrelly, J. (2003) 'Developmental psychology and knowledge of being', in T.V. Doan, V. Shen and G.F. Mclean (eds) *Chinese foundations for moral education and character development*, Washington, DC: Council for Research in Values and Philosophy (www.crvp.org).

Finn, D. (1998) 'Labour's New Deal for the unemployed and the stricter benefit regime', in E. Brunsdon, H. Dean and R. Woods (eds) *Social Policy Review 10*, London: Social Policy Association, pp 105–22.

Flaherty, J., Veit-Wilson, J. and Dornan, P. (2004) *Poverty: The facts*, London: Child Poverty Action Group.

Forsberg, E., Kantakeisu, U., Kalander-Blomqvist, M., Lofgren, U. and Starrin, B. (2002) *National report Sweden: Innovative institutional responses to youth unemployment and social exclusion*, Bremen: Institute for Psychology of Work, Unemployment and Health, University of Bremen.

Friedman, M. (1982) *Capitalism and freedom*, Chicago, IL: University of Chicago Press.

Fu, P.J. (1991) 'Human nature and human education: on human nature as tending toward goodness in classical Confucianism', in T.V. Doan, V. Shen and G. F. Mclean (eds) *Chinese foundations for moral education and character development*, Washington DC: Council for Research in Values and Philosophy (www.crvp.org/book/Series03/III-2/chapter_ii_human_nature_and_huma.htm).

FUIF (Federation of Unemployment Insurance Funds) (2002) *Unemployment insurance*, Helsinki: FUIF.

Gay, R. (2003) 'Sweden backs off US-style child support reforms', *Fathering Magazine*, 6 May (www.canadiancrc.com/articles/ Sweden_Backs_Off_US_child_support_06May03.htm).

Geneva Convention (1950) *Geneva Convention Relative to' the Treatment of Prisoners of War Adopted on 12th August 1949 by the Diplomatic Conference for the Establishment of International Conventions for the Protection of Victims of War*, held in Geneva from 21 April to 12 August, 1949, entry into force 21 October, Geneva: Office of the High Commissioner for Human Rights (www.unhchr.ch/html/menu3/ b/91.htm).

Giddens, A. (2000) *The Third Way: The renewal of social democracy*, Cambridge: Polity Press.

Giertz, A. (2004) *Making the poor work: Social assistance and activation programs in Sweden*, Lund Dissertation in Social Work, No 19, Sweden: Lund University.

Ginsburg, N. (1992) *Division of welfare: A critical introduction to comparative social policy*, London: Sage.

Goolam, N.M. (2001) *Human dignity – Our supreme constitutional value*, Johannesburg: the Konrad-Adenauer-Stiftung (KAS) (www.kas.de/ proj/home/pub/32/2/year-2001/dokument_id-4904).

Gordon, D, Levitas, R., Pantazis, C., Patsios, D., Payne, S., Townsend, P., Adelman, L., Ashworth, K., Middleton, S., Bradshaw, J. and Williams, J. (2000) *Poverty and social exclusion in Britain*, York: Joseph Rowntree Foundation (www.jrf.org.uk/knowledge/findings/socialpolicy/ 930.asp).

Government Offices of Sweden (2002) 'The budget for 2003: welfare reforms, jobs and health' (press release), 8 October.

Government Offices of Sweden (2003a) 'Spring fiscal policy bill: responsible policies for unsettled times' (press release), 15 April.

Government Offices of Sweden (2003b) 'The budget for 2004: investing in growth, jobs, and welfare' (press release), 22 September.

Government Offices of Sweden (2004a) 'A labour market policy to promote participation and growth', Stockholm: Government Offices of Sweden (www.sweden.gov.se/sb/d/2192/a/19783).

Government Offices of Sweden (2004b) 'Public health objectives', Stockholm: Government Offices of Sweden (www.sweden.gov.se/ sb/d/2942/a/17044).

Government Offices of Sweden (2004c) 'Financing family policy', Stockholm: Government Offices of Sweden (www.sweden.gov.se/sb/d/2197/a/15259;jsessionid=alhJTiBd_5ca).

Granerud, A. and Severinsson, E. (2003) 'Preserving integrity: experiences of people with mental health problems living in their own home in a new neighbourhood', *Nursing Ethics*, vol 10, no 6, pp 602–23.

Green, H., Marsh, A. and Connolly, H. (2001) *The short-term effects of compulsory participation in ONE. Survey of clients: Cohort 2 Wave 1*, Research Report No. 156, London: DWP (www.dwp.gov.uk/asd/asd5/156summ.asp).

Green-Pedersen, C. and Linbom, A. (2002) *Employment and unemployment in Denmark and Sweden: Success or failure for the universal welfare model?*, Aarhus: Department of Political Science, University of Aarhus.

Guardian (2002) 'Brown £40bn "kiss of life" for NHS', 18 April (http://society.guardian.co.uk/nhsfinance/story/0,8150,686196,00.html).

Guardian (2004a) 'US military in torture scandal', 30 April (www.guardian.co.uk/Iraq/story/0,2763,1206725,00.html).

Guardian (2004b) 'Poor get less help with school uniform costs', 9 September (http://education.guardian.cu.uk/social/exclusion/story/0,11499,130034,00.html).

Guardian (2004c) 'Lone parents offered £40 a week back to work bonus', 2 December (http://society.guardian.co.uk/publicfinances/story/0,12671,1364861,00.html).

Hang, T.C. (1994) 'Confucian Hsin and its twofold functions: psychological aspects of Confucian moral philosophy, with an excursus on Heidegger's later thought', in V. Shen, R. Knowles and T.V. Doan (eds) *Psychology, phenomenology and Chinese philosophy*, Washington, DC: Council for Research in Values and Philosophy (www.crvp.org/book/Series03/III-6/chapter_viii.htm).

Harman, H. (1997) 'Harriet Harman sets our her goals for steering social security towards the millennium' (press release), 2 June, London: DSS.

Harris, G. (1997) *Dignity and vulnerability*, Berkeley, CA: University of California Press.

Heritage Foundation (2005) 'Hong Kong', *2005 index of economic freedom*, Washington, DC: Heritage Foundation (www.heritage.org/research/features/index/country.cfm?id=HongKong).

Heyd, D. (1999) *Reflection on the concept of dignity*, Los Angeles, CA: Program on Medicine, Technology and Society, UCLA School of Medicine (http://research.mednet.ucla.edu/pmts/germline/Psychosocial%20Dangers/pdcdhvid1.htm).

Hill, T. (1991) *Autonomy and self-respect*, Cambridge: Cambridge University Press.

Hillyard, P., Kelly, G., McLaughlin, E., Patsios, D. and Tomlinson, M. (2003) *Bare necessities: Poverty and social exclusion in Northern Ireland: Key findings*, Belfast: Democratic Dialogue.

Hirsh, D. (1999) *Welfare beyond work: Active participation in a new welfare state,* York: Joseph Rowntree Foundation.

HM Treasury (2002) 'Joint Ministerial Committee on Poverty' (press release), 18 September (www.hm-treasury.gov.uk/newsroom_and_speeches_/press/2002/press_90_02.cfm).

HM Treasury (2004a) Child poverty review, 12 July 2004 (www.hm-treasury.gov.uk/media/250/91/childpoverty_chap6_290704.pdf).

HM Treasurey (2004b) '2004 spending review: record health funding means shorter waits, more choice and better care and advice', press notices, 12 July (www.hm-treasury.gov.uk/spending_review/spend_sr04/press/spend_sr04_press13.cfm).

Ho, C.W (2002) 'Improving Hong Kong's health care system', *Harvard Medical International* (http://hmiworld.org/past_issues/March_April_2002/forum.html).

Holmlund, B. (1997) 'Unemployment insurance in theory and practice', Paper presented at the Scandinavian Journal of Economics 100th anniversary symposium on Public Policy and Economic Theory, Lysebo, Oslo, 31 January–2 February.

Holmlund, B. (2003) *The rise and fall of Swedish unemployment*, Uppsala: Department of Economics, Uppsala University.

Hong Kong Council of Social Service (2001a) *A study on the employment situation of middle and old aged persons in Hong Kong*, Hong Kong: Hong Kong Council of Social Service.

Hong Kong Council of Social Service (2001b) '"Support for Self-Reliance Scheme" needs improvement' (press release), 11 June, Hong Kong: Hong Kong Council of Social Service (www.hkess.org.hk/press/11060/e.htm).

Hong Kong Government (1977) *Help for those least able to help themselves* (Green Paper), Hong Kong: Government Printer.

Hong Kong Government (1979) *Social welfare into the 1980s* (White Paper), Hong Kong: Government Printer.

Hong Kong Government (1996) *Report on review of Comprehensive Social Security Assistance (CSSA) Scheme*, Hong Kong: Hong Kong Government Printer.

Hong Kong Policy Viewers (1998) *A study of Hong Kong people's attitudes on CSSA unemployed cases*, Hong Kong: Hong Kong Policy Viewers.

Hong Kong Polytechnic University (1995) *A study of CSSA special grants users*, Hong Kong: Department of Applied Social Studies, Hong Kong Polytechnic University (in Chinese).

House of Commons (2002) *Jobcentre Plus, 14 February, col 637w* (www.publications.parliament.uk/pa/cm200/02/cmhansrd/vo020214w32.html).

House of Commons (2004a) *Work and Pensions – Written Evidence*, 14 January (www.parliament.the-stationery-office.co.uk/pa/cm200304/cmselect/cmworpen/85/85we01.htm).

House of Commons (2004b) *New Deal, Hansard written answers for 12 March 2004, col 1805w* (www.publications. parliament.uk/pa/cm200304/cmhansrd/vo040312/text/40312w15.htm#40312w15.html_sbhd1).

Human Resource Management (2004) *Unemployment*, 11 August, Alan Price and HRM Guide Network Contributors (www.hrmguide.co.uk/jobmarket/unemployment.htm).

ILO (International Labour Organisation) (2004) 'Unemployment benefit systems benefit few of the unemployed and virtually none of the working poor', Geneva: ILO (www.ilo.org/public/english/bureau/inf/pkits/wlr2000/wlr00ch3.htm).

IMF (International Monetary Fund) (2003) 'Sweden – 2003 Article IV Consultation Concluding Statement', 15 May, Washington: IMF (www.imf.org/external/np/ms/2003/051503.htm).

Information Office of the State Council (2002) 'Labour and social security in China', 29 April (www.china.org.cn/english/2002/Apr/31774.htm).

Information Office of the State Council (2004) 'China's social security and its policy (full text)', 7 September, *People's Daily* (http://english.people.com.cn/200409/07/eng20040907_156193.html).

Jacobs, J. (2004) 'Paleoanthropology in the 1990s: a comparison of some similar chimpanzee and human behaviours', (www.jqjacobs.net/anthro/paleo/primates.html).

Jewell, C. (2002) 'Responding to need in the "Three Worlds": how welfare state traditions and social service organizations impact the role caseworkers play in shaping welfare policy in Sweden, Germany and the United States', Paper presented at the Comparative Research Seminar, Center for Comparative Research, Yale University, 4 April.

Jobcentre Plus and DWP (2004a) 'Jobseeker's Allowance', (www.jobcentreplus.gov.uk/cms.asp?Page=/Home/Customers/ WorkingAgeBenefits/497).

Jobcentre Plus and DWP (2004b) 'Customer's charter', (www.jobcentreplus.gov.uk/cms.asp?Page=/Home/Customers/ OurCharter).

Jones, K. (1994) *The making of social policy in Britain 1830–1990* (2nd ed), London: Athlone Press.

Julkunen, I. (2002) 'Social and material deprivation among unemployed youth in Northern Europe', *Social Policy & Administration*, vol 36, no 3, pp 235–53.

Kant, I. (1964) *Groundwork of the metaphysic of morals* (translated and analysed by H.J. Paton), New York, NY: Harper & Row, Publishers.

Kant, I. (2004) *Introduction to the metaphysic of morals* (translated by W. Hastie), The University of Adelaide Library Electronic Texts Collection (http://etext.library.adelaide.edu.au/k/k16m/)

Kapor-Stanulovie, N. (2003) 'Psychological well-being and dignity', Paper presented at the Fifty-sixth Annual Conference of Non-Governmental Organisations associated with the United Nations Department of Public Information: 'Human security and dignity: Fulfilling the promise of the United Nations', New York, NY: United Nations headquarters, 8 September.

Kelleher, J. et al (2002) *Delivering a work-focused service: Final findings from ONE case studies and staff research*, Research Report No 166, London: DWP (www.dwp.gov.uk/asd/asd5/166summ.asp).

Kempson, E. (1996) 'Life on a low income' (press release), York: Joseph Rowntree Foundation (www.jrf.org.uk/knowledge/findings/social/ policy/sp97.asp).

Kennett, P. (2001) *Comparative social policy*, Buckingham: Open University Press.

Klein, D. (1998) 'Liberty, dignity, and responsibility: the moral triad of a good society', in D. Klein (ed) *Three libertarian essays*, New York, NY: Foundation for Economic Education, pp 25–59 (http:// lsb.scu.edu/~dklein/papers/libertyDignity.html).

Klemme, D. (1999) 'The concept of "self" in Confucian thought', *Unification News for August 1999* (www.tparents.org/UNews/ unws9908/Klemme_confucian.htm).

Kvist, J. (2000) *Activating welfare states: Scandinavian experiences in the 1990s*, Working Paper 7: 2000, Copenhagen: Danish National Institute of Social Research (www.sfi.dk/graphics/SFI/Pdf/Working_papers/ workingpaper2000_7.pdf).

Kvist, J. (2001) 'Nordic activation in the 1990s', *Benefits*, vol 5, pp 5–9.

Labour Department (2003) *The Labour Department annual report*, Hong Kong: Hong Kong Labour Department.

Labour Department (2004a) *Joint application of Youth Pre-employment Training Programme and Youth Work Experience and Training Scheme*, Labour Department of the HKSAR (http://yptp.com.hk/joint_app/index_eng.htm).

Labour Department (2004b) *Re-Employment Training Programme for the Middle-Aged* (RETPMA) Labour Department of the HKSAR (www.jobs.gov.hk\\eng\\rtp/index.asp).

Labour Department (2004c) 'Job training schemes provide over 20,000 places for youths', 4 August (press release), Labour Department of the SAR (http://www.info.gov.hk/gia/general/200408/04/0804091.htm).

Labour Department (2004d) *The Youth Self-Employment Support Scheme Office*, Labour Department of the HKSAR (www.labour.gov.uk/eng/service/content7.htm).

Lakey, J., Barnes, H. and Parry, J. (2001) *Getting a chance: Employment support for young people with multiple disadvantages*, York: Joseph Rowntree Foundation.

Lau, A. (2000) 'Motion on "Encouraging people to achieve continuous self-improvement" moved by Hon Ambrose Lau on 10 May 2000', Hong Kong: Hong Kong Legislative Council (http://sc.info.gov.hk/gb/www.hwfb.gov.hk/hw/english/archive/speech/SP0510.htm).

Learndirect (2004) *Adult learning grants*, Ufi Limited 2000, UK (www.learndirect-advice.co.uk/featured/alg).

LegCo Panel on Manpower (2004) 'Extension of temporary jobs in the public sector' (discussion paper), 12 February, Hong Kong: Legislative Council.

LegCo Panel on Welfare Services (2002) 'An update on the Support for Self-Reliance Scheme', Paper No CB(2)569/02-03(04), 9 December, Hong Kong: Legislative Council (www.legco.gov.hk/yr02-03/english/panels/ws/papers/ws1209cb2-569-4e.pdf).

Leung, A. (2003) *The 2003–2004 budget by the Financial Secretary to the Legislative Council on 5 March 2003*, Hong Kong: Government Printer.

Lin, H.Y. (1988) 'A Confucian theory of human development', in T. Murray (ed.) *Oriental theories of human development*, New York, NY: Peter Lang Publishing, Inc, pp 117–33.

Liu, Y., Rao, K. and Fei, J. (1998) 'Economic transition and health transition: comparing China and Russia', *Health Policy*, vol 44, pp 103–22.

LO (Swedish Trade Union Confederation) (2003) *The Swedish Trade Union Confederation, LO Sweden* (www.lo.se).

Long, R.T. (2004) 'Immanuel Kant: the Metaphysics of Morals', *Praxeology.net: The website of Roderick T. Long* (www.praxeology.net/philosophy.htm).

Loumidis, J., Stafford, B., Young, R., Green, A., Arthur, S., Legard, R., Lessof, C., Lewis, J. and Walker, R. (2001) *Evaluation of the New Deal for disabled people personal adviser service pilot*, London: DWP (www.dwp.gov.uk/asd/asd5/rrep144.asp).

Lund, B. (1999) 'Ask not what your community can do for you: obligation, New Labour and welfare reform', *Critical Social Policy*, vol 19, no 4, pp 447–62.

Lundin, M. and Skedinger, P. (2000) *Decentralisation of active labour market policy: The case of Swedish local employment service committees*, Stockholm: Office of Labour Market Policy Evaluation.

Ma, F. (2001) *Social protection as a factor of national cohesion: The practice and experience of China*, Bonn, Germany: Capacity Building International (www.dse.de/ef/social/fenghzi.htm).

Ma, K. (2004) *Report on the implementation of the 2003 plan for national economic and social development and on the 2004 draft plan for national economic and social development*, delivered at the Second Session of the Tenth National People's Congress, 6 March (http://english.people.com.cn/features/sco-ecoplan/plan04.html).

Mabbett, D. and Bolderson, H. (1999) 'Theories and methods in comparative social policy', in C. Jochen (ed) *Comparative social policy: Concepts, theories and methods,* Oxford: Blackwell, pp 34–56.

Macleod, D. (2003) *The welfare system and post-16 learning: Breaking down the barriers*, London: Learning and Skills Development Agency.

MacPherson, S. (1994) *A measure of dignity: Report on the adequacy of Public Assistance rates in Hong Kong*, Hong Kong: Department of Public and Social Administration, City University of Hong Kong.

Major, J. (2005) 'Labour's half-truths and spin are a cancer in the body politics', *Daily Telegraph*, 22 February (www.opinion.telegraph.co.uk/opinion/main.jhtml?xml=/opinion/2005/02/22/do2201.xml&sSheet=/opinion/2005/02/22/ixopinion.html).

Malik, K. (2002a) 'In defence of human agency', paper presented to the Engelsberg Seminar on Consciousness, Genetics and Society, Avesta, Sweden, 14–16 June (www.kenamalik.com/papers/engelsberg_nature.html).

Malik, K. (2002b) 'Human nature, human differences and the human subject', paper presented at 45th Annual Symposium of the Society for the Study of Human Biology, Institute of Education, London, 20–22 September (www.kenamalik.com/papers/sshb_universal.html).

Margalit, A. (1996) *The decent society* (translated by N. Goldblum), Cambridge, MA: Harvard University Press.

Marshall, B. and Macfarlane, R. (2000) *The intermediate labour market: A tool for tackling long-term unemployment,* York: Joseph Rowntree Foundation (www.jrf.org.uk/knowledge/findings/socialpolicy/970.asp).

Médecins Sans Frontières (2004) 'China:The socialist market economy takes a toll on public health' (www.msf.org/content/page.cfm?articleid=6589C0D3-DC2C-11D4-B2010060084A6370).

Medical.Net (2004) 'Computers can't compete with humans in the ability to recognize patterns or images' (www.news-medical.net/?id=1390).

Mendes, E. (2000) 'Taking equality into the 21st century: establishing the concept of equal human dignity', Ottawa: Human Rights Research and Education Center, University of Ottawa (www.cdp-hrc.uottawa.ca/publicat/dignity.html).

Midgely, J. (1997) *Social welfare in global context,* London: Sage.

Miguel, C. (2002) 'Human dignity: history of an idea', *Jahrbuch des öffentlichen Rechts der Gegenwart,* vol 22, pp 281–99 (http://web.usc.es/~ruizmi/pdf/dignity.pdf).

Millar, J. (2000) *Keeping track of welfare reform:The New Deal programmes,* York: Joseph Rowntree Foundation (www.jrf.org.uk/bookshop/eBooks/1859353436.pdf).

Minas, R. (2005) *Administrating poverty: Studies of intake organisation and social assistance in Sweden,* Stockholm: University of Stockholm.

Ming Pao (2001a) 'Contracted evening secondary schools increased tuition fees', 21 June.

Ming Post (1998) 'Millionaire abused the CSSA, Social Welfare Department evaluates home visits to prevent welfare frauds', 28 June.

Ming Pao (2001) 'Poor service quality of the Social Welfare Department', 8 October.

Ming Pao (2003a) 'Unemployed man cheated supermarkets', 18 January.

Ming Pao (2003b) 'Government's efforts on consulting voluntary organisations are inadequate', 3 March.

Ming Pao (2003c) 'Last year nearly half suicide cases were related to unemployment', 19 June.

Ming Pao (2003d) 'An unemployed man committed suicide, unwilling to live on CSSA', 22 October.

Ming Pao (2003e) '60 per cent CSSA respondents were unhappy during Chinese New Year', 16 February.

Ming Pao (2004a) '8 years old collecting rubbish for 2 years', 19 January.

Ming Pao (2004b) 'Unemployed person kissed his son before jailed', 11 May.

Ming Pao (2004c) 'One member missed voluntary work, the whole family's CSSA benefit was deducted by 14 days', 2 June.

Ming Pao (2004d) 'A woman committed suicide, refused to apply for CSSA', 3 June.

Ming Pao (2004e) 'Unemployed man stole bread, unwilling to apply for CSSA', 2 November.

Ming Pao (2004f) '40 percent patients lacked of money to receive treatment', 23 November.

Ming Pao (2005) '25 percent population do not have money to receive treatment', 28 February.

Ministry of Civil Affairs (2004a) 'Ministry of Civil Affairs' statistics in February 2004', 18 March (www.mca.gov.cn/news/content/recent/2004318163846.html).

Ministry of Civil Affairs (2004b) 'Ministry of Civil Affairs urges enhancing and developing the Minimum Standard of Living System for urban residents', 7 April. (www.mca.gov.cn/news/content/recent/200447141037.html).

Ministry of Education (2004) 'Basic education in China', Ministry of Education of the PRC (www.moe.edu.cn/baze/zonghe/04/htm).

Ministry of Finance (2005) *Local government in Sweden: Organisation, activities, and finance*, Stockholm: Ministry of Finance.

Ministry of Health and Social Affairs (2003a) *Sweden's action plan against poverty and social exclusion 2003-05*, Stockholm: Ministry of Health and Social Affairs.

Ministry of Health and Social Affairs (2003b) 'Swedish family policy', *Fact Sheet* no 14, September, Stockholm: Ministry of Health and Social Affairs, pp 1–2.

Ministry of Justice (2002) 'Democracy in the new century', *Fact Sheet*, February, Stockholm: Ministry of Justice.

Ministry of Labour and Social Security (1998) *Issues about the management of state enterprises' laid-off workers and the establishment of Re-employment Service Centres*, Document no 8, Ministry of Labour and Social Security of the PRC (www.molss.gov.cn/index_zcwj.htm).

Ministry of Labour and Social Security (2001) *Special measures for laid-off workers*, Training and Employment Unit, Ministry of Labour and Social Security of the PRC (www.molss.gov.cn/).

Ministry of Labour and Social Security (2004a) 'Second quarter of 2004', press release, Ministry of Labour and Social Security of the PRC (www.molss.gov.cn/news/20040722a.htm).

Ministry of Labour and Social Security (2004b) *What are 'community services business?'*, Training and Employment Unit, Ministry of Labour and Social Security of the PRC (www.molss.gov.cn/colimn/page6.htm).

Morris, L. and Ritchie, J. (1994) *Income maintenance and living standards*, London: Social and Community Planning Research.

Moss, B. (2001) 'Party life under New Labour: the untold story', *What Next?* No 19 (www.whatnextjournal.co.uk/Pages/Back/Wnext19/Bernie.html).

Multiple Sclerosis Society (2005) 'Am I entitled to Jobseekers' Allowance?' (www.mssociety.org.uk/what_is_ms/faqs/benefits_or_grants/jsa.html).

Nardi, M., Ren, L. and Wei, C. (2000) *Income inequality and redistribution in five countries – Sweden, Finland, Canada, Germany*, Federal Reserve Bank of Chicago & Gale Group (www.chicagofed.org/publications/economicperspectives/2000/29epl.pdf).

National Agency for Education (2003) *Descriptive data on childcare, schools and adult education in Sweden 2003*, Stockholm: National Agency for Education.

National Board of Health and Welfare (2000) 'Social services in Sweden 1999' (www.sos.se/fulltext/0077-018/0077-018/kap4.htm).

National Board of Health and Welfare (2002) 'Social assistance: 2002', (www.sos.se/fulltext/44/2003-44-8/Summary.htm).

National Board of Health and Welfare (2003) *Health care: Status report 2003*, Stockholm: National Board of Health and Welfare (www.socialstyrelsen.se/NR/rdonlyres/1DA644DE-5036-43C5-A186-3DC31171F021/2519/summary.pdf).

National Board of Health and Welfare (2004) *Social services in Sweden 1999*, Stockholm: National Board of Health and Welfare (www.sos.se/fulltext/0077-018/kap6.htm).

NCSR (National Centre for Social Research) and DWP (Department for Work and Pensions) (2004) *Families and children in Britain: Findings from the 2002 families and children study (FACS)*, London: DWP (www.dwp.gov.uk/asd/asd5/rports2003-2004/rrep206.asp).

Nordic Social-Statistical Committee (2003) *Social Protection in the Nordic Countries 2001: Scope, expenditure and financing*, Copenhagen: Nordic Social Statistical Committee (www.nom-nos.dk/Nosbook/public.pdf).

Novak, M. (1998) 'The Judeo-Christian foundation of human dignity, personal liberty, and the concept of the person', *Journal of Market and Morality*, vol 1, no 2 (www.acton.org/publicat/m_and_m/1998_oct/novak.html)

Osgood, J., Stone, V. and Thomas, A. (2002) *Delivering a work-focused service: Views and experiences of clients*, Research Report No 167, London: DWP (www.dwp.gov.uk/asd/asd5/167summ.asp).

Palme, J. (2002) *How is the Swedish model faring?*, Stockholm: the Swedish Institute (www.sweden.se/templates/Article_2891.asp).

Palme, J., Bergmark, A., Backman, O., Estrade, F., Fritzell, J., Lundberg, O., Sjoberg, O. and Szebehely, M. (2002) 'Welfare trends in Sweden: balancing the books for the 1990s', *Journal of European Social Policy*, vol 12, no 4, pp 329–46.

Peck, J. and Theodore, N. (2000) 'Work first: workfare and the regulation of contingent labour markets', *Cambridge Journal of Economics*, vol 24, pp 119–38.

People's Daily (2002a) 'New term: Re-employment Service Centre', 26 February.

People's Daily (2002b) 'Problem solving: the implementation of the minimal standard of living system in our country', 26 June.

People's Daily (2002c) 'Urban needy: The new concern of Chinese government', 3 November.

People's Daily (2003a) 'What are "community beneficial jobs"?', 7 April.

People's Daily (2003b) 'Information Office of the State Council: further promoting re-employment measures', 22 May.

People's Daily (2003c) 'The national employment seminar held in Beijing', 17 August.

People's Daily (2003d) 'Strategies supporting the unemployed worker', 18 August.

People's Daily (2003e) 'The re-employment of laid-off workers: tax exemption', 10 January.

People's Daily (2003f) 'Shanghai social workers to get official status', 7 December.

People's Daily (2004a) 'China is working to improve the quality of workforce', 26 April.

People's Daily (2004b) '0.8 billion yuan for unemployed workers', 9 May.

People Daily's (2004c) 'The Ministry of Work and Social Security asks all local governments to implement "new three directions" on services', 2 July.

People's Daily (2004d) 'Premier addresses global conference on poverty', 26 May.

Perkins, N. (2001) 'Poor attitudes? Unemployment and the dependency culture', Department of Policy Studies, University of Lincoln, Unpublished Master of Philosophy Thesis.

Plomin, R. (1990) *Nature and nurture: An introduction to human behavioural genetics*, Pacific Grove, CA: Brooks/Cole Publishing Company.

Post, R. (2000) *Dignity, autonomy, and democracy*, Berkeley, CA: Institute of Government Studies, University of California.

Powell, M. (1999) *New Labour, new welfare state?*, Bristol: The Policy Press.

Richardson, K. (2000) *Developmental psychology: How nature and nurture interact*, London: Macmillan.

Riley, G. (2003) *Living standards and poverty in the European Union*, tutor2u (www.tutor2u.net/Case_Study_European_Living_Standards.pdf).

Rocca, J. (2003) 'The invention of social policies in marketizing China: the cases of migrant workers and precarious urban workers', Shanghai Conference 11–13 September (www1.msh-paris.fr/reseauemploi/Shanghai/RoccaShanghaiENG/RoccaShanghaiEn1.html).

Rothstein, B. (1998) *The universal welfare state as a social dilemma*, Goteborg: Department of Political Science, University of Goteborg.

Sainsbury, D. (1999) 'Gender regimes and welfare state regimes', in D. Sainsbury (ed) *Gender and welfare state regimes*, Oxford: Oxford University Press, pp 245–75.

Saunders, T., Stone, V. and Candy, S. (2001) *The impact of the 26 week sanctioning regime*, Employment Service Report 100, Sheffield: Employment Service.

Secretary of State for Social Security (1998) *A new contract for welfare: Principles into practice,* London: The Stationery Office.

Shang, X. and Wu, X. (2004) 'Changing approaches of social protection: social assistance reform in urban China', *Social Policy & Society*, vol 3, no 3, pp 259–71.

Shanghai Daily and China Internet Information Center (2004) 'Residence card open to Shanghai migrants', 9 October (www.china.org.cn/english/Life/108857.htm).

Shanghai Labour and Security Bureau (2003) *Government's subsidy training,* Shanghai Labour and Security Bureau (www.83666.gov.cn/wsbs/zypxjd/zfbtpx/index.shtml).

Shanghai Labour and Security Bureau (2004a) *Shanghai Labour and Security Bureau's notification about the implementation of medical subsidy for unemployed workers*, document no (2004)15 (www.12333.gov.cn/xxgk/zcfg/zcfg_detail.shtml?mes_oid= 939905).

Shanghai Labour and Security Bureau (2004b) *Career placement scheme,* Shanghai Labour and Security Bureau (www.83666.gov.cn/wsbs/zypxjd/zyjx/jxjd/index.shtml).

Shanghai Labour and Security Bureau (2004c) *Issues about labour and security administrative review* (www.12333.gov.cn/bszn/detail.jsp?mes_oid=125640).

Shanghai Ministry of Civil Affairs (1996) *Shanghai social assistance measures* (www.shmzj.gov.cn/node2/node8/node30/userobjectlai141.html).

Shanghai Ministry of Civil Affairs (2004) *Application for five groups in countryside* (www.shmzj.gov.cn/node2/node6/node15/userobject1ai2040.html).

Shanghai Ministry of Civil Affairs and Shanghai Municipal Education Committee (2001) *Issues about the implementation of education assistance for primary and secondary school children from the MLSG,* document no 2001(39) (http://shmzj.gov.cn/node2/node8/node30/userobjectlai976.html).

Shanghai Ministry of Civil Affairs, et al (2003) *Take a further step to do good work for the poor,* document no 2003(55), 22 December (www.shmzi.gov.cn.node2/node8/node30/userobject1ai2337.html).

Shanghai Ministry of Civil Affairs, Shanghai Ministry of Finance, Shanghai Ministry of Employment and Social Security and Shanghai Trade Unions (2003) *Issues about the calculation of the incomes of the Minimum Living Standard Guarantee's applicants,* document no (2003)75, 31 December (www.shmzj.gov.cn/node2/node396/node403/node428/node482/userobject8ai207.html).

Shanghai Municipal Government (1996) *Shanghai social assistance measures,* document no (1996)60 (www.shmzj.gov.cn/node2/node8/node30/userobject1ai141.html).

Shanghai Municipal Government (1999) *Shanghai unemployment insurance measures,* document no (1999)7.

Shanghai Municipal Government (2003) *Han Zheng: Task strong measures to accomplish the yearly task of employment promotion,* Office of the Mayor, Shanghai Municipal Government (www.sh.gov.cn/gb.shanghai/node8059/node10471/node10472/userobject22ai83...).

Shanghai Municipal Government (2004a) *Notification from the Shanghai Employment and Social Security Bureau about adjusting the level of monthly minimum age* (www.83666.gov.cn/dtxx/zxdt/t20040302_2288.htm).

Shanghai Municipal Government (2004b) *Employment support workers to be more professional* (www.83666.gov.cn/dtxx/zxdt/t20040511_2853.htm).

Shanghai Municipal Government (2004c) *Shanghai city officially starts 'Hundreds of Enterprises with Thousands of Jobs Go to Community'* (www.83666.gov.cn/dtxx/zxdt/t20040412_2647.htm).

Shanghai Municipal Government (2004d) *Free to choose subsidized vocational training* (www.83666.gov.cn/dtxx/zxdt/t20040427_2758.htm).

Shanghai Municipal Government (2004e) *The requirement of setting up business*, document no (2004)22 (www.83666.gov.cn/rxdh/index.jsp).

Shanghai Municipal Government (2004f) *Solving the employment problems of rural workers: Shanghai employment assistant workers go to villages* (www.83666.gov.cn/dtxx/zxdt/t20040405_2567.htm).

Shanghai Municipal Government (2004g) *Unemployed workers have four types of benefits* (www.8366/gov/cn/dtxx/zxdt/t20040209_2142.htm).

Shanghai Star (2004) 'Crushing burden of sickness', 26 September (www.chinadaily.com.cn/english/doc/2004-09/26/content_377827.htm).

Shanghai Star (2005) 'Awkward occupation', 13 January (http://app1.chinadaily.com.cn/star/2005/0113/fo5-1.html).

Shen, V. (2003) 'Existential relationships and optimal harmony: philosophical foundations for values in a time of change', in B. Kirti, F. Liu, X. Yu and X. Yu (eds) *The bases of values in a time of change: Chinese and Western*, Chinese philosophical studies XVI, Washington, DC: Council for Research in Values and Philosophy (www.crvp.org/book/Series03/III-16/chapter_xix.htm).

Shipman, W. (1995) 'Retiring with dignity: social security vs. private markets', *Social Security Privatization*, no 2, 14 August (www.cato.org/pubs/ssps/ssp2.html).

Social Welfare Department (1996) *Report on review of Comprehensive Social Security Assistance (CSSA) Scheme*, Hong Kong: Government Printer.

Social Welfare Department (1998) *Support for self-reliance: Report on review of the Comprehensive Social Security Assistance Scheme*, Hong Kong: Government Printer.

Social Welfare Department (1999) 'Support for self-reliance scheme' (leaflet), Hong Kong: Government Printer.

Social Welfare Department (2004a) *A guide to Comprehensive Social Security Assistance*, Hong Kong: HKSAR Printer.

Social Welfare Department (2004b) *Gainful employment and self-reliance,* Hong Kong: Government Printer.

Social Welfare Department (2004c) *Social security* (www/info.gov.hk/swd/html_eng/ser_sec/soc_secu).

Social Welfare Department (2004d) 'Second round of Intensive Employment Assistance Projects invites applications' (press release), 16 June.

Socialism Today (2002) 'The union link with New Labour', Issue 73, March (www.socialismtoday.org/63/unions.html).

Solear, C. (1999) *Income transfers and support for mothers' employment: The link to family poverty risks,* Badia Fiesolana: European University Institute.

SSAC (Social Security Advisory Committee) (2005) *About SSAC,* (www.ssac.org.uk/res.htm).

Standard (2003) 'New CSSA rules "will lead to tragedies"', 5 June.

Standard (2004) 'Hong Kong pays dearly for suicides', 11 September.

State Council (1997) 'State Council's announcement on establishing a national minimum living system for urban residents', (www.mca.gov.cn/article/content/WDB_ZCWJ/2003/22484945.htm).

State Council (1999) *Unemployment Insurance Ordinance*, Ordinance No 258, State Council of the PRC (www.molss.gov.cn/correlate/sybxTL.htm).

State Council (2001) *Issues on strengthening the work of the Minimum Standard of Living System,* 12 November (www.mca.gov.cn/artical/content/WDB_ZCWJ/2003122484526.htm).

Statistics Sweden (2005) *Unemployment 1999-2005*, Stockholm: Statistics Sweden (www.scb.se/templates/tableOrChart____23319.asp).

Steinfeld, E. (1998) *Forging reform in China: The fate of state-owned industry,* Cambridge: Cambridge University Press.

Stetson, B. (1998) *Human dignity and contemporary liberalism*, London: Praeger.

Sullivan, R.J. (1989) *Immanuel Kant's moral theory*, Cambridge: Cambridge University Press.

Sweden Information Smorgasbord (2004a) 'Compulsory education' Stockholm: Swedish Tourism Trade Association (www.sverigeturism.se/smorgasbord/smorgasbord/society/education/compulsory.html).

Sweden Information Smorgasbord (2004b) *Democratic reforms* Stockholm: the Swedish Tourism Trade Association (www.swerigeturism.se/smorgasbord/smorgasbord/society/history/reforms.html).

Swedish Association of Local Authorities and Federation of Swedish County Councils (2003) *Levels of local democracy in Sweden*, Sweden: Swedish Association of Local Authorities and Federation of Swedish County Councils.

Swedish Institute (2003) *Fact sheets on Sweden: The health care system in Sweden*, Stockholm: Swedish Institute.

Swedish Institute (2004a) *The health care system in Sweden*, Stockholm: Swedish Institute (www.sweden.se/templates/FactSheet____ 6856.asp).

Swedish Institute (2004b) *Swedish labour market policy*, Stockholm: Swedish Institute (www.sweden.se/templates/FactSheet__ 4020.asp).

Swedish National Board of Health and Welfare (1999) 'Social service in Sweden 1999' (www.sos.se/fulltext/0077_018/kap6.htm).

Tang, J. (2002) *Establish a comprehensive minimum living security system*, Beijing: Research Center of Social Policies, Chinese Academy of Social Science (www.cass.net.cn/chinese/s09_shx/zlk/39.htm).

Tang, J. (2003) *Social exclusion and the living conditions of urban poor people*, Beijing: Research Center of Social Policies, Chinese Academy of Social Science (www.cass.net.cn/chinese/s09_shx/zlk/39.htm).

Tang, K. W. (2004) 'Developing a sustainable welfare system', Paper presented at The United Nations Asian-Pacific Leadership Forum on Sustainable Development for Cities, 26 February, HKSAR.

The Basic Law of the Hong Kong SAR of the People's Republic of China (1990), the Consultative Committee for the Basic Law of the Hong Kong SAR of the People's Republic of China.

Titmuss, R. (1974) *Social policy: An introduction*, London: George Allen & Unwin.

Tong, Y.L. (2004) *2004 Budget*, Hong Kong: Government Printer.

Tsang, Y.K. (1998) *The 1998-99 Budget by the Financial Secretary to the Legislative Council*, Hong Kong: Hong Kong Government Printer.

Tu, W. M. (1982) 'Core values in Confucian thought' (www.trinity.edu/rnadeau/FYS/TU%20Wei-ming.htm).

Tu, W.M. (1993) *Way, learning, and politics: Essays on the Confucian intellectual*, Albany, NY: Sate University of New York Press.

Tung, C.H. (1998) *Policy address by the Chief Executive to the Legislative Council*, 7th October 1998, Hong Kong: Government Printer.

Tung, C.H. (2000) *Policy Address by the Chief Executive to the Legislative Council, 11 October 2000*, Hong Kong: Government Printer.

Tung, C.H. (2003) *Policy address by the Chief Executive to the Legislative Council*, 8 January 2003, Hong Kong: Government Printer.

Tung C.H. (2004) *Policy address by the Chief Executive to the Legislative Council*, 7 January 2004, Hong Kong: Government Printer.

Tung, C.H. (2005) *The 2005 policy address: Working together for economic development and social harmony*, 12 January, Hong Kong: Government Printer.

United Kingdom Parliament (2004) 'Making new law' (www.parliament.uk/works/newlaw.cfm).

United Nations (1948) *Universal declaration of human rights*, adopted and proclaimed by General Assembly Resolution 217A(III) of 10 December 1948.

United Nations Children's Fund (2000) *A league table of child poverty in rich nations*, Florence: UNICEF Innocenti Research Centre.

United Nations Development Programme (2004) *Human development report 2004*, New York, NY: UNDP (http://hdr.undp.org/reports/global.2004).

Veit-Wilson, J. (1999) 'Poverty and the adequacy of social security', in J. Ditch (ed) *Introduction to social security: Policies, benefits and poverty*, London: Routledge, pp 78–107.

Veit-Wilson, J. (2004) 'Memorandum submitted by Professor John Veit-Wilson', Select Committee on Work and Pensions Written Evidence, United Kingdom Parliament (www. parliament.the-stationery-office.co.uk/pa/cm200001/cmselect/cmsocsec/72/1011702.htm).

Walker, A. and Wong, C. K. (1996) 'Rethinking the western construction of the welfare state', *International Journal of Health Services*, vol 26, no 1, pp 67–92.

Wang, J. (1998) 'The Confucian filial obligation and care for aged parents', Paper presented at the 20th World Congress of Philosophy in Boston, Massachusetts from 10–15 August, 1998 (www.bu.edu/wcp/Papers/Comp/CompWang.htm)

Welfare Watch (1996) 'Alternatives to workfare', vol 1, issue 2 (www.welfarewatch.toronto.on.ca/wrkfrw/wrkwtch2.htm).

Wennerberg, T. (1995) 'Undermining the welfare state in Sweden', *Zmagazine*, June (www.zmag.org/zmag/articles/june95wennerberg.htm).

Wen Wei Po (2004) 'Our country implements international business training courses', 22 July.

Wilensky, H. (1975) *The welfare state and equality: Structural and ideological roots of public expenditures*, Berkeley, CA: University of California Press.

Williams, F. (1989) *Social policy: A critical introduction*, Cambridge: Polity Press.

Wilson, D. (1987) *Policy address by the Governor to the Legislative Council,* 7 October 1987, Hong Kong: Government Printer.

Wilson, J. (1994) *Dignity not poverty: A minimum income standard for the UK*, London: Institute of Public Policy Research.

Wong, H. and Chua, H. W. (1998) *Exploration study on termination and re-activation of CSSA cases*, Hong Kong: HKCSS and Oxfam.

Wood, A. (2003) 'Kant and the problem of human nature', in B. Jacobs and P. Kain (eds) *Essays on Kant's anthropology*, Cambridge: Cambridge University Press, pp 38–59.

Word I.Q.Com (2004) *Thinking* (www.wordiq.com/definition/thinking).

World Bank Group (2005) 'Data by country' (www.worldbank.org/data/countrydata/countrydata.html).

Woronoff, J. (1980 *Hong Kong: Capitalist paradise*, Hong Kong: Heinemann Asia.

Worth, S. (2003) 'Adaptability and self-management: a new ethic of employability for the young unemployed?', *Journal of Social Policy*, vol 32, no 4, pp 607–21.

Xinhua News Agency (2002) 'Re-employment centers aid redundant urban employees', 22 July (http://211.147.20.14/chinagate/focus/relief/news/i006/20020722saos.htm).

Xinhua News Agency (2004a) 'Pilot health scheme for urban poor', 28 April (www.chinadaily.com.cn/english/doc/2004-04/28/content_326947.htm).

Xinhua News Agency (2004b) 'Shanghai begins certifying community service workers', 17 May.

Xinhua News Agency (2004c) 'To increase farmers' income, a new challenge for China's poverty reduction endeavor', 17 May.

Xinhua News Agency (2004d) 'China's rural poverty declines, urban poverty rises', 8 September (http://service. china.org.cn/link/wcm/Show_Text?info_id=106452&p_qry=china and educ...).

Xinhua News Agency (2005) 'China experiences rising school dropout rate', 4 March (http://english.people.com.cn/200503/04/eng20050304_175476.html).

Index

Added to a page number 'f' denotes a figure and 't' denotes a table.